33 bodies were unearthed but Gacy's lawyers say they have a good defence

John Wayne Gacy, a cordial man who donned costume and grease paint to play clown at children's parties, has been charged with more murders than any person in American history. Prosecutors say he lured 33 young men to his middle class Chicago home and killed them, burying 29 in a crawlspace.

JOHN WAYNE GACY

The Pursuit, Arrest, and Confession

By John Borowski

Waterfront Productions

JOHN WAYNE GACY:
HUNTING A PREDATOR

Copyright ©2020 by John Borowski
johnborowski.com

All rights reserved.

Published By:
Waterfront Productions
Chicago, IL
U.S.A.

ISBN 978-0-9976140-6-0

OTHER BOOKS BY AUTHOR JOHN BOROWSKI

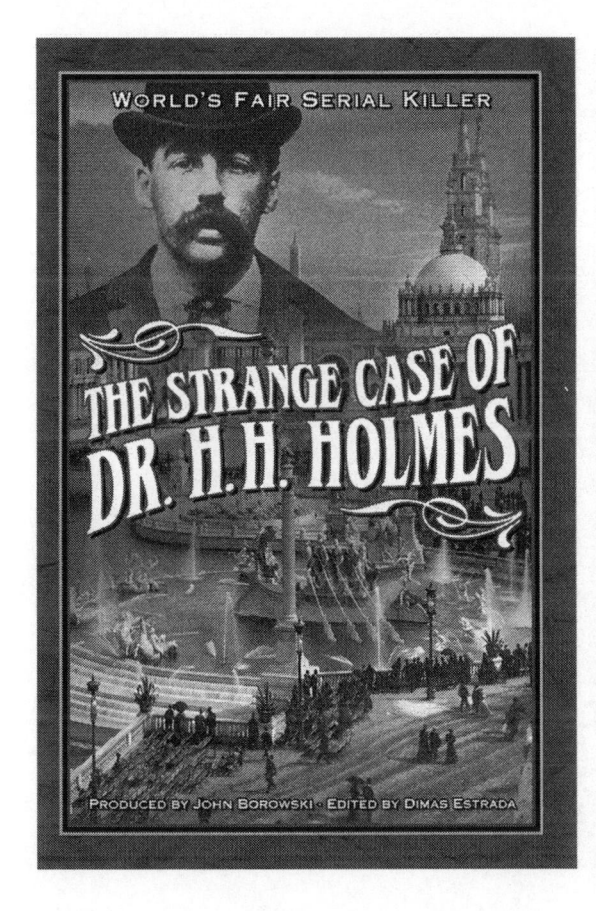

THE ED GEIN FILE: A PSYCHO'S CONFESSION AND CASE DOCUMENTS
PRODUCED AND EDITED BY JOHN BOROWSKI

ALBERT FISH IN HIS OWN WORDS
THE SHOCKING CONFESSIONS OF THE CHILD KILLING CANNIBAL
PRODUCED AND EDITED BY JOHN BOROWSKI

THE STRANGE CASE OF DR. H.H. HOLMES
WORLD'S FAIR SERIAL KILLER
PRODUCED BY JOHN BOROWSKI · EDITED BY DIMAS ESTRADA

DAHMER'S CONFESSION: The Milwaukee Cannibal's Arrest Statements
John Borowski

Available on Amazon.com, JohnBorowski.com and Ebay.

OTHER FILMS BY FILMMAKER JOHN BOROWSKI

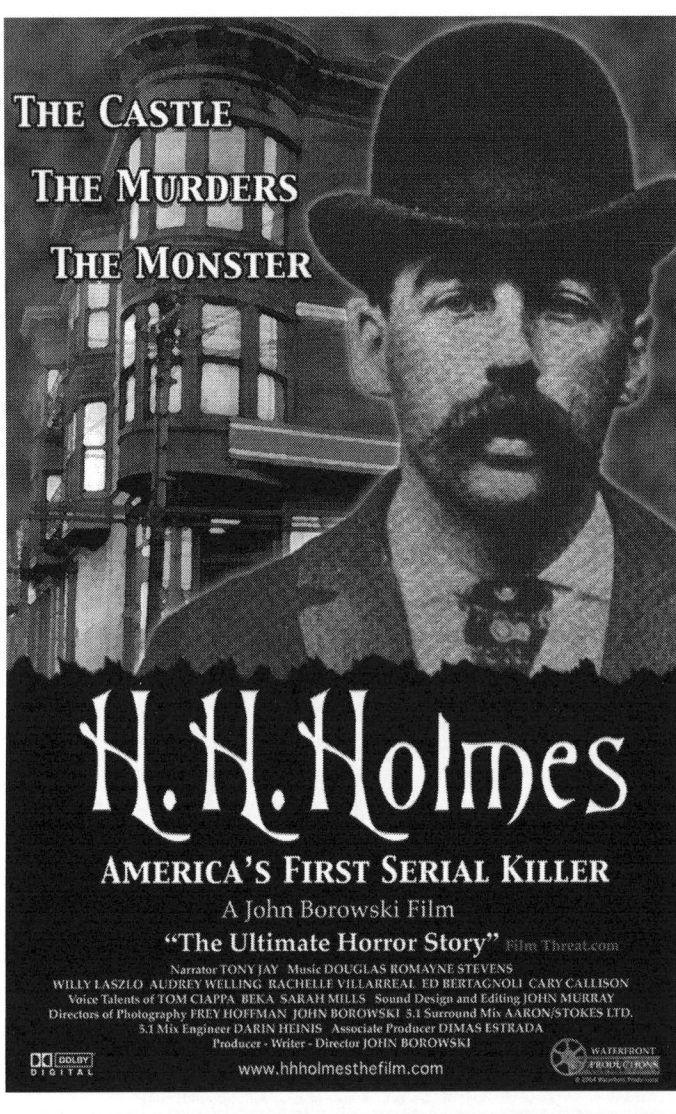

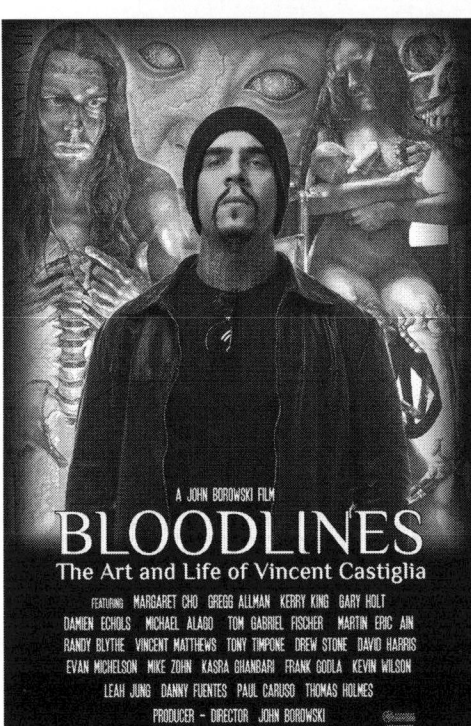

SERIAL KILLER CULTURE TV
A TV Show by filmmaker John Borowski.

Serial Killer Culture TV is an episodic true crime TV series featuring intimate interviews with those involved in the culture of serial killers and true crime. Included are collectors, artists, survivors, authors, forensic psychologists, museums, universities, and more.

CONTENTS

FOREWORD
1

OFFICIAL STATEMENT OF THE FACTS
3

ROB PIEST AND THE DES PLAINES P.D.
15

EVIDENCE RECOVERED FROM FIRST SEARCH WARRANT
37

SURVEILLANCE CONTINUES
65

DAVID CRAM INTERVIEW
73

SURVEILLANCE AND MORE EVIDENCE
93

THE CONFESSION
147

EXCAVATION AND AFTERMATH
169

IMPRISONMENT & SUPPLEMENTAL MATERIALS
267

AFTERWORD: THE RIPPER CREW
281

Gacy as Pogo the clown.

The poster for John Borowski's film. Poster design by Claudio Bergamin.

Anamosa State Penitentiary, Anamosa, IA, where Gacy was imprisoned in 1968.

The front of Gacy's house at 8213 W. Summerdale Avenue in Norwood Park Township, IL.

The rear of Gacy's house at 8213 W. Summerdale Avenue in Norwood Park Township, IL.

OWNER(S) NAME LAST FIRST INITIAL		T2937430
P.D.M. CONTRACTORS	PURCHASE DATE	NEW USED
LEGAL ADDRESS 8213 Summerdale	9 16 78	XX
CITY Norwood Park ILL. ZIP CODE 60656	COUNTY Cook	
VEHICLE IDENTIFICATION NUMBER 3N69R9X105706	YEAR 1979	MAKE AND MODEL OF VEHICLE Oldsmobile	BODY STYLE 4 Dr. Sedan

DATE ISSUED: Dec. 13, 1973

PASSENGER NO. 8 — TAX HP 52.7

I/We hereby affirm that the information provided is true and correct.

SIGNATURE OF OWNER(S): X PDM Contractors

OWNER'S ILLINOIS DRIVER'S LICENSE NO. G 200-4794-2079

LIEN(S) IN FAVOR OF:
Northwest National Bank
LEGAL ADDRESS 3985 Milwaukee Ave.
CITY Chicago STATE Ill ZIP CODE 60641

LIEN DATE: 9 / 16 / 78

STATE OF ILLINOIS
CERTIFICATE OF TITLE OF A VEHICLE

I, Alan J. Dixon, Secretary of State of the State of Illinois, do hereby certify that application has been made to me for a certificate of title for the vehicle described above.

Applicant has stated under oath that said applicant is the owner of said vehicle and that it is subject to the above liens and encumbrances and no others.

IN WITNESS WHEREOF, I HAVE HERETO AFFIXED MY SIGNATURE AND THE GREAT SEAL OF THE STATE OF ILLINOIS, AT SPRINGFIELD

Alan J. Dixon
ALAN J. DIXON, Secretary of State

RELEASE OF LIEN

By _____ Date 9/1/79
Firm Name / Signature of Authorized Agent

By _____ Date _____
Firm Name / Signature of Authorized Agent

The above holder of Lien on the vehicle described in this Certificate does hereby state that the lien described in said Certificate of Title is released and discharged.

(Do not accept title showing any erasures, alterations or mutilations.)

1431483

Gacy's car info and release of lein after arrest. (Courtesy of Ed Dymitrowicz)

ASSIGNMENT OF TITLE

The undersigned hereby certifies that the vehicle described in this title has been transferred to:

whose address is _____

with warranty to be free of all encumbrances except as follows:

Amount $_____ Kind of Lien _____

In favor of _____

whose address is _____

Signature of Seller X *John W Gacy P.124*

Subscribed and Sworn to before me this 28th day of August
19 71. Notary Public _____ (Seal)

FIRST RE-ASSIGNMENT BY DEALER

The undersigned dealer hereby certifies that the vehicle described in this title has been transferred to:

_____

whose address is _____

with warranty to be free of all encumbrances except as follows:

Amount $_____ Kind of Lien _____

In favor of _____

whose address is _____

Dealer's Plate No. _____ Firm Name _____

Signature of Authorized Agent _____

Subscribed and Sworn to before me this _____ day of _____
19_____ Notary Public _____ (Seal)

SECOND RE-ASSIGNMENT BY DEALER

The undersigned dealer hereby certifies that the vehicle described in this title has been transferred to:

_____

whose address is _____

with warranty to be free of all encumbrances except as follows:

Amount $_____ Kind of Lien _____

In favor of _____

whose address is _____

Dealer's Plate No. _____ Firm Name _____

Signature of Dealer or Agent _____

Subscribed and Sworn to before me this _____ day of _____
19_____ Notary Public _____ (Seal)

Gacy's car title transfer to his attorney. (Courtesy of Ed Dymitrowicz)

FOREWORD

by John Borowski

Researching for the making of a true crime film or book is like detective work. Ultimately, both are the search for truth. The definitive truth. Wading through the sea of sensational news reports and books, discovering the definitive truth becomes problematic. Ultimately, it is my function as a true crime filmmaker and author to dig up as much of the truth as possible, even if it has been buried and sensationalized for decades.

I chose to open this book with the Official Statement of Facts in the John Wayne Gacy Case. So much information in true crime cases is either sensationalized, inaccurate, or both. Many times, the sensational aspects of cases actually transforms into inaccurate facts. One of the sensational aspects of Gacy's case is the desire for the proof of more victims beyond the thirty-three/thirty-four. The public wants more victims! When I interviewed an officer of the Cook County Sheriff's department for my film on Gacy, he stated "Isn't thirty-three victims enough?" The public loves a good true crime story and Gacy's is one of the greatest serial killer cases ever, mostly due to his cunning nature by evading the Chicago and suburban authorities for six years.

Because Gacy retracted his confession and ultimately denied almost everything, there are aspects of Gacy's case which we may never know the answers to. This book includes information by the Des Plaines police force, detectives and Illinois law enforcement who diligently tailed Gacy for twenty-four hours for ten days in December of 1978, which led to his apprehension, trial, and execution. These documents are an excellent example of tried and true detective work which will go down in history along with Detective Frank Geyer's (The H.H. Holmes case.) and Detective William King's (The Albert Fish case.) amazing detective work. What these three cases have in common is the lack of DNA typing. When I imagine how difficult it was for all of these detectives, I am in awe of what they accomplished. This book is dedicated to all of the Des Plaines detectives and the Illinois law enforcement/legal system who apprehended, imprisoned, and executed John Wayne Gacy.

A note on the materials: The majority of files are photocopies. I did not have access to the original files, so I utilized the resources and materials which are publicly available. Also, there is a missing page (Page 1 of the excavation report, p. 180) which I could not locate. I did my best job cleaning up these files. I am sure, like myself, you will squint and read every word in this book!

OFFICIAL STATEMENT OF THE FACTS

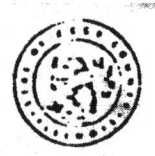

OFFICE OF THE STATE'S ATTORNEY
COOK COUNTY, ILLINOIS
CHICAGO 60608

BERNARD CAREY
STATE'S ATTORNEY

CRIMINAL DIVISION
2600 SOUTH CALIFORNIA AVE.

April 11, 1980

DEFENDANT: JOHN W. GACY   AGE: 38

I.R. NO.: 273632

INDICTMENT NO.	CHARGE	SENTENCE
79-69	Murder Deviate Sexual Assault Indecent Liberties	Death

JUDGE: Louis B. Garippo

DATE SENTENCED: March 14, 1980

TYPE OF TRIAL: Jury - (Also Jury on Death Penalty Sentencing Hearing)

REPRESENTED BY: Sam Amirante & Robert Motta -
Attorneys-at-Law

PREVIOUS RECORD: See attached

COMPLAINING WITNESS(ES): Mr. & Mrs. Harold Piest
2722 Craig Drive
Des Plaines, Illinois
(Deceased: Robert Piest, 15)

ARRESTING OFFICERS:

Captain Joseph Kozenszak
Des Plaines Police Department

Investigator Gregory Bedoe
Cook County Sheriff's Police Department
c/o 2650 South California Avenue
Chicago, Illinois 60608

ASSISTANT STATE'S ATTORNEYS: William J. Kunkle, Jr.
Robert R. Egan
John T. Sullivan
James Varga

IN RE: JOHN WAYNE GACY
INDICTMENT NOS.:

79-69	79-2382	79-2393
79-70	79-2383	79-2394
79-71	79-2384	79-2395
79-72	79-2385	79-2396
79-73	79-2386	79-2397
79-74	79-2387	79-2398
79-75	79-2388	79-2399
79-2378	79-2389	79-2400
79-2379	79-2390	79-2401
79-2380	79-2391	79-2402
79-2381	79-2392	79-2403

OFFICIAL STATEMENT OF FACTS

The facts in these Indictments are briefly as follows:

John Wayne Gacy, I.R. #273632, F.B.I. #585 181 G, I.S.B. #1377836, was born on March 17, 1942 in Chicago, Illinois.

He stands convicted by a jury of thirty-three (33) murders of young men and boys. Twenty-nine (29) of the victims were buried on the defendant's property and four (4) were recovered from the Des Plaines - Illinois River system. To date, twenty-four (24) of these victims have been identified and nine (9) remain unidentified.

The defendant was sentenced on March 14, 1980, by the Honorable Louis B. Garippo, to twelve (12) sentences of death by electrocution and twenty-one (21) sentences of life without possibility of parole. John Gacy has been charged, convicted and sentenced for more murders than anyone in the history of this nation. It was the plain intent of the jury and the Court that this man should never be free to kill again under any circumstances, and should in fact be removed permanently from society by execution.

On December 11, 1968, John Gacy, was received at Anamosa Mens' Reformatory, Anamosa, Iowa, having been sentenced to ten (10) years in the penitentiary for sodomy after a plea of guilty to that charge in Blackhawk County, Iowa, on December 3, 1968.

Using his abilities as a manipulative con-man he was viewed as a "model prisoner" and was paroled to Chicago, Illinois on June 19, 1970.

On or about January 2, 1972 John Gacy resided at 8213 West Summerdale Avenue, in unincorporated Norwood Park Township, Illinois. On that night he picked up and unidentified young man at the Greyhound bus station in Chicago's loop. He took his victim to his home and there they performed various cousensual homosexual acts.

According to the defendant's statements, when he awoke on the morning of January 3, 1972, he saw the victim coming at him with a knife. He struggled with the victim, gained control of the knife, and stabbed him to death in the chest. He

IN RE: JOHN WAYNE GACY
         (CONTINUED......)

buried this first murder victim in the crawl space under his home.

Later in 1972 he married his second wife. She complained about the odor in the basement and while she was on an out-of-town visit, the defendant poured concrete over this first grave.

During statements made after his arrest on December 21, 1978, John Gacy made a sketch or diagram of his crawl space showing the locations of most of the bodies. He specifically identified his first victim as being buried in a location consistent with body number nine (9), recovered later.

Unidentified body number 9 (Indictment No. 79-2384) was in fact the only body in the crawl space covered with a layer of concrete. Further, radiological examination of the chest of these skeletal remains showed evidence of lacerations or nicks in two ribs, consistent with a cause of death of stabbing.

On an unknown date and time, unidentified body number 28 (Indictment No. 79-2402) was killed by strangulation. According to John Gacy's statements, he placed this dead body, head down in a bedroom closet for storage before burial. He noted that blood and other fluids from the mouth of this victim had stained the carpet. (Laboratory testing of a stain in this carpet confirmed that it was human blood.) Thereafter he used cloth or other materials to stuff in the mouths and throats of his victims to prevent any further inconvenience to him from the life-blood of his victims.

On July 31, 1975, John Butkovich, 20, came to Gacy's house with some friends and demanded that Gacy pay him wages owed for work on the defendant's construction crew. After an unresolved argument, Butkovich and his friends left.

Later that night the defendant, while "cruising" in his black Oldsmobile sedan, picked up John Butkovich. He took his victim to the house on Summerdale and had a few drinks with him. After getting the victim handcuffed (purportedly a demonstration of a "handcuff trick"), they began arguing again. Butkovich said that if he got out of the cuffs he would kill Gacy. Gacy then showed Butkovich his "rope trick". The rope is placed around the victim's neck from behind and two knots are tied tight to the back of the neck. A loop is made after the knots and tied with a third knot. A stick is inserted in the loop, tightening the noose like a tourniquet.

Butkovich was buried out back at the end of the tool shed addition to the garage in a trench previously dug for drain tile. Again, the body was covered with concrete. After his arrest, Gacy specifically pointed out the location and orientation of the body. These remains were body number 2 and related to Indictment Number 79-70.

In April of 1976, Gacy killed body number 29, identified as Darryl Sampson, and buried him under the dining room addition to his house. His second wife and step-children had moved out in February. He was convicted of the murder of Darryl

IN RE: JOHN WAYNE GACY
(CONTINUED . . .)

Sampson in Indictment Number 79-2403.

On May 14, 1976 Gacy committed his first "double." Samuel Stapleton, 14, and Randall Reffett, 15, were neighbors. Their lives ended together at 8213 Summerdale and they were buried in a common grave in the crawl space. They were recovered as bodies number 6 and number 7, respectively. Gacy was convicted of their murders in Indictments 79-2380 and 79-2381.

On June 3, 1976 Gacy strangled 17 year old Michael Bonnin to death and buried him in the crawl space. He was recovered as Body Number 18 and was the victim in Indictment Number 79-2393.

On June 13, 1976, the defendant killed 17 year old William Carroll. He was recovered as Body Number 22. This murder conviction bore Indictment Number 79-2397.

Probably during the summer of 1976, based on their locations in the crawl space, Gacy killed and buried unidentified young males referred to as Body Numbers 24, 26, 21 and 13. He was convicted of these murders in Indictments Number 79-2398, 79-2400, 79-2396 and 79-2388.

On August 6, 1976, Gacy picked up 17 year old Rick Johnston near the Aragon Ballroom after a rock concert. The victim was recovered from the crawl space as Body Number 23. Gacy was convicted of this murder in Indictment Number 79-73.

On October 25, 1976 the defendant committed another double murder, killing 14 year old Michael Marino and 16 year old Albert Parker, burying them in a common grave in the crawl space, with a single plastic garbage bag covering both of their heads and upper bodies. They were recovered as Body Number 14 and Body Number 15. Gacy was convicted of these murders in Indictments 79-2389 and 79-2390.

On December 12, 1976 Gacy killed 16 year old Gregory Godzik, a part time construction employee of his, who he picked up after Greg had dropped his steady girlfriend off at home. This victim was Body Number 4 and this murder resulted in a conviction on Indictment Number 79-72.

John Szyc, a nineteen year old graduate of Maine West High School was killed by Gacy on January 20, 1977. He was identified as Body Number 3. His class ring was recovered from the top of Gacy's bedroom dresser. Szyc's car title was forged and the car was sold to an employee of Gacy's. Gacy's conviction for this murder was on Indictment Number 79-71.

Most probably during 1977, due to the location of Bodies Number 5, Number 10, and Number 19, these unidentified young males were strangled and buried by John Gacy. He was convicted of their murders in Indictment Numbers 79-2379, 79-2385, and 79-2394.

IN RE: JOHN WAYNE GACY
(CONTINUED . . .)

On March 15, 1977 Gacy picked up Jon Prestige, age 20, who was visiting Chicago from Michigan. His remains were labeled Body Number 1 and Gacy was convicted of his murder in Indictment 79-2378.

On July 5, 1977 the prisoner, convicted of this murder in Indictment Number 79-2382, killed Matthew Bowman, age 19, and buried him in the crawl space where he was recovered as Body Number 8. Since this murder took place after the enactment of the current Illinois death penalty statute and the jury found the existence of multiple homicides, the sentence for this murder was death.

On September 15, 1977, 18 year old Robert Gilroy was on his way from his home, near Gacy's, to a riding stable. He never returned. He was identified as Body Number 25. Gacy was sentenced to death for this murder in Indictment Number 79-2399.

John Mowery was 19 when John Gacy strangled him on September 25, 1977. His remains were recovered from the crawlspace as Body Number 20. Gacy was sentenced to death in Indictment Number 79-2395.

Russell Nelson was 22 when Gacy killed and buried him on October 17, 1977. He was recovered as Body Number 16. A death sentence was issued on Indictment Number 79-2391.

Robert Winch, from Kalamazoo, Michigan, was 16 when Gacy killed him and buried him in grave number 11 on November 11, 1977. The defendant was sentenced to death from this murder in Indictment Number 79-2386.

Twenty-one year old Tommy Boling, living with his wife and child in Chicago, disappeared on November 18, 1977. He was recovered from Gacy's graveyard as Body Number 12. On Indictment Number 79-2387 Gacy was sentenced to death.

On December 9, 1977, ex-marine David Talsma, 19, was strangled to death at 8213 Summerdale. He was identified as Body Number 17 and a death sentence was issued on Indictment Number 79-2392.

The last victim buried in the crawl space was William Kindred, who disappeared in February of 1978 at age 19. He was removed as Body Number 27. His murder was charged in Indictment Number 79-2401 and the verdict and sentence was death.

Gscy had often used unsuspecting young employees, some of whom were consenting homosexual partners as well, to dig "drain tile trenches" in the crawl space, to be used later as graves. Now, however, the crawl space was "full."

In June, 1978, Timothy O'Rourke, age 20, was killed by Gacy at 8213 Summerdale. He disposed of this body by throwing it off of the I-55 bridge over the Des Plaines River. The body was recovered near the Dresden Island Lock and Dam. The verdict and sentence on Indictment Number 79-2383 was death.

IN RE: JOHN WAYNE GACY
(CONTINUED . . .)

You will be dealing with an intelligent (129 to 135 I.Q.) devious, glib, articulate, engaging and sadistic person. John Gacy learned in the Iowa Reformatory in Anamosa that he couldn't risk allowing a homosexual victim to live if he threatened blackmail, exposure or appeared to be a person who would "beef to the police."

As far back as 1967 in Iowa, he was capable of using anyone, in any way, to accomplish his evil purposes. Young men would be rewarded with sex with Gacy's first wife in return for oral sex with Gacy. When a sodomy victim reported him to the authorities, Gacy hired another young man to beat him up and convince him not to testify.

You are dealing with a man capable of the cruelest sexual sadism imaginable and who now truly has nothing to lose.

He is a con-man, a malingerer, a manipulator, a skilled torturer and an equally skilled killer. Accept his word at your peril. Allow him contact with other inmates at their peril.

Over and above the statutory notice requirements, I respectfully ask to be personally notified of _any_ proposed change of status for this prisoner.

Respectfully submitted,

BERNARD CAREY
State's Attorney of Cook County

By: *William J. Kunkle, Jr.*
William J. Kunkle, Jr.
Chief Deputy State's Attorney

Robert R. Egan
Robert R. Egan
Assistant State's Attorney

John Terry Sullivan
John Terry Sullivan
Assistant State's Attorney

James Varga
James Varga
Assistant State's Attorney

WJK:ab

Attachment

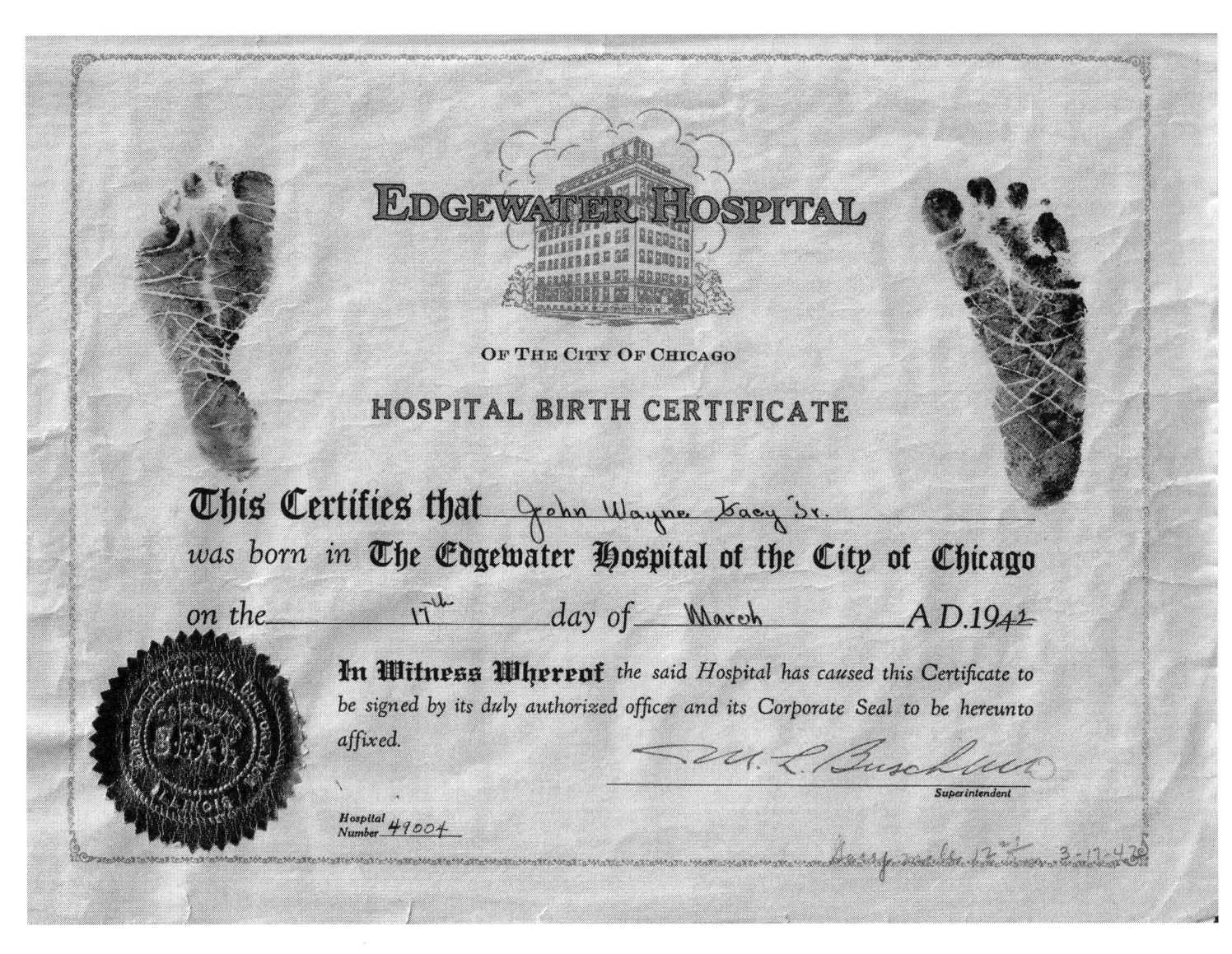

Birth certificate of John Wayne Gacy Jr.

THE GACY PRODUCTION CO.

3309 Normandy Road • Springfield, Illinois

JOHN W. GACY, JR.	DR. VICTOR H. BEINKE	MARLYNN LEE GACY
Designing Engineer	*Technical Superintendent*	*Producing Engineer*

ANNOUNCES

A new 1966 Model Boy—Michael-John. Weight 7 pounds, 13 ounces. Released February 24, 1966, 9:33 A.M. now on display at 3309 Normandy Road. Two-Lung Power, Free Squealing, Knee Action, Economical Feed, Screamlined Body, and Changeable Seat Covers. The management cannot assure the public of a new Model during the balance of the year.

Gacy's son's birth announcement with his first wife.

The Gacy's Christmas card. Gacy is with his second wife and her daughters.

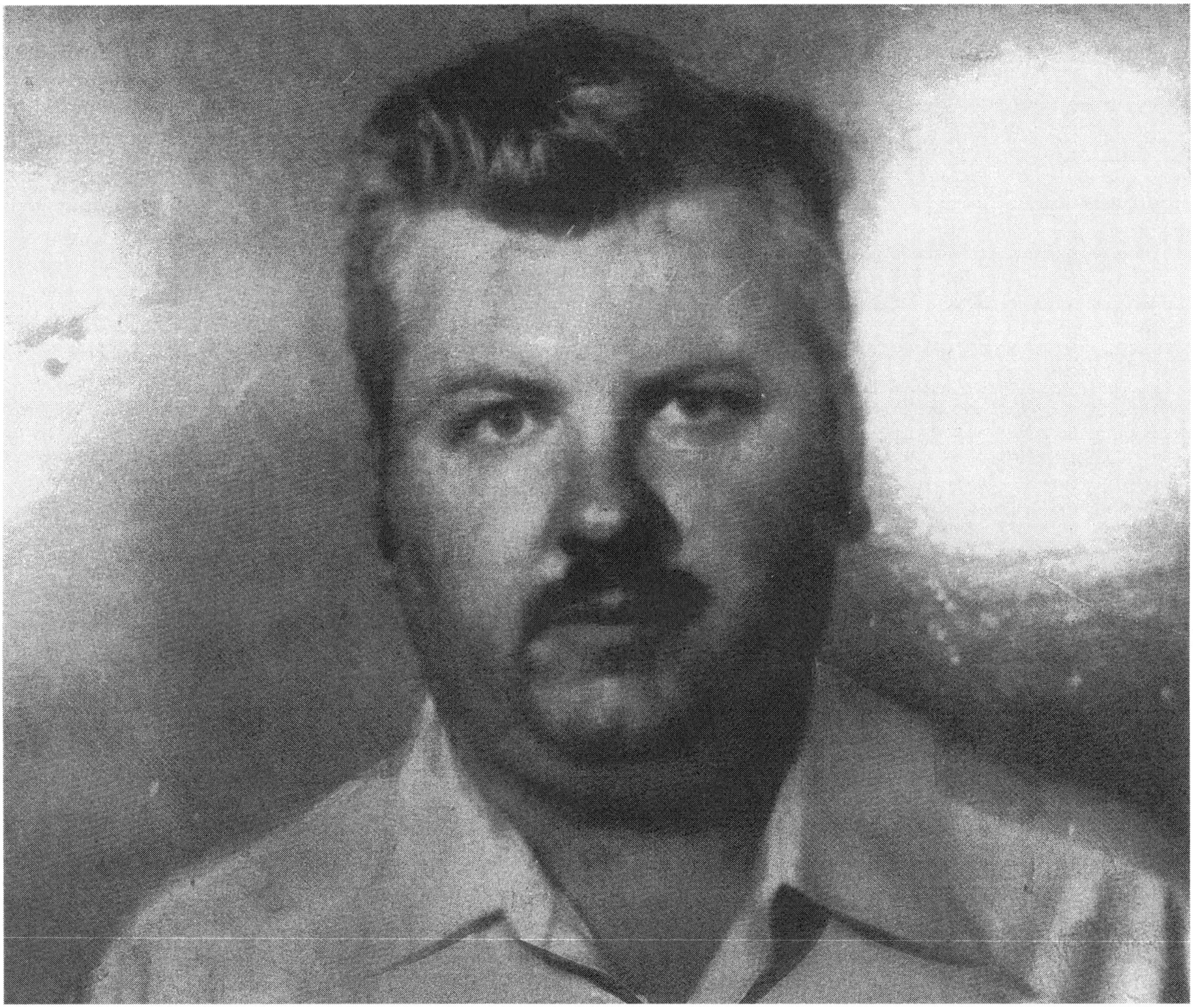

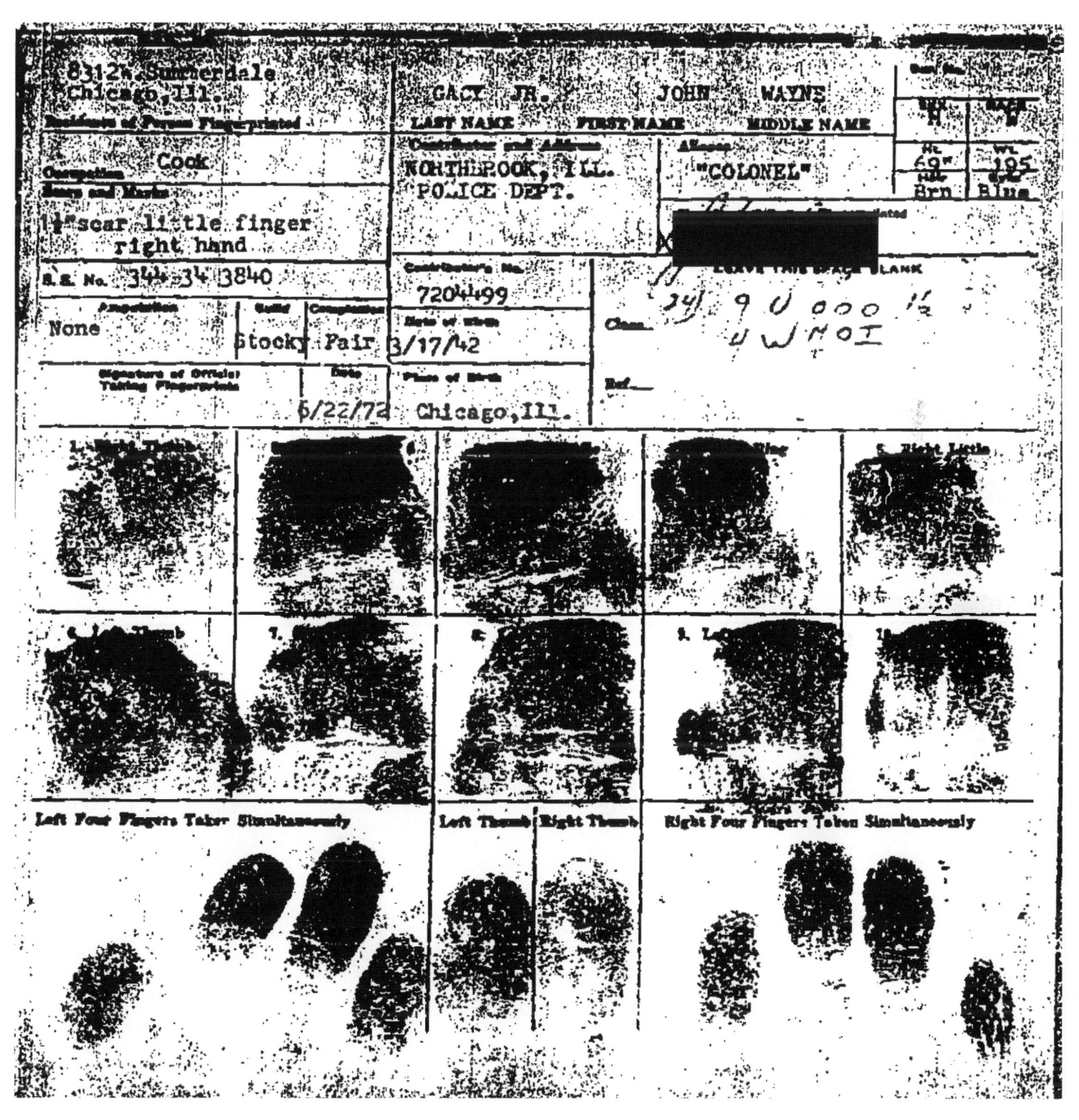

Gacy's Northbrook, IL arrest on 6/22/72. Gacy had murdered one victim by this point.

ROB PIEST AND THE DES PLAINES P.D.

Missing Youth

Piest,

NARRATIVE:

At approximately 0845 hours this date Mrs. Piest came to the police station with her son, Kenneth, and daughter to discuss the above captioned incident. In essence Mrs. Piest indicated that at approximately 2100 hours on December 11, 1978 she went to Nisson Pharmacy, 1920 Touhy Avenue, to pick up her son, at which time she spoke briefly with the missing youth and, because of the fact that he did not re-enter the store by 2120 hours, she left the area of the pharmacy and returned home. At approximately 2140 hours Mrs. Piest again contacted Nisson Pharmacy, at which time she was advised that as of that time the youth had not returned to the store. Mrs. Piest contacted the store on a second occasion at approximately 2155 hours, at which time Robert had not yet returned to work. At 2329 hours Mrs. Piest filed the missing person's report with this department.

At 0907 hours I contacted Larry Torf, at Nisson Pharmacy, tx 827-4700, and was advised that Phillip Torf might be able to provide this Officer with additional information regarding the missing youth.

I then contacted Phillip Torf at home, tx ███████, and received the following information. Phillip Torf stated that a contractor named John Gacy had entered the pharmacy on two occasions, the first being at 1800 hours and the second being at approximately 2000 hours. During the time Mr. Gacy was in the pharmacy, apparently a conversation between John Gacy and Phillip Torf took place, in which case Gacy had mentioned that he hires high school ___ for his business which is referred to as P D M. The P D M stands for Painting, Decorating & Maintenance. Phillip Torf was unable to state for certain that John Gacy had any specific conversation with the missing youth, although it is possible that Robert Piest may have overheard the conversation regarding the hiring of youths between Gacy and Phillip Torf. Mr. Torf stated that the reason Mr. Gacy was in their establishment, was he had done some remodeling approximately two years ago and at the present time Gacy works at two pharmacies. Phillip Torf stated that on December 11, 1978 after the store had received the calls from Mrs. Piest, he contacted the message service for John Gacy, tx 457-1614, although Gacy never recontacted him. During my conversation with Larry Torf, Larry indicated that Phillip Torf made a statement to Kim Byers to the effect that Rob was talking to the guy about a job.

At approximately 0915 hours I contacted P.D.M. Contractors and spoke with John Gacy. Mr. Gacy indicated that he had been in the pharmacy and had questioned Mr. Torf about some fixtures in the backyard. When asked if he had spoken with the missing youth, Mr. Gacy replied no and, when again asked if he had any personal contact with the youth, he stated no.

At 0932 hours I again contacted Larry Torf and determined that Kim Byers lives on Gregory Lane and that Kim may have additional information regarding the incident. I then determined that Kim Byers resides at 8704 D Gregory Lane, tx 824-1612.

At approximately 0942 hours I contacted Kim Byers and I was advised that Rob Piest had left the store at approximately 2100 hours and prior to leaving he made a statement to the effect "That contractor guy wants to talk to me." Upon questioning the Byer youth further, she stated that he had left some of his personal belongings in the store and she had described the youth as kind of spacey at times and indicated that on occasion he has a tendency to forget things. Kim Byers indicated that she did not observe the missing youth talking to John Gacy and did not observe the two together in the pharmacy.

At 1035 hours I went to Maine West and, in the presence of Assistant Principal Eldon Burke and Boys Dean Jurinek, I interviewed Ken Collier, tx ███████. The Collier youth stated that he had last spoken with the missing youth at approximately 1800 hours on 12-11-78 and at that time had no indication that the missing youth had any problems at home, in school or at the pharmacy. The Collier youth did indicate that at about the time of the homecoming Rob broke up with his girlfriend, Cary Gibbons, tx ███████ although he does not feel that would be sufficient reason for the youth to leave home. Upon terminating the interview with the Collier youth, I then went to Nisson Pharmacy and spoke with Todd Schludt, tx ███████ to determine if he could provide this Officer with any information.

Todd stated that he had contacted Cary Gibbons between 1000 and 1030 hours this date, although she had no information that would indicate the whereabouts of the youth.

I then went to Wall's Liquors and spoke with Stanley Wall, as it is common knowledge that the youths employed at the pharmacy purchase soda from the liquor store. Kenneth Piest advised this Officer that his brother usually purchased A & W Root Beer in bottles from Wall's, and that perhaps an employee of the liquor store might have observed Rob in the store. Upon speaking with Mr. Wall, it was determined that Timmy Kehl, tx ███████ worked until 2200 hours on December 11, 1978 and that Steve Mortowski, tx ███████ started at 2000 hours and that, although neither of the employees were present at that time, Timmy Kehl will begin work at approximately 1600 hours this date. Mr. Wall was advised to have Timmy Kehl contact this Officer as soon as he reports to the liquor store.

At approximately 1334 hours I contacted ... Byers, at which time he advised this Officer that his daughter, Kim, was presently attending school at Maine North. He had no objection if we interviewed her at school.

At approximately 1357 hours I went to Maine North High School and, in the presence of Gloria Mazone, Kim Byers, DOB: 08-22-61, was interviewed from 1357 until approximately 1425 hours. Miss Byers stated that she did not remember John Gacy leaving the store, although he had been in making some measurements and was rearranging items. She further advised this Officer that in her opinion Rob has no reason to leave home. Upon questioning the Byers youth further, she indicated that Rob had left the store between 2100 and 2102 hours and she is relatively certain of the time, as he had called her to the front of the store stating "Come watch the register," at which time she asked where are you going and he stated "The contractor guy wants to talk to me. I'll be right back." Kim Byers stated that during the time Rob made that statement, Mrs. Piest was in the store. Kim further advised this Officer that Rob had been in and out of the store a few times to take out the garbage and at least on one occasion he had entered the store through the back door. She believes that he took the garbage out at approximately 2000 hours, as during that time he was struck by snowballs which were allegedly thrown by little kids. Upon further questioning her about other statements which she allegedly made, specifically the statement regarding a big boy, she advised this Officer that she had made a statement to the effect that Rob is a big boy he can take care of himself and, although she is not certain that statement may have been directed to Phil Torf. Ms. Byers stated that she doubts that the individuals at the liquor store could be of any assistance, because Rob did not enter that establishment to purchase any soda on 12-11-78. Ms. Byers was advised to contact this Officer in the event she should develop any information that would

DES PLAINES POLICE DEPARTMENT
DAILY BULLETIN

CONFIDENTIAL - FOR POLICE USE ONLY

14 DECEMBER 78

MISSING YOUTH

RD# 78-35203   LEADS W7857880

Robert J. PIEST, DOB 031663, 5'8", 140 lbs, brown/brown, hair worn shag style, slim build, wearing light blue hooded down filled jacket, tan T-shirt, tan levi pants, brown leather belt, brown suede type tie shoes.

Youth last seen at approximately 2100 hrs, on 11 December 78. Youth disappeared from the area of 1920 Touhy Avenue, Des Plaines.

Any information, contact the Youth Bureau immediately, TX 297-2131, ext. 222.

Missing youth resides at 2722 Craig Drive.

BEAT

A-11	BURGLARY F/ VEHICLE 78-35373	12-13 DEC 78 - 1700-0800 HRS - 1870 BUSSE - PARKING LOT. Door & window lock forced open.
A-21	BURGLARY F/ VEHICLE 78-35338	11-13 DEC 78 - 1715-1400 HRS - 750 NORTHWEST HWY - DEALER LOT. (2) silver bucket seats taken from 1978 Ford van.
	BURGLARY F/ VEHICLE 78-35359	13 DEC 78 - 1200-1530 HRS - CENTRAL @ DES PLAINES RIVER - ROAD SHOULDER. Miscellaneous items taken.
31	BURGLARY F/ VEHICLE 78-35367	12-13 DEC 78 - 1700-0730 HRS - BEHREL CITY LOT - PARKING GARAGE. Taken: Radio Shack 40 Channel C.B. and antenna.

(OVER)

MISSING YOUTH

Robert J. PIEST, DOB 031663, 5'8", 140 lbs. brown/brown, hair worn shag style, slim build.

Youth last seen at approximately 2100 hrs, on 11 DEC 78. Youth disappeared from the area of Nisson Pharmacy.

Youth disappeared under suspicious circumstances.

Any information, contact the Youth Bureau immediately, Tx. 297-2131, ext. 222.

Missing youth resides at ███████████ Des Plaines.

indicate the whereabouts of the missing youth.

The Dean of Students at Maine West, Fred Bancriscutto, and the Dean of Boys, George Jurinek, have been advised of the reported missing youth. Gloria Mazzoni, the Dean of Girls at Maine North, having been present during the conference with Kim Byers, is also aware of the missing youth and will contact this Officer in the event she should develop any information. It has been determined that the teletype message is active and a special message was placed on the Daily Bulletin dated 12 December 1978.

R.D. # 78-35203

C.I.D. CONTINUATION REPORT

Missing Youth

Piest, Robert

13 December 1978 1500

On December 12, 1978 at 0915 hours reporting officer as the Commander of the Criminal Investigation Division, had occassion to review report 78-35203 which was a missing person report on a young boy who was identified as:

Robert J. Piest M/W 15 YOA 5'8" 140 Bro/Bro
Present address:
D.O.B.

This report was subsequently assigned to a youth officer for further investigation as the background information on this boy warranted further attention by this department. Youth Officer Ronald Adams was assigned by this reporting officer to gather more information on this matter.

At 1200 hours this date (12-12-78) Sgt. R. Fredricks, Supv. of the Youth Bureau and reporting officer had occassion to meet with Det. Adams and upon receiving a summary report of this case, reporting officer directed Sgt. Fredricks to bring in more man-power to assist Det. Adams in his investigation. Det. Adams was advised by this R/O to make periodic reports into R/Os office so the case could be evaluated on an hour to hour basis.

At this time the following two officers were assigned to this case by R/O:

Det. Michael Olsen
Det. James Pickell

At approximately 1330 hours this date R/O had received information that a construction worker by the name of John W. Gacy had been in the drug store and that his address of business was not immediately available. His current TX is 457-1614. At this time R/O with the cooperation of the telephone company was able to locate a business in Norridge by the the name of PDM Contractors and the address given by the telephine company was 8213 West Summerdale, Norridge, IL.

R/O assigned Det. Pickell to proceed to the above location of John W. Gacy's residence and try to obtain further information from Mr. Gacy as to what he observed at the drug store on the night of the boys disappearence.

13 December 1978

R.D. # 78-35203

| | 28 Dec 78 | 1215 Hours |

Missing

Piest, Robert

NARRATIVE

On the above time and date Mr. Boso was contacted at the Salvation Army Warehouse, 2258 North Kilbourn, Chicago, Il. 477-1300, in reference to pick up boxes which might be owned by their organization. We specifically requested information regarding the pick up boxes at the following locations; Harlem and Irving, Harlem and Golf, Belle Plaine Avenue, and 4880 North Milwaukee Avenue. Mr. Boso stated that the boxes at those locations are emptied every evening, in which case the items collected at those locations are moved to their warehouse and are shipped from the warehouse on the following morning. The items that are of some value are shipped to the Salvation Army Outlet Stores and the articles of clothing which are of no value are packaged in large bundles and are used as rags. Mr. Boso stated that he would direct a memo to their various stores in an attempt to locate the items which had been worn by the missing youth and were allegedly discarded by Mr. Gacy in a collection box at either Harlem and Irving or Lawrence and Cumberland.

28 Dec 78

C.S.D. SUPPLEMENTARY REPORT / DES PLAINES POLICE 12 Dec 78 2350 Hours

Missing Person

Piest, Robert

CONFIDENTIAL

At approximately 1330 hours this date Reporting Officer Pickell arrived at the Des Plaines Station and was briefed by Detective Adams in reference to the above incident. Reporting Officer was advised that a person who may have last had conversation with the above missing youth was Mr. John W. Gacy, tx 457-1614. Lt. Kozenczak traced this telephone number through the telephone company and learned that the number was registered to John W. Gacy, 8213 West Summerdale, Norridge, Illinois. Information was also received from Robert Piest's employer, Mr. Phillip Torf, of Nisson Pharmacy, 1920 Touhy, that Mr. John Gacy has a Christmas Tree lot on Cumberland Avenue between Foster and Lawrence. The Christmas Tree lot was reportedly on the west side of Cumberland next to a church with five steeples.

Reporting Officer Pickell proceeded to that location and located a Christmas Tree lot just north of St. Joseph's Ukrainian Church, 5000 North Cumberland. Reporting Officer proceeded to the Christmas Tree Lot Office and spoke with the gentleman inside, asking for Mr. John Gacy. The gentleman indicated that no John Gacy was involved with that particular Christmas Tree Lot. He indicated, however, that there was a lot further north on Cumberland and he might be associated with that Christmas Tree Lot. Two vehicles were parked in the Christmas Tree Lot. The first vehicle was a brown over tan '73 Plymouth 4 door with Illinois '78 license 566-101, which registers to Richard Fugiel, 6634 North Ogallah, Chicago. The second vehicle was a '76 red Dodge Van with Illinois '78 license ███████, which registers to Louis Pietlos, of ███████.

Reporting Officer next proceeded to a Christmas Tree Lot which was located on the east side of Cumberland just south of Bryn Mawr. Reporting Officer spoke with a middle aged couple in the trailer located at that lot and neither party admitted knowing or hearing of Mr. John Gacy. They referred Reporting Officer to the Christmas Tree Lot next to the Ukrainian Church which had just been checked.

Reporting Officer Pickell next proceeded to the home of Mr. Gacy, 8213 West Summerdale in Norridge. Reporting Officer knocked at both the front and back doors, but there was no one apparently home.

Reporting Officer next went to the next door neighbor west of the Gacy residence and inquired of the neighbor if she knew where Mr. Gacy's Christmas Tree Lot was located. She stated that she did not. She further advised that since Mr. Gacy's 1979 Oldsmobile 4 door sedan license ███████ was in his driveway, he was probably out in his truck. She advised that the truck would be easy to spot, since it had PDM Maintenance painted on the side. A 10-28 for ███████ is attached to this report.

Reporting Officer Pickell next returned to the station and attempted to collect some information on Mr. Gacy which might be useful in this investigation. Reporting Officer ran a name check through the Chicago Police Department and it was learned that he was arrested in Chicago reference I.R. 273632. Mr. Gacy's Date of Birth is 17 March 1942.

Reporting Officer next contacted the Records Section of the Chicago Police Department and spoke with Officer Washington, tx 744-5565. Officer Washington gave Reporting Officer the following information:

#1: 20 May 1968 - Waterloo, Iowa - Sodomy - 10 years
#2: 9 September 1968 - Conspiracy - Assault With Attempt To Commit Felony - C.D.3036939.
#3: 12 September 1968 - Burglary and Entry
#4: 11 December 1968 (Reference 26526 Blackhawk County)
#5: 18 June 1970 - Paroled To Chicago
#6: 19 October 1971 - Parole Discharge (Served 18 months 10 #26426)
#7: 12 February 1971 - Disorderly Conduct - Discharged
#8: 9 March 1971 - D/P (Refers To Above Disorderly Conduct Charge)
#9: 22 June 1972 - Northbrook, Illinois - Aggravated Battery, Reckless Conduct - SOL (Northbrook Case #7204499).
#10: 15 July 1978 - Battery - Officer Burke, 16th District, Chicago Police Department. No Disposition.

A check was then made on John W. Gacy, M/W, DOB: 03-17-42, through LEADS, NCIC, and CCH. No record indicated.

Reporting Officer Pickell next contacted Northbrook Police Department, Detective Dick Adamek, tx 564-2060, in reference to their reported arrest of Mr. John Gacy on 22 June 1972. Detective Adamek advised that Mr. John Gacy was a Male/White, 5'9", 195 pounds, brown hair, blue eyes, and he resided at 8213 West Summerdale, Norridge, tx 457-1614. Illinois D.L.#. G200-4794-2079. He further advised that Mr. Gacy attended Prosser Vocational High School in Chicago. Reporting Officer requested Detective Adamek to furnish a copy of the original case report #7204499, a copy of the fingerprint card of John W. Gacy and a copy of Mr. Gacy's mug shot. Reporting Officer proceeded to Northbrook Police Department and picked up the aforementioned items, see attached.

At 1640 hours on 12 December 78 Reporting Officer spoke with Kevin Martin, ████████████████, a friend of Robert Piest. Kevin advised that he last saw Robert about one week ago and Robert said nothing and gave no indication of any kind of a problem either at home or at school. Kevin stated that he did not inquire of Robert whether or not there were any problems, since they were not that close in friendship. Kevin advised that Robert was a very straight young man as far as he was concerned.

At 1645 hours on 12-12-78 Reporting Officer Pickell spoke with Georgene Ketchum, ████████████████. Georgene advised that she had seen Rob within the past few days, but she didn't remember exactly when. She advised that she was quite a good friend of Rob's and up to a couple of months ago she knew for certain that Rob had no problems either at home or at school. She stated that within the past two months she has not had a conversation with Rob relating to any problems he might have had, but she did not believe that he had any.

Reporting Officer attempted to contact another named friend, Joseph Jones, ████████████████. Reporting Officer spoke with the father of Joseph, who advised that Joseph is at school in Champaign, Illinois, and the last time that he was home was Thanksgiving. Investigation to continue.

C.I.D. CONTINUATION REPORT ☐

C.I.D. SUPPLEMENTARY REPORT / DES PLAINES POLICE

13 DECEMBER 1978

Missing Youth

Piest, Robert

NARRATIVE:

At 1730 hours on December 12, 1978 R/O was contacted at his residence regarding an update on the Piest investigation. Det. Adams advised R/O that at this time there were no further paths of investigation left and Det. Adams requested direction regarding what further steps should be taken regarding the missing boy.

R/O advised Det. Adams to stand-by at the Youth Bureau, while R/O contacted Cook County States Attorney/Felony Review at 26th & Califirnia, Chicago, IL. At this time R/O contacted the Night Duty States Attorney and advised him of the facts surrounding this case. R/O told the on-duty S/A that Mr. Gacy was in the drug store on the night that the boy disappeared and that Mr. Gacy also had a long rap sheet that contained a conviction for Sodomy in the state of Iowa.

The S/A was advised by Lt. Kozenczak that R/O wanted to go to Mr. Gacys residence and question him in regard to the boy disappearing on the same night that Mr. Gacy was in the drug store. The on-duty S/A told this R/O that I should be very careful regarding the questioning of this subject as the subject could refuse to admit R/O into his residence and it would be to R/Os advantage to possibly discuss this case with States Attorneys in Dist. 3. R/O explained that he had tried to reach the 3rd District S/A but none were available for a conferance.

At this time R/O decided to go to the Gacy house and advised Det. Pickell to stand-by at HQ and to have Det. Olsen and Det. Sommerschield prepare to accompany R/O to Mr. Gacys residence.

At 2100 hours on 12 December 1978 R/O returned to the Des Plaines Police HQ. and held a briefing with Det. Pickell, Det. Olsen and Det. Sommerschield. R/O advised that a decision was made that we would all proceed to the residence of John W. Gacy and would utilize two squads. All officers concerned were told that this would be a informal type interview and we would be asking Mr. Gacy for his cooperation in this matter and R/O would then ask Mr. Gacy to accompany us back to the Des Plaines Police HQ. for further queastioning.

At 2130 hours all of the aforementioned officers and R/O proceeded to the home of John W. Gacy, 8213 W. Summerdale, Norridge, IL. Upon arrival R/O directed Det. Olsen and Det. Sommerscheild to go to the rear of the residence and R/O and Det. Pickell went to the front door. At this time R/O knocked on the front door and after several minutes it was noted by R/O that the shadow of a subject could be seen staring out of a small window in the front door, but whoever this subject was he would not resond to R/O s knocking. At this time a van type vehicle pulled inot the driveway of the Gacy residence and the driver identified himself as Michael Rossi, an employee of PDM Contractors. Mr. Rossi advsied R/O that Mr. Gacy would not answer the front door and that R/O should go to the East side of the residence and knock on the side door.

R.D. # 78-35203

J. Kozenczak   Commander/CID

Upon proceeding to the East side of the residence R/O stopped in front of a large picture window and upon looking into the window R/O observed a subject who was identified by Mr. Rossi, as John W. Gacy. Mr. Gacy was sitting in a recliner chair watching television.

R/O knocked on the back door and Mr. Gacy responded by opening the door and prior to R/O identifying himself as a Police Officer Mr. Gacy staed " I heard you knocking at the front door, but I was in the bathroom". R/O identified himself as a police officer and told him that we were at his home to ask him some questions regarding a missing boy from the City of Des Plaines. R/O advised Mr. Gacy that we had information that he was in the drug store on the same night that R.Piest was in there.

At this time Mr. Gacy stated that he had been in the drug store (Nisson Pharmacy) on the night in question and that he came to the drug store after being called by one of the owners (Mr. Phil Torf) to do an estimate for work inside of the drug store. Mr. Gacy denied that he even saw anyone in the drug store who would match the missing boys description, however he vaguely recalled two younger people who were employees of the drug store. He denied having any conversation with these youths , but may have asked one of them if there were any old shelving at the outside rear of the drug store.

Mr. Gacy told R/O that he left the drug store around 2045 hours and went directly home. Mr. Gacy advised R/O that upon his arrival at home he had received information that his uncle had died, at which time he had gone to Northwest Hospital which is located at Central & Addison,Chicago,IL. for the purpose of talking with his Aunt, who was the wife of the deceased uncle.

R/O advised Mr. Gacy that R/O would like Mr. Gacy to accompany him to the Des Plaines Police Headquarters for the purpose of him writing a witness statement out regarding what he remembered about the night at the Nisson Drug Store when the boy disappeared. Mr. Gacy stated that he would not be able go right at this time as he was expecting a long distance call from his mother in Arkansas, regarding the death of his uncle. At the prompting of R/O, Mr. Gacy called his mother and conversed with her for about 10 minutes. At the end of the conversation on the phone. Mr. Gacy was about to get his coat when the side door opened and Michael Rossi entered the residence. (Mr. Rossi had been detained out side of the house by Det. Olsen & Det. Sommerschield) Once Mr. Rossi entered, Mr. Gacy appeared to gain some confodence and told R/O that he would not go with him as he had more important things to do. R/O advsied Mr. Gacy that the missing boy was also an important issue and that the boys parents were very concerned about his disappearence.

Mr. Gacy told R/O that he had some other things to do and he would try to come into the station later this evening. R/O gave his business card to Mr. Gacy and told him that I would stay at the station waiting for his arrival.

Upon leaving the residence R/O assigned Det. Sommerschield & Det. Olsen to stake out the Gacy residence and to keep R/O advised of any activity that might take place once R/O and Det. Pickell left the area. Det.S & Det.O. set up an observation point about a ½ block east of the residence on Summerdale St.

Upon leaving the area of Mr. Gacys residence R/O and Det. Pickell were proceeding North on Cumberland Ave at the Kennedy Expressway when radio traffic was received from Det. Sommerschield that they had lost Mr. Gacy who was driving his private vehicle, in the area of Summerdale & Cumberland Ave. The R/O then advised the stake-out team to proceed to the Des Plaines Police HQ. for further instructions.

While at the CID HQ. R/O received a call from Mr. Gacy around 2300 Hrs. at which time Mr. Gacy asked this R/O if Lt. Kozenczak still wanted to talk with him. R/O advised Mr. Gacy that I did want to talk with him and that I would wait for him at the Des Plaines Police HQ. R/O waited for Mr. Gacy until around 0100 Hrs. and at this time R/O left word with the 11/7 Desk Officer that if Mr. Gacy shows up tell him that he is to report to the DPPD in the morning of 13 December 1978.

R.D. #78-35203

C.I.D. CONTINUATION REPORT

FIELD SUPPLEMENTARY REPORT / DES PLAINES POLICE

Date/Time: 13-DEC-78 0330

Original Offense: MISSING PERSON
Offense Changed To: SA-2

Victim: PIEST, ROBERT

NARRATIVE:

At 0050 hours, Lt. J. Kozenczak advised the R/O that he had been expecting a Mr. John Gacey to come into the station and talk with him, but Mr. Gacey was late. Lt. Kozenczak stated he could not wait any longer and advised the R/O that if Mr. Gacey showed up, the R/O was to tell Mr. Gacey to come back first thing in the morning.

At 0320 hours, 13-Dec-78, a man identifying himself as Mr. John Gacey entered the station. The R/O told Mr. Gacey that Lt. Kozenczak could not wait and had to leave, and that he, Mr. Gacey, was to come back first thing in the morning. Mr. Gacey appeared somewhat apprehensive and asked the R/O what Lt. Kozenczak wanted to see him about. The R/O told Mr. Gacey that the R/O had no information. Mr. Gacey then told the R/O that the reason he was late was because he had been involved in some sort of automobile accident. Mr. Gacey then left the station.

The R/O observed that Mr. Gacey's eyes were glassy and he had fresh mud on his pants and shoes.

Date/Time Report Completed: 0358 HRS. 13-DEC-78

SUPPLEMENTARY REPORT / DES PLAINES POLICE
13 DECEMBER 1978

Missing Youth

Piest, Robert

NARRATIVE:

Upon R/O arriving at work at 0800 Hrs. 13 December 1978 it was observed that a note had been left for R/O by the 11/7 Desk officer, which stated that Mr. Gacy had shown up at the DPPD asking for R/O at about 0330 Hrs. The D/O stated that Mr. Gacys clothes were disarrayed and tha he had a glassey look in his eyes. The D/O advsied Mr. Gacy that R/O had gone home for the day and that R/O had requested Mr. Gacy to come back in the morning of 13 December 1978 for an interview with R/O.

After reviewing the total amount of evidence in this case R/O called the States Attorneys office in the Des Plaines Civic Center in order to have a S/A review R/Os case packet on this matter as R/O felt that a search warrant should be obtained to search the residence of Mr. Gacy. At this time R/O felt that because of Mr. Gacys background in sex crimes dealing with boys of similar age as Robert Piest that their was a possibility that Mr. Gacy was holding the Piest boy as a prisoner in his residence.

R/O was advised by the secretary in the D.P. S/A office that no one was available for review of this matter for a search warrant, but that around 1200 Hours the 3rd Dist. Supervisor Terry Sullivan might be stopping by from the Niles office.

At 1100 Hours R/O received a call from Mr. Gacy and Mr. Gacy again asked R/O if he still wanted to talk with Mr. Gacy. R/O advsied Mr. Gacy that it would still be necessary that he come to our station for a witness statement and Mr. Gacy stated that he would be in prior to 1200 Hours.

R/O prepared all of the necessary documents to present to the states attorney for a search warrant request. At this time R/O assigned Det. Pickell to stand-by the station and in the event that Mr. Gacy shows up he is to have Mr. Gacy fill out a witness statement. Det. Pickell was assisted in this assignment by Sgt. K. Fredricks.

At 1200 Hrs. R/O met with S/A Terry Sullivan and advised him that I wanted a search warrant for Mr. Gacys residence and vehicles. The total case was explained to Mr. Sullivan and he agreed to help in this case by approving the request and assisting with having the warrant approved by Judge Marvin Peters. S/A Sullivan assigned S/A Investigator Bedoe to assist R/O in drawing up the Request for Search Warrant & the Search Warrant itself

During the time period that the Search Warrant was being obtained by R/O, information was received that Mr. Gacy had shown up and had written a witness statement. During the course of his writing this statement, Sgt. K. Fredricks asked Mr. Gacy if he would like to take a polygraph regarding the missing boy and Mr. Gacy flatly refused and asked to call his attorney.

At this time Mr. Gacy was advised that he was being held by our department for further investigation and that R/O was in the process of obtaining a search warrant for his residence. At this time R/O asked Mr. Gacy for the keys to his residence and he stated that he wanted to talk with his attorney before giving up the keys. After some discussion R/O obtained the keys for Mr. Gacys residence.

Date/Time Report Completed: 13 DECEMBER 1978

R.D. #78-35203

J. Kozenczak, Commander/CID

Upon the completion of typing the Request for and the Warrant (Search) itself, R/O in the company of S/A Sullivan went in front of Judge Marvin Peters and presented these documents for Judge Peters approval. At 1540 hours the Search Warrant was approved and R/O called next door to the DPPD to advise Det. Pickell not to release Mr. Gacy.

R/O called a meeting of all available investigative staff and advised them that we would be proceeding to 8213 W. Summerdale to search the residence of Mr. Gacy. The officers who participated in this search process were: Lt. Kozenczak(R/O), Det. Pickell, Det. Kautz, Det. Tovar, Det. Adams, Det. Olsen and and assisting with evidence processing would be Off. Karl Humbert of the C.C.S.P., as Mr. Gacys house is located within the jurisdiction of the Cook County Sheriff. The search warrant that was authorized is S.A. 78-1-003792

Initial entry was made into the residence by R/O and it was noted that the residence was in complete darkness. Upon completion of the search Mr. Gacys residence was secured and all items of evidence secured were returned to the DPPD for processing and inventory. The search was culminated at around 1900 Hrs. 12/13/78.

At 2200 Hours 12/13/78, Mr. Gacy was interviewed briefly by Lt. Kozenczak & Inv. Bedoe. Prior to this interview and in the presence of his attorney Mr. Stevens, Mr. Gacy was given his Miranda warnings and was asked to sign the Miranda sheet. After some discussion with his attorney Mr. Gacy signed the Miranda sheet in the presence of his attorney, Lt. Kozenczak & Inv. Bedoe.

Mr. Gacy refused to answer any questions and asked R/O if he was under arrest. R/O advised Mr. Gacy that he was not under arrest and at this time Mr. Gacy was released from the DPPD in the company of his attorney.

R.D. # 78-35203

C.I.D. CONTINUATION REPORT

CONFIDENTIAL

At 1600 hours Reporting Officer was informed of the circumstances surrounding Robert Piest's disappearance by Detective Adams. He requested this Officer to contact a group of youths whose names were underlined in Robert's Maine West High School Telephone Directory to determine if they had any pertinent information. Reporting Officer interviewed the following youths by telephone:

James C. Penkala,
Yolanda Quille,
Gundalupe Reyes,
Karen L. Roehrig,
James E. Rosner,
Diane Sakal,
Janet L. Schuldt,
Joanne Scelsa,
Edmund Williams,
Kathy Winiecki,
Katherine R. Kramer,
David B. Blessing,
Michael L. Miller,

All youths questioned, with the exception of Yolanda Quille, who stated she did not know Robert Piest, had the highest opinion of the boy. All stated that he was definitely not the type of boy who would run away or do things on impulse. They stated that to their knowledge the boy was not involved with drugs. None of them had any idea where he might be at this time. The last youth to have seen the victim was Michael Miller. He saw the boy at Nisson Pharmacy at approximately 1930 hours on 11 December 78. He had no conversation with Robert, outside of saying hello. He seemed to be in good spirits at that time.

Reporting Officer was not able to contact two of the names Detective Adams assigned him. James Rosner and Kenneth Quinn, were both out of town in college and, according to their parents, probably would have not been in contact with the victim. Reporting Officer also interviewed a Pat Horndasch, Steven P. Bahr, and Venessa Berry, Pat Horndasch related that he last saw the victim at gymnastics practice at Maine West High School. This was on 11 December 78 at approximately 1730 hours. He had had conversations with the victim during practice, but noticed nothing unusual. Steven Bahr states he is no longer a close friend of the victim. He has no ideas as to the youth's whereabouts. Venessa Berry related that she hasn't seen the victim since last summer. Reporting Officer also attempted to contact Randy J. Uidl, He wasn't at home, but a message was left for him to contact this Officer. As of this time he has not done so.

Reporting Officer also interviewed Tim Harris, ███████████████ Tim had no pertinent information.

R.D. # 78-35203

C.I.D. CONTINUATION REPORT ☐

SUPPLEMENTARY REPORT / DES PLAINES POLICE	13 Dec 78 0955 Hours
Missing Person	
Piest, Robert	2722 Craig Drive, Des Plaines

CONFIDENTIAL

At 0935 hours this date Reporting Officer contacted the Missing Persons Section of the Chicago Police Department to get information on the proper procedure for having information and photograph of the above missing person placed on the Chicago Daily Bulletin. Reporting Officer was advised that first of all a teletype message should be sent from Des Plaines to the Missing Persons Section of the Chicago Police Department giving name of the missing person and all pertinent information. After this is done, a letter should be sent to the Commander of the Missing Persons Section, along with a photograph of the missing person, and a request should be made that the photograph and information of the missing person should be placed on the Chicago Daily Bulletin. Reporting Officer Pickell will see that this is done.

Reporting Officer Pickell next contacted Mr. Valdez, the Supervisor at the Admitting Desk at the Cook County Morgue, tx 443-6161. He was advised that Reporting Officer was running a routine check with various agencies to determine if any information relative to the above missing person could be learned. Mr. Valdez advised that at this time they have no unknown male/white subjects. He advised that he would collect information relative to the above missing person and post it at the admitting desk so that if any unknown male/white should come in matching the description of the above missing person, he will immediately contact this department.

R.D. # 78-35203

13 Dec 78

Directed Message

Det. J. Pickell 229

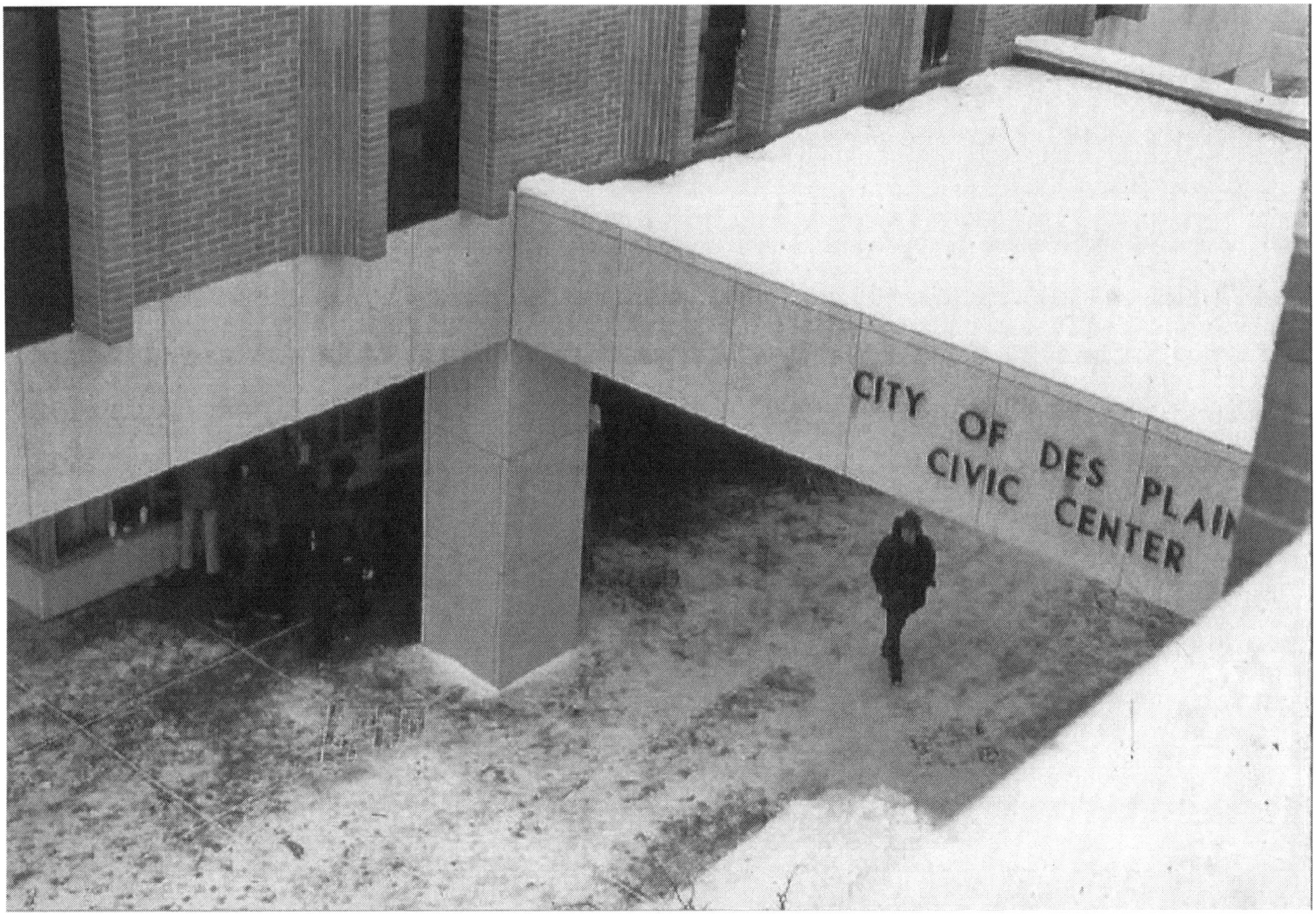
CITY OF DES PLAIN
CIVIC CENTER

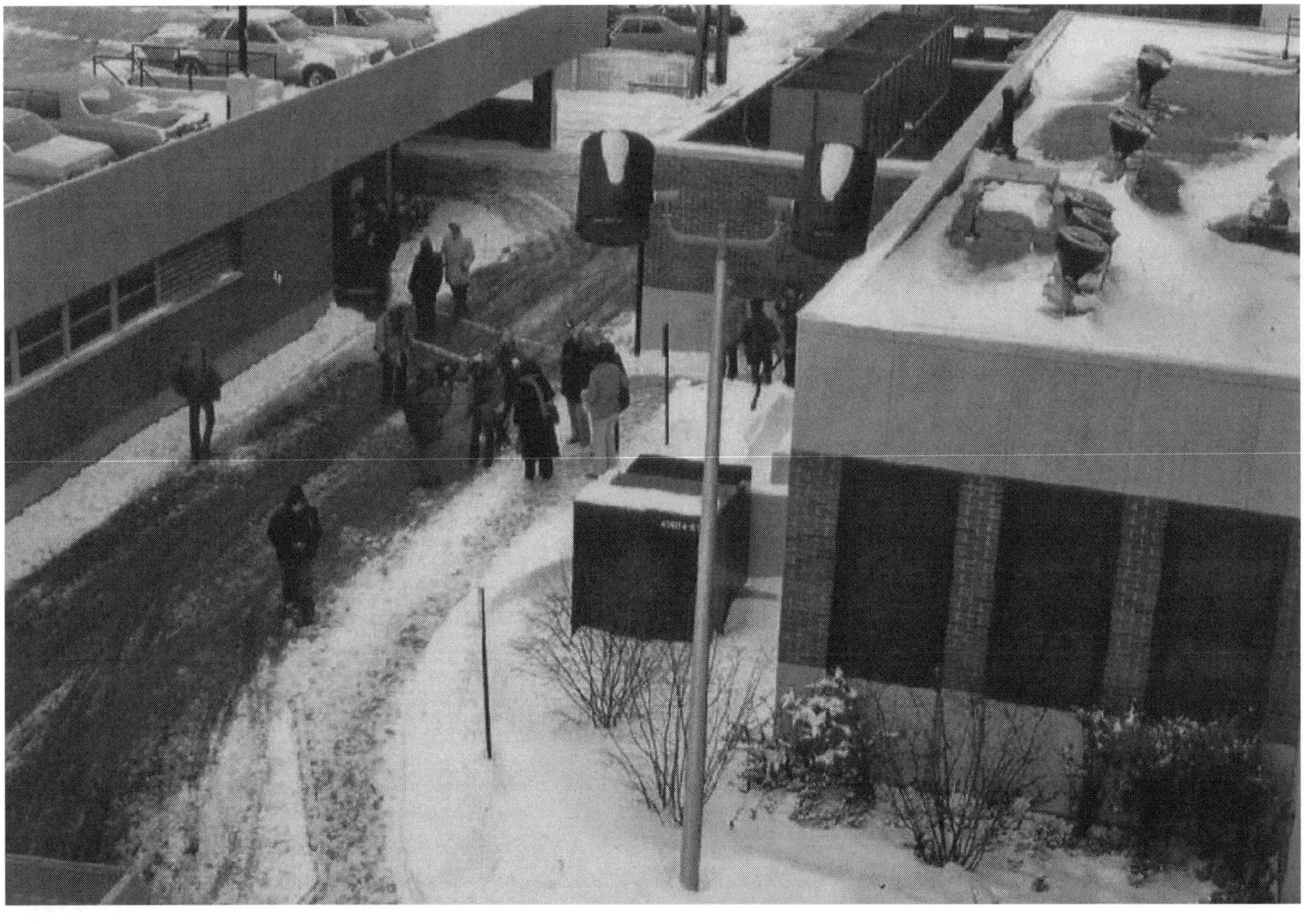

Lieutenant Kozenczak (center) and the Des Plaines, IL Detectives who investigated the disappearance of Rob Piest.

The Des Plaines, IL Police Department. (opposite page)

EVIDENCE RECOVERED FROM FIRST SEARCH WARRANT

VEHICLE TOW REPORT / DES PLAINES POLICE

Time: 1256 **Date:** 13 DEC. 78 **1403**

A-11	155	A-11	1403	WED

8. REASON FOR TOW:

1. ☐ ABANDONED — CITY CODE 10-14-2 / 7-DAY NOTICE ISSUED _____ DATE _____ TIME _____
2. ☐ ILLEGAL PARKING - PRIVATE PROPERTY — CITY CODE 10-13-1 / CITATION NO _____
3. ☐ RECOVERED STOLEN VEHICLE   LOCAL ☐   FOREIGN ☐
4. ☒ HOLD FOR INVESTIGATION - EXPLAIN IN NARRATIVE
5. ☐ TRAFFIC HAZARD — OBSTRUCTING TRAFFIC - CITATION NO _____ / EXPLAIN IN NARRATIVE
6. ☐ UNDER ARREST - VEHICLE CONTROLLED BY ARRESTEE

Location of Vehicle: 1454 HINES ☒ STREET **Towed by:** SCHIMKA **To:** SECURITY GARAGE **Date/Time Heads Checked:** 13 DEC 78 1615

Color: BLK **Year:** 1979 **Make:** OLDS **Body:** ROYALE **License:** [redacted] **State:** ILL **Year:** 78

VIN: 3N69R9X105704 **Vehicle Tag No:** U49727 **Year:** 78 **Issuing Agency:** COOK COUNTY

Owner: PDM CONTRACTORS **Address:** 2213 SUMMERDALE, NORWOOD PARK

Towing Officer's Signature: K. Byrne

NARRATIVE:

VEHICLE TOWED TO SECURITY GARAGE PER THE REQUEST OF THE INVESTIGATION DIVISION. VEHICLE WAS NOT ENTERED OR SEARCHED BY R/O

Date/Time Report Completed: 13 DEC 78 1840 **Date/Time Vehicle Towed:** 13 DEC 78 1825

Signature: K. Byrne 251

R.D. # 78-35349

TOW REPORT / DES PLAINES POLICE

1. Offense Code: 6056
2. Date/Time Occurred: 13 Dec 78
5. Beat Assigned: /02
7. Date of Occurrence: 13 Dec 78

8. REASON FOR TOW:

1. ☐ ABANDONED — CITY CODE 10-14-2, 7-DAY NOTICE ISSUED _____ DATE _____ TIME _____
2. ☐ ILLEGAL PARKING - PRIVATE PROPERTY — CITY CODE 10-13-1, CITATION NO: _____
3. ☐ RECOVERED STOLEN VEHICLE   LOCAL ☐   FOREIGN ☐
4. ☒ HOLD FOR INVESTIGATION - EXPLAIN IN NARRATIVE
5. ☐ TRAFFIC HAZARD — OBSTRUCTING TRAFFIC - CITATION NO. _____ EXPLAIN IN NARRATIVE
6. ☐ UNDER ARREST - VEHICLE CONTROLLED BY ARRESTEE

9. Location of Vehicle: 8213 W. Summerdale
10. Towed By: DNA
13. Color: Black
14. Year: 1978
15. Make: Chev.
16. Body: Pick-Up
18. Year: 1979
19. State: IL
20. Appears Drivable: YES ☒ NO ☐
21. VIN: CKL248J182155
25. Vehicle Searched By: CCSPD
28. Evidence Tech Processed: YES ☒ NO ☐
29. Name (Owner): Gacy, John W.
30. Address: 8213 W. Summerdale, Norridge
31. Home Phone: 457-1614
32. Business Phone: 457-1614
Star #: 167

NARRATIVE: Vehicle driven from 8213 W. Summerdale, Norridge, to 1420 Miner St., Des Plaines, by Det. Tovar. Vehicle held for investigation and for processing. Vehicle in Police Garage.

40. Date/Time Report Completed: 13 Dec 78

R.D. # 78-3520

	Job Number	Case Report Number	Date Received
	12510B	801160	13 December 78

Assignment	Time Assigned	Time Arrived
Missing Person-Assist Other Agency, Des Plaines PD	1400	1400

Location	Agency	Beat
Des Plaines Police Station garage	Des Plaines Police	35

Victim	Sex	Race	Age	D.O.B.
Robert J. PIEST	M	W	15	

Victim's Address / Telephone Number

#	Photographs or Evidence Description and Location	P	L	E	Inventory
1	Vacuumed trace evidence from passenger seat and floor of truck			X	2369-78
2	Vacuumed trace evidence from driver's seat and floor of truck			X	2369-78
3	Broken hammer handle from under passenger seat of truck			X	2369-78
4	Rope recovered from left side of bed of truck			X	2369-78
5	Photo of front of truck showing 1979 license plate	BW			
6	Photo of right side of truck from right front corner	BW			
7	Photo of right side of truck from cab	BW			
8	Photo of interior of truck from right side	BW			
9	Photo of rope attached to left side of truck from right	BW			
10	Photo of rope attached to left side of truck from rt. rear	BW			
11	Last item				

Photographs B&W [X] C [ ] S [ ] Print Cards [ ] Palm [ ] Blood [ ] Hair [ ] Nails [ ] Swabs [ ] Bile [ ]
Urine [ ] Clothing [ ] Ammo [ ] Glass [ ] Soil [ ] Paint [ ] Safe Material [ ] Scene Plat [ ]
Latents [X] Firearms [ ] Serology [ ] Chemistry [ ] Trace [X] Arson [ ] ToolMarks [ ] Spectro [ ]
Gunshot Residue [ ] Handwriting-Type Analysis [ ] Other

Make-Yr-Mileage	Model	Color	Via	Lic-Yr-St	
Chevrolet	Scottsdale 20 Pickup	black	CKL248J182155, Il. '79		5642.5 mi.

R/ET was requested by Lieutenant Joseph Kozenzak, Des Plaines Police Department, to process a pickup truck in reference to a missing Des Plaines youth, Robert J. PIEST. The vehicle was processed in the heated secure garage at the Des Plaines Police Station. The vehicle is a black Chevrolet Scottsdale 20 pickup truck with a red Western brand snowplow attached to the front. It bears Illinois 1979 license plates 1146793, VIN CKL248J182155 and has a milage of 05642.5 miles. The interior of the truck was vacuumed for trace evidence (items 1 and 2) which will be submitted to the State lab for analysis. A broken hammer handle was recovered from under the passenger seat of the truck (item 3) and a section of rope was removed from the left side of the bed of the truck, (item 4). These items will be inventoried for future comparison. The interior and exterior of the truck were processed for latent prints with negative results. The vehicle was photographed as

	Investigator-Agency
Karl A Humbert, 424	Lt. Joseph Kozenzak
Daniel J. Genty, 366	Des Plaines Police Department

PAGE TWO FOM 1-1510B   78-35203

listed under item numbers 5 through 10.

No further action at this time.

PROPERTY INVENTORY No. 2318-78

ETU Humbert

No. 2318-78

	X 1	Bag containing section of beige rug with possible blood.	
	X 1	Bag containing green long sleeve shirt with possible blood.	
	X 1	Bag containing blue parka	
		Bag containing yellow undershorts with possible blood.	
		Bag containing plastic card holders.	
	X 1	Bag containing section of nylon rope.	
	X 1	Bag containing glass slide with blood from victim.	
	X 1	Bag containing hat and brush from victim.	
		Last Item.	

PRINT VERY HARD

Recovered from 8213 Summerdale, Norwood Park Twp.

R/ET

Lt. J. Kozenzak, Des Plaines Police

Karl A Humbert 424
ETU

78-35203

PROPERTY INVENTORY No. 2369-78

COOK COUNTY
SHERIFF'S POLICE DEPARTMENT — 2316-78, 2343-78, 2368-78 — ETU — Humbert/Genty

DATE RECOVERED: 14 December 78 | 12510B/801160 | Il. '79 plate [redacted] Process Chev. Pick-up

#	QTY	DESCRIPTION OF PROPERTY		
1	1	Sealed bag containing sealed box containing trace evidence,	pass.	front
2	1	Sealed bag containing sealed box containing trace evidence,	Driv.	front
3	1	Sealed bag containing broken handle of hammer, front of truck.		
4	1	Sealed bag containing rope removed from bed of truck.		
5		Last item.		

PRINT VERY HARD

Recovered from: Black Chevrolet pick-up truck, '79 Il plate [redacted]

R/ETs

Lt. Joseph Kozenzak, Des Plaines PD

Karl A Humbert — 424 — ETU
D. J. Genty — 366 — ETU

C.I.D. SUPPLEMENTARY REPORT / DES PLAINES POLICE	1. DATE/TIME THIS REPORT 15 Dec 78 1200 Hours
2. ORIGINAL OFFENSE: Surveillance	3. OFFENSE CHANGED TO:
4. VICTIM: Piest, Robert J.	5. ADDRESS: 2722 Craig Drive, Des Plaines

NARRATIVE:

On 15 December 78 at 0130 hours Reporting Officer began surveillance on 8213 West Summerdale, Norwood Park Township, the house of John W. Gacy. Reporting Officer observed this residence from 0130 hours until 0845 hours with no activity. At 0845 hours a 1968 Oldsmobile black vinyl over light yellow pulled into the driveway. The plate number was US 2154. This plate checked to a Gordon Nebel, 7950 West Lawrence, Norridge, Illinois. The driver got out of his car, looked around the house, picked up the newspaper and he then entered the house with a set of keys that he had on his person. At 0950 hours a black in color van with writing P.D.M. Construction pulled into the driveway. A male/white teenager was driving the vehicle. He entered the house. At 1010 hours a Ford pickup truck with a camper on the back, license plate number 20066RV, followed by a silver Plymouth Valiant, license plate number DK 9923, pulled up in front of the area of 8213 West Summerdale. The Plymouth pulled in the driveway. The pickup truck went to the next intersection, made a U-Turn and doubled back. It appeared as though both vehicles were together. The driver of the Plymouth fit the description of John W. Gacy. That subject entered the house. At approximately 1100 hours Reporting Officer was relieved by Officer Schultz.

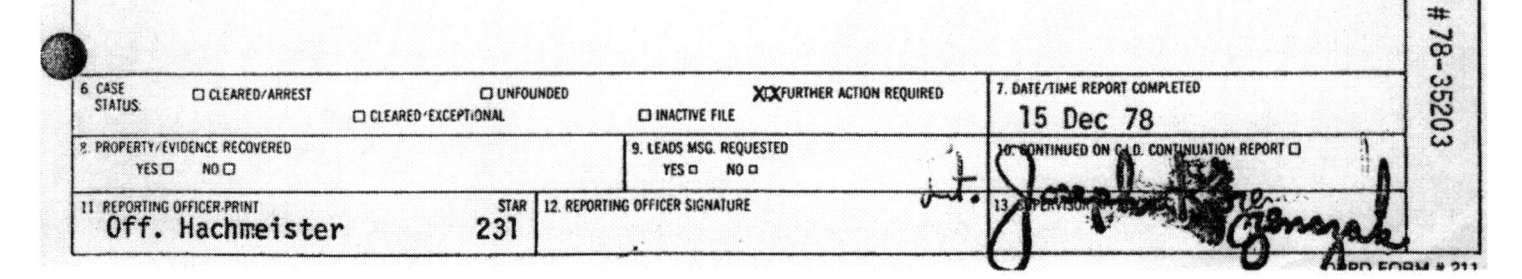

6. CASE STATUS: ☒ FURTHER ACTION REQUIRED	7. DATE/TIME REPORT COMPLETED: 15 Dec 78
11. REPORTING OFFICER-PRINT: Off. Hachmeister STAR 231	

R.D. # 78-35203

C.I.D. SUPPLEMENTARY REPORT / DES PLAINES POLICE		1. DATE/TIME THIS REPORT 16 Dec 78 1400 Hours
ORIGINAL OFFENSE Surveillance		3. OFFENSE CHANGED TO
4. VICTIM Piest, Robert J.		5. ADDRESS 2722 Craig Drive, Des Plaines

NARRATIVE:

At 0100 hours Reporting Officer and Officer Albrecht observed John Gacy enter a house at 4920 Clifton in Norridge, Illinois. This house is owned by Ron Rohde. Gacy spent the night at the house and there was no further activity until 0930 hours when Rohde left for work. Reporting Officers observed no further activity and were relieved at 1300 hours.

R.D. #78-35203

CASE STATUS: ☐ CLEARED/ARREST ☐ UNFOUNDED ☒ FURTHER ACTION REQUIRED
☐ CLEARED/EXCEPTIONAL ☐ INACTIVE FILE

7. DATE/TIME REPORT COMPLETED
16 Dec 78

PROPERTY/EVIDENCE RECOVERED YES☐ NO☐
9. LEADS MSG. REQUESTED YES☐ NO☐
10. CONTINUED ON C.I.D. CONTINUATION REPORT ☐

11. REPORTING OFFICER-PRINT
Officer D. Hachmeister   STAR 231

12. REPORTING OFFICER SIGNATURE

13. SUPERVISOR APPROVING
Lt. Joseph Kozenczak

DATA

(11) Victim(s), Sex, Race, D.O.B.
Robert J. PIEST, M/W/15

(12) Signature of Submitting Officer

(13) Printed Name of Submitting Officer

EVIDENCE INVENTORY

(14) Lab Exhibit Number	(15) Agency Exhibit Number	(16) Description of Evidence (See Instructions)
	1	Brn. bag alleged to contain section of rug with possible blood.
	2	Brn. bag alleged to contain grn. shirt with possible blood.
	3	Brn. bag alleged to contain blue parka.
	4	Brn. bag alleged to contain yellow undershorts with possible blood.
	5	Brn. bag alleged to contain plastic card holders.
	6	Brn. bag alleged to contain section of nylon-like rope.
	7	Brn. bag alleged to contain a glass slide with blood from Piest.
	8	Brn. bag alleged to contain a brush and hat owned and used by Piest.

EVIDENCE CHAIN

RECEIVED

(20) Lab Exhibit Number(s)	(21) Date	(22) Signature of Laboratory Employee	(20) Lab Exhibit Number(s)	(21) Date	(22) Signature of Laboratory Employee

RELEASED

(23) Lab Exhibit Number(s)	(24) Date	(25) Laboratory Employee	(26) Released to:

REQUEST

(27) Case Summary and Questions to be Resolved:

A 15 year old M/W disappears after keeping an appointment with a subject who wanted to talk with him about a summer job. A search warrant is issued to search the subjects house for evidence of a homicide. The above items were removed from the house by R/ET. Items 7 and 8 recovered at the Des Plaines Police Department.

Item 1: Are the spots on the carpet blood? Type?
Item 2: Is stain under left arm (or other) blood? Type?
Item 3: Is trace evidence on the parka recoverable?
Item 4: Is stain at front of shorts blood? Type?
Item 5: Can the letter and number impressions on the first case be read?
  (They appear to be from a Des Plaines library card. Impressions
    at lower left will be upside down and will start with letter
    D. Robert J. Piest had an old library card number DP 85104 and
    a new card with number DP 94883.)
Item 6: Is any trace evidence present on the rope?
Item 7: This blood was drawn from the finger tip of victim Piest by himself
    to observe and attempt to type as a self interest project. His
    brother witnessed him draw it.   CONTINUED

DEPARTMENT OF LAW ENFORCEMENT
STATE OF ILLINOIS
SCIENTIFIC SERVICES
EVIDENCE RECEIPT

(TYPE OF USE BLACK BALL POINT PEN ONLY — INSTRUCTIONS ON BACK)

78-35203

Item 8: This brush and hat were owned and used by victim Piest. Hair found on them to be used as a standard.

Last item.

COOK COUNTY SHERIFF'S POLICE DEPARTMENT
EVIDENCE TECHNICIAN'S REPORT

Job Number	Case Report Number	Date Received
12510(C)	801160	16 Dec 78

Assignment	Time Assigned	Time Arrived
Assist Other Agency - Missing Person	1515	1610

Location	Agency	Beat
Des Plaines P.D. - Garage	Des Plaines P.D.	35

Victim	Sex	Race	Age	D.O.B.
Robert J. Piest	M	W	15	Unk.

#	Photographs or Evidence Description and Location	P	L	E	Inventory
1	White env with hairlike fiber, Rec'd from Lt. Kozenzak			X	2343-78
2	Paper towel from Chev. Van CGL2584118817			X	2343-78
3	Overall Chev van, right rear	X			
4	Overall Chev van, left front	X			
5	Overall interior of van thru drivers door	X			

Photographs B&W[X] C[ ] S[ ] Print Cards[ ] Palm[ ] Blood[X] Hair[X] Nails[ ] Swabs[ ] Bile[ ]
Urine[ ] Clothing[ ] Ammo[ ] Glass[ ] Soil[ ] Paint[ ] Safe Material[ ] Scene Plat[ ]
Latents[ ] Firearms[ ] Serology[ ] Chemistry[ ] Trace[ ] Arson[ ] ToolMarks[ ] Spectro[ ]
Gunshot Residue[ ] Handwriting-Typo Analysis[ ] Other

Make-Yr-Mileage	Model	Color	Vin	Lic-Yr-St
Chev/78/29701.8	Van 20	Black	CGL2584118817	219 114B/79/Ill

R/ET was requested by Inv. Bedoe to process the above listed vehicle at the DesPlaines P.D. garage reference a missing juvenile. Upon arrival R/ET met with Lt. Kozenzak of the D.P.D. who turned over to R/ET item 1, a hairlike fiber he had observed and recovered from a suspects auto, black Oldsmobile VIN 3N69R9X105706. R/ET then examined a 1978 black Chevrolet Van 20 with the lettering P.D.M. Construction and the vehicle number 4 written on the side. R/ET photographed the van as listed above and recovered item 2, a blood spotted paper towel, from the drivers door step. Examination of the rest of the van revealed various construction tools and materials consistant with the stated use of the vehicle. No other evidence was found in the truck. No further action taken at this time.

D.J. Genty 366

Investigator-Agency: Lt. Joseph Kozenzak Des Plaines P.D.

COOK COUNTY SHERIFF'S POLICE DEPARTMENT
EVIDENCE TECHNICIAN'S REPORT

78-35203

Job Number	Case Report Number	Date Received
12510A	801160	11 Dec. 78

Assignment	Time Assigned	Time Arrived
Missing Person-Assist Other Agency, Des Plaines PD	1930	2000

Location	Agency	Beat
Des Plaines Police Department, Garage	Des Plaines Police	35

Victim	Sex	Race	Age	D.O.B.
Robert J. Piest	M	W	15	

Victim's Address: [redacted]   Telephone Number: [redacted]

#	Photographs or Evidence Description and Location	P	L	E	Inventory
1	Vacuumed trace evidence from passenger front of '79 Olds			X	2368-78
2	Vacuumed trace evidence from driver front of '79 Olds			X	2368-78
3	Vacuumed trace evidence from passenger rear of '79 Olds			X	2368-78
4	Vacuumed trace evidence from driver rear of '79 Olds			X	2368-78
5	Vacuumed trace evidence from trunk of '79 Olds			X	2368-78
6	Soil and grass from jack base from trunk of '79 Olds				-78
7	Soil and grass from right rear outside corner of '79 Olds			X	2368-78
8	Spool of silver colored tape from trunk of '79 Olds			X	2368-78
9	Photo of rear of '79 Olds showing Il. 78 plate PDM 42	C			
10	Photo of right rear corner of Olds showing soil	C			
11	Photo of front of Olds showing red spotlight on right	C			
12	Photo of front interior of Olds	C			
13	Photo of interior of front of Olds	C			
14	Photo of interior of trunk from right side	C			
15	Photo of interior of trunk from rear.	C			

Photographs B&W [ ] C [X] S [ ] Print Cards [ ] Palm [ ] Blood [ ] Hair [ ] Nails [ ] Swabs [ ] Bile [ ]
Urine [ ] Clothing [ ] Ammo [ ] Glass [ ] Soil [ ] Paint [ ] Safe Material [ ] Scene Plat [ ]
Latents [ ] Firearms [ ] Serology [ ] Chemistry [ ] Trace [X] Arson [ ] ToolMarks [ ] Spectro [ ]
Gunshot Residue [ ] Handwriting-Typo Analysis [ ] Other

Make-Yr-Mileage	Model	Color	Vin	Lic-Yr-St
Oldsmobile, 1979, 7398.5 Mi.	Delta 88	Black	3N69R9X105706	PDM 42 Il. 78

R/ET was requested by Lieutenant Joseph Kozenzak, Des Plaines Police Department, to process an automobile at their station in reference to a missing person, Robert J. Piest. The auto is a black 1979 Oldsmobile Delta 88 four door, bearing 1978 Illinois license plates PDM 42, VIN 3N69R9X105706. The auto is equipped with two front spotlights, white on the drivers side, red light on the passenger side. The interior of the auto contained miscellaneous papers, parking tickets, a Realistic 40 channel CB radio, grape candy, a flashlight and a tape measure. The exterior and interior were dusted for latent prints with negative results. The interior was vacuumed for trace evidence (items 1 through 4) which will be submitted to the State lab for analysis. The trunk of the auto was opened and vacuumed for trace evidence (item 5), which will be submitted for trace analysis. The trunk contained a wet and muddy spear tire, a jack and base, the base having a quantity of wet mud

Karl A Humbert, #424
William K. Dado, #338

Investigator-Agency: Lt. Joseph Kozenzak, Des Plaines Police Department

Supervisor: [redacted]

PAGE TWO—Job 12510A

on it, a white construction helmet, jumper cables, flares, red rubber mats, brown cloth gloves, and a spool of silver colored tape. R/ET took a sample of the mud and grass from the base of the jack (item 6) and the spool of tape (item 8) to use in future comparisons. The floor of the trunk was covered with a orange and black carpet. R/ET observed mud and grass adhering to the right rear quarter panel of the auto. A sample of the material was collected for future comparison (item 7). Color photographs of the interior and exterior of the auto are listed as items 9 through 15 on this report. (Items 12 and 13 are the same).

No further action at this time.

PROPERTY INVENTORY

No. 2368-78

Related: 2318-78, 2343-78, 2369-78

Unit: ETU — Humbert/Dado

Date Recovered: 13 December 78

Location: 12510A/801160 (Process '79 Olds 4 dr)

#	Qty	Description of Property	Case #
1	#1	Sealed bag containing sealed box containing trace evidence, passenger front	
2	#1	Sealed bag containing sealed box containing trace evidence, driver front	
3	#1	Sealed bag containing sealed box containing trace evidence, passenger rear	
4	#1	Sealed bag containing sealed box containing trace evidence, drivers rear	
5	#1	Sealed bag containing sealed box containing trace evidence, trunk	
6	1	Sealed bag containing two sealed boxes of soil and grass from jack base	
7	1	Sealed bag containing box with soil from outside right rear of Olds	
8	1	Sealed bag containing spool of silver colored tape from trunk of Olds	
9		Last item.	

PRINT VERY HARD

Recovered from: Black 1979 Oldsmobile 4 dr, bearing 78 Il. ▮▮▮▮▮
R/ETs

Lt. Joseph Kozenzak, Des Plaines Police

Karl A Humbert — 424 ETU
William Dado — 338 ETU

		Job Number	Case Report Number	Date Received
		12510	801160	13 December 78

Assignment: Missing Person-Assist Other Agency, Des Plaines PD
Time Assigned: 1555 **Time Arrived:** 1700
Location: 8213 Summerdale, Norwood Park Township
Agency: Des Plaines Police **Beat:** 40
Victim: Robert J. PIEST
Sex: M **Race:** W **Age:** 15 **D.O.B.:**

#	Photographs or Evidence Description and Location	P	L	F	Inventory
1	Section of beige rug with possible blood stains			X	2318-78
2	Long sleeve green shirt with possible blood stains			X	2318-78
3	Blue parka jacket			X	2318-78
4	Yellow undershorts with possible blood stains			X	2318-78
5	Plastic card holders as from a wallet with impressions			X	2318-78
6	Approximately one yard section of rope			X	2318-78
7	Box alleged to contain glass slide with victim's blood			X	2318-78
8	Plastic bag containing a hairbrush and a brown hat.			X	2318-78
9	Photo of blood spots on hall floor next to bathroom		C		
10	Photo of hall between kitchen and bedrooms, E to W.		C		
11	Photo of hall between kitchen and bedrooms, W to E		C		
12	Photo of laundry room showing green shirt and blue parka		C		
13	Photo of bathroom N to S		C		
14	Photo of yellow shorts in bathroom closet, E to W		C		
15	Photo of NE corner of kitchen with trash container		C		

Photographs B&W[ ] C[X]S[ ] Print Cards[ ] Palm[ ] Blood[X] Hair[ ] Nails[ ] Swabs[ ] Bile[ ]
Urine[ ] Clothing[X] Ammo[ ] Glass[ ] Soil[ ] Paint[ ] Safe Material[ ] Scene Plat[ ]
Latents[ ] Firearms[ ] Serology[X] Chemistry[ ] Trace[X] Arson[ ] ToolMarks[ ] Spectro[ ]
Gunshot Residue[ ] Handwriting-Type Analysis[ ] Other

Make-Yr-Mileage Model Color Vin Lic-Yr-St

R/ET was advised at 1555 hours 13 December 1978 by ET Rossi to respond to 8213 Summerdale, Norwood Park Township and assist Des Plaines Police Department investigators in executing a search warrant at that location. Upon arrival R/ET met Lieutenant Joseph Kozenzak who advised that the search was for evidence concerning a Robert J. Piest, a fifteen year old white male missing from Des Plaines. It was believed that the youth was last in the company the resident of 8213 Summerdale, and that the youth had met with violence.

R/ET entered the residence through a rear kitchen door in the southeast corner of the building an toured the residence with Lt. Kozenzak. Spots of suspected blood were observed on the carpeting in a hall running between the kitchen and bedrooms. The spots were to the left of the entrance to a bathroom near the south wall of the hall. That section

Investigator-Agency: Lt. Joseph Kozenzak, Des Plaines Police Department

of carpet (item 1) was photographed in place and removed by R/ET and will be submitted to the State lab for evaluation. A green, long sleeve button shirt (item 2) and a blue parka jacket (item 3) believed to have been the garments worn by the suspect on the night Piest disappeared, were found in the laundry room. They were photographed and collected by R/ET and will be submitted to the State lab for analysis of possible blood stains and trace evidence. Yellow jockey-type shorts (item 4) found in a closet in the bathroom were photographed and collected by R/ET. They will be submitted to the State lab for analysis of a possible blood stain at the inside front. A plastic card holder (as found in wallets) (item 5) with card impressions was recovered from a trash basket in the kitchen by Detective Ron Adams, #167 Des Plaines Police. The case will be submitted to the State lab for examination of the impressions. A section of rope approximately a yard long was recovered by R/ET from the trash basket and will be submitted for trace examination and future comparison. Interior and exterior color photographs of the residence taken by R/ET are listed as items 9 through 23. Printed material removed from the residence by Des Plaines officers was photographed at the Des Plaines Police station and is listed as item 24. Items 7 and 8 were turned over to R/ET by Lt. Kozenzak, and are to be submitted to the State lab as standards of blood and hair of Robert J Piest.

No Further action at this time.

COOK COUNTY
SHERIFF'S POLICE DEPARTMENT
Criminalistics Section

		Job No.	Case Report No.			Date
		A2510	801160			13 Dec, 78

Item	Description and Location	P	L	E	Invent. No.
16	Photo of bedroom in NW corner of building, SE to NW	C			
17	Photo of bedroom in NW corner of building, N to S	C			
18	Photo of bedroom in NW corner of building, SW to NE	C			
19	Photo of back (south side) of house, S to N	C			
20	Photo of garage south of the house, N to S	C			
21	Photo of east side of house, NE to SW	C			
22	Photo of west side of house, NW to SE	C			
23	Photo of front of house, N to S	C			
24	Photo of printed material taken by Des Plaines Police	C			
	Last item.				

OFFENSE		DATE AND TIME PROPERTY RECOVERED		
MISSING PERSON INVESTIGATION		18 DEC 78 1700		
LOCATION				
2?22 CLARK		FOUND ☐ RECOVERED ☐ EVIDENCE ☒		
OWNER		ADDRESS		
JOHN W. GACY		8213 W. SUMMERDALE NORWOOD PK. TOWNSH.		
RECOVERED FROM				
From # 7 Closet				

ITEM	QUANTITY	DESCRIPTION	VALUE	RELEASED TO (SIGNAT)
inv # 1	1	ONE BROWN ENVELOPE CONTAINING 3 PAPER BACK BOOKS "THE SEEDS OF SPRING" "THE CURIOUS		
2.		NURSE" "21 ABNORMAL SEX CASES"		
Ex. # 2	1	ONE BROWN ENVELOPE CONTAINING 2 BOOKS "MASTURBATION AND THE HOMOSEXUAL"		
		"A STUDY OF ADULT/CHILD SEXUAL RELATIONS PEDOPHILIA"		
in # 3	1	ONE BROWN ENVELOPE CONTAINING 4 BOOKS "SELECTED SHORTS" "BREAKING IT" "MORE		
		THAN 7 INCHES" "HARD"		
In # 4	1	ONE BROWN ENVELOPE CONTAINING 3 BOOKS "COMING ON" "SUPER SEX ADULTS ONLY"		
		"MORE THAN 7 INCHES"		
Ex. # 5	1	ONE BROWN ENVELOPE CONTAINING 3 BOOKS "THE PHALLUS" "MORE THAN 7 INCHES NO. 3"		
10.		"COME SWEET COME"		
Ex. # 6	1	ONE BROWN ENVELOPE CONTAINING 3 BOOKS "PHALLIC PHACTS NO 1" "SODOM AND		
12.		GOMORRAH" "THE GREAT WHITE SWALLOW"		

REPORTING OFFICERS: DET. S. KAUTZ # 717

	QUANTITY	DESCRIPTION	VALUE	RELEASED TO / SIGNATURE
	1	Brown envelope containing 4 books "Teacher's Broken" "The Lonely Boy"		
		"Jock Man" "The Anal Lovers"		
	1	One brown envelope containing 5 books "Rogue" "Girls-Guys-Gimmicks"		
		"Young Stars" "Swank" "The Reel Thing"		

Det. Kautz #21

1. STATUS: MISSING PERSON INVESTIGATION		2. DATE AND TIME PROPERTY RECOVERED: 13 DEC 78 1700		
		3. CHECK ONE: FOUND ☐ RECOVERED ☐ EVIDENCE ☒		
8. RECOVERED FROM NAME: John W. Gacy	ADDRESS: 8213 W. Summerdale Norwood Pk. Township			
From #7 Residence				

ITEM	QUANTITY	DESCRIPTION	VALUE	RELEASED TO (SIGN)
Exh #9	1	One Brown Paper Bag containing "Heads & Tails" - Book		
		Swedish Erotica Film Pamphlet		

14. REPORTING OFFICERS: Det. J. Kautz #217

Missing Person Investigation — 12 DEC 78 1700

☐ FOUND ☐ RECOVERED ☒ EVIDENCE

8213 W. Summerdale, Norwood Pk. Township
Floor #1 Residence

	QTY	DESCRIPTION	VALUE	RELEASED TO/SIGNAT
		Brown paper bag containing the following		
		"Gay Boy" – book "Pederasty: Sex Between Men and Boys" – book "The Rights of Gay People" – book "The American Bicentennial Gay Guide" – book		
	1	One brown paper bag containing the following films		
		Swedish Erotica #119		
		Swedish Erotica #131		
		Swedish Erotica #134		
		Swedish Erotica #40		
		Swedish Erotica #107		
		Swedish Erotica #137		
		Swedish Erotica #23		

Missing Person Investigation — 15 Dec 78 1700

EVIDENCE [X]

... W. Summerdale Norwood Pk Township

ITEM	QUANTITY	DESCRIPTION	VALUE	RELEASED TO
Knife	ONE	ONE 2th approx 39" long with two holes ... old		

Det. ...

Offense	Date and Time Property Recovered
Missing Person	13 December 78 1700 Hrs

Recovered From: John W. Gacy — 8213 W. Summerdale Norwood Twnshp, Ill.

Residence of the above #1

Item	Quantity	Description	Value	Released To
1.	One (1)	white plastic bottle containing 21 pink pills		
2.		suspected Preludin*		
3.	One (1)	brown plastic bottle containing seven (7) un-		
4.		identified pills, one red/blue capsule *tunial*		
5.		10 yellow pills *valium*, 3 blue pills *valium*		
6.	One (1)	Clear plastic bottle containing 3 blue pills		
7.		*valium* and 4 capsules of amyl nitrite		
8.	One (1)	Marlboro flip top pack containing cannabis		
9.	One (1)	Clear plastic baggie containing cannabis		
10.	One (1)	Hypo-dermic syringe		

Reporting Officer: t. James Kautz #213

			13 December 78, 1700 Hrs	FOUND ☐ RECOVERED ☐
		8213 W. Summerdale Norwood Park Twnshp, Ill		

	QUANTITY	DESCRIPTION	VALUE	
	One (1)	Glass vial containing four (4) green pills suspected Papaver	✓	
	One (1)	Brown bottle containing Atropine Sulfate	✓	
	One (1)	silver 100 gr scale	✓	
	One (1)	white handle switchblade	✓	
	One (1)	Expired Ill DL ▮▮▮ to James O. O'Toole	✓	
	One (1)	Expired Temporary DL Michael B. Raker	✓	
	One (1)	Maine West High School class ring 1975 (JAS)	✓	
	One (1)	Silver (No brand) set of handcuffs and 2 keys	✓	
	Two (2)	Polaroid photos of unidentified M/W youth		

REPORTING OFFICERS AND STAR NOS.
Det James Kautz #217

			13 December 78 1700 Hrs	
			FOUND ☐ RECOVERED ☒	

John W. Gacy   8213 W. Summerdale Norwood Pk Twnshp, Ill.

Same as above

ITEM	QUANTITY	DESCRIPTION	VALUE	REF
	One (1)	Brevettata 1949 cal 6mm starter pistol and box		
	One (1)	Pack of e-z wider cigarrette rolling paper		
	One (1)	plastic bag containing possible starter pistol blanks		
	Four (4)	polaroid photos of unidentified buildings	✓	
	One (1)	Pocket Book ("Tight Teenagers")	✓	
	One (1)	Plastic ID (Rapael Charo)	✓	
	One (1)	Red Address Book	✓	
	Three (3)	Unidentified Buildings (Polaroid Pics.)	✓	
	—	Dirt + grass samples - (12-16-78)		

Det. James Kautz #217

OFFENSE: MISSING PERSON		DATE/TIME PROPERTY RECOVERED: 13 DEC 78 2130		
		CHECK ONE: FOUND ☐ RECOVERED ☐ EVIDENCE ☒		
OWNER: PIEST, ROBERT T.				
RECOVERED FROM: MRS. PIEST		ADDRESS: S/A #7		
QUANTITY	DESCRIPTION		VALUE	RELEASED TO (SIGNA
1	HAIR BRUSH — GREEN HANDLE, BLACK BRISTLES — USED BY 3 OTHER FAMILY MEMBERS			
1	BROWN HAT			
	"IF NEEDED FOR COMPARISONS"			

R NOS. 242

SURVEILLANCE CONTINUES

C.I.D. SUPPLEMENTARY REPORT / DES PLAINES POLICE

Date/Time This Report: 15 Dec 78 1030 Hours

Original Offense: Missing Person

Victim: Piest, Robert J.

NARRATIVE:

On December 14, 1978 I contacted Mr. Eldon Burk, the Assistant Principal at Maine West, in an attempt to determine the owner of a 1975 class ring which had been recovered at the residence of John Gacy, 8213 West Summerdale, while executing the search warrant at the Gacy residence. Mr. Burk was advised the ring was made of a gold metal material, contained a blue stone, was from the 1975 graduating class at Maine West and had the initials J.A.S. engraved on the inside of the band. In addition to the initials J.A.S., this Officer observed the following letters and digits, H.J. - 10K. Mr. Burk stated that he would check the 1975 issue of the Dial-Tone, the Maine West High Telephone Directory, and attempt to determine the owner of the ring. Upon terminating my conversation with Mr. Burk, this Officer checked the '75 issue of the Dial-Tone and the 1975 issue of The Legend and noticed that two students who would have graduated in 1975 from Maine West had the initials J.A.S. The two youths were John A. Schimmel, and John A. Szyc,

At approximately 1830 hours on December 14, 1978 I received a call from Mr. Burk, at which time he stated that 1975 was the only year that salesmen were not allowed to come into Maine West to sell rings to the graduating class, therefore the ring would have been purchased from Herf Jones, a jewelry store on Miner Street next to the Des Plaines Theatre.

On December 15, 1978 at 1030 hours I received a call from Mr. Burk, at which time he stated the 1975 graduating class of Maine West did not purchase their rings through the school. The rings for the '75 graduating class were purchased through Herf Jones on Miner Street next to the Des Plaines Theatre probably in the fall of 1972 or 1973. The H.J. - 10K on the inside of the band denotes Herf Jones - 10 Carat. According to Mr. Burk, Herf Jones does not have records dating back to 1972 or 1973. In Mr. Burk's opinion, the ring was purchased by either John A. Schimmel or John A. Szyc. Upon receiving the information from Mr. Burk, this Officer made numerous unsuccessful attempts to contact either someone at the Schimmel residence or at the Szyc residence.

At 1855 hours on December 15, 1978 I called the Szyc residence and spoke with Mrs. Szyc. Mrs. Szyc stated that her son had purchased a 1975 class ring, although the youth had been reported missing to Chicago approximately two years ago. Upon further speaking with Mrs. Szyc, it was determined that John Szyc had been reported missing to the Shakespeare Avenue District and that subsequently John A. Szyc's automobile was found in the possession of a boy that stated he bought the automobile in February of 1977. Mrs. Szyc indicated that she had reported her son missing on/or about January 25, 1977 and felt the incident was somewhat unusual, because her son never picked up his check and the check contained an unspecified amount of overtime. To the best of Mrs. Szyc's knowledge, John A. Szyc's paycheck, including the overtime, still remains at his former employer and, as indicated by Mrs. Szyc, because the youth was of legal age she cannot pick up her son's paycheck.

Date/Time Report Completed: 15 Dec 78

R.D. # 78-35203

C.I.D. CONTINUATION REPORT / DES PLAINES POLICE

At approximately 2210 hours I contacted Patti Schimmel, at which time she stated that she believed her brother, John's, class ring had been lost in a lake, although she did not have any additional details. Ms. Schimmel was advised to inform her parents and her brother that we would like to speak with John as soon as possible to determine if, in fact, his ring had been lost or misplaced and if, in fact, the youth had a 1975 class ring from Maine West which contained a blue stone.

Missing Person

Biesta, Robert J.

NARRATIVE:

The following report reflects the combined activities of Detectives Tovar and Ryan on 15 December 78 while at 11th and State, the Chicago Police Department Headquarters.

On today's date Detectives Ryan and Tovar went to Chicago Police Department Headquarters and obtained a copy of the Chicago Rap sheet of John W. Gacy, whose Date of Birth is 03-17-42, IR# 273632, F.B.I. #: 5851816, ISB Number is 1377836, and received a copy of said criminal history. Two items were blanked out, as they indicated they were Federal Bureau of Investigation charges. Indicated as the last arrest for 15 July 78, Officer Burk making the arrest in the 16th District for Battery under CB Number 5289230 was John W. Gacy of 8213 West Summerdale. We then obtained a copy of the report under that C.B. number and Report Bureau #7094622. Also attached find the copy of the arrest report of John Gacy under the C.B. Number and signed by Investigator Edward McCleske. Also attached you will find a copy of the photograph of John Gacy, dated 15 July 78 C.B. Number 5289230 and IR# 273632. This report is for a battery of a sex nature involving a victim Jeffrey D. Rignell of home phone Area Code . The date of the incident is 22 March 1978.

15 Dec 78

C.I.D. SUPPLEMENTARY REPORT / DES PLAINES POLICE

Date/Time Reported: 16 Dec 78, 2030 Hours

Offense: Missing Person

Victim: Piest, Robert J.

NARRATIVE:

The following report reflects my activities of December 16, 1978 on the above mentioned missing person case.

On today's date I had a conversation with Investigator Harry Belluomini, of Area 5, General Assignment, Chicago Police Department, reference to a letter that he wrote to the mother of John A. Szyc. In this letter he made reference to the vehicle that belonged to John Szyc had been involved in an incident, whereas that had led the police department to believe that the subject, Szyc, must still be alive; as the vehicle had been involved in an incident. I questioned Investigator Belluomini about it and he indicated that his only contact with this case was that back at the time of the letter, approximately December of '76, the vehicle in question that belonged to Szyc had pulled into a gas station, obtained gasoline and left without paying. The attendant apparently copied down the license plate number of the vehicle which checked out to John Szyc's vehicle and, upon his going to the residence at ▓▓▓▓▓▓▓▓▓▓▓▓▓▓▓▓▓▓▓▓▓ he found out that this subject, Szyc, was missing. He further advised me that he checked around the area and that the information he had received was that the subject John Szyc was, in fact, gay. He also indicated that information received by him indicated that possibly he might have moved to Colorado and was living there at this time. I further checked this out by checking with the Department of Motor Vehicles in Colorado and ascertained that there is no driver's license or a car issued to any John A. Szyc, which would refer to this missing person. I also asked Investigator Belluomini if he had ever seen the car or the subject that the car belonged to, and he indicated negative to this. At approximately 9:35 I concluded the interview with Investigator Belluomini.

At approximately 1000 hours I telephoned Cicero Police Department and spoke to Investigator William Baldwin reference Michael A. Rossi, M/W, DOB: ▓▓▓▓▓▓▓ who had indicated to me that he had committed a battery upon John Gacy in Cicero and subsequently had been placed on probation for the offense. In checking with Investigator Baldwin, I learned that the only arrest that they showed for Michael Rossi were three charges for traffic related offenses and that this occurred on December 4, 1977, and the facts of this were that Rossi apparently did not stop for a stop sign and tried to elude the police department when they attempted to stop him. The chase was started in Cicero and was concluded at 3130 North Albany in Chicago and he subsequently was charged with the stop sign violation, eluding and reckless driving. At this time Rossi gave his home address as ▓▓▓▓▓▓▓▓▓▓▓▓▓▓▓▓▓▓▓▓▓▓▓▓▓▓▓ He pled not guilty, was found guilty, got a two year suspension of his license, but according to his 10-27 it shows that he does have a valid license, so it would probably be a supervision and a $50 fine.

At approximately 1220 hours I then went to ▓▓▓▓▓▓▓▓▓▓▓▓▓▓▓▓▓▓▓▓▓▓▓▓ to locate one Carol Hoff, which is the second ex wife of John Gacy, and spoke to one Rose Dussias, who lives in the building where Ms. Hoff is allegedly living. I was told that Carol no longer lives there, that she recently had been married and only her mother, one Jean Cienciwa, lived upstairs at the moment. Her telephone number is ▓▓▓▓▓▓▓

I then went to a location that we directed to by Ms. Dussias, which would be at the corner of Higgins and Normandy in Chicago at a beauty shop where we met and spoke to

Date/Time Report Completed: 16 Dec 78

R.D. # 78-35203

C.I.D. CONTINUATION REPORT / DES PLAINES POLICE PAGE 2

Carol Hoff's mother and we were given the address and phone number of her daughter. Her daughter is now married to one Bruce Lofgrn and they live at ▓▓▓▓▓▓▓▓▓▓▓▓▓▓▓▓▓▓▓▓▓▓▓▓. Detective Lt. Kozenczak was called and he in turn called Mrs. Lofgrn, who indicated she would call and come in at approximately 1500 hours. The license plate number for Mrs. Lofgrn's mother is ▓▓▓▓▓ which checks out to the ▓▓▓▓▓▓▓▓▓▓▓▓▓▓▓▓▓▓▓▓▓▓▓.

At approximately 1400 hours I then called the Chief of Police, one Larry Mitchell in Riverton, Illinois, this in reference to a map found in the vehicle of John Gacy which had a route outlined to that location. I called him at Area Code 217-629-9800 and inquired as to the possibility of them having found any floaters in any of the rivers around their area. Chief Mitchell indicated that they are right along side the Sangamon River, but no one has been located in their river in the last year or so. I asked him to further check in the telephone book for the name of Itullo, or any name similar to that, but he was unable to locate any. He did indicate that we should call the Sangamon County Sheriff's Police at 753-6666 for any further information.

At approximately 1900 hours date I was assigned to go pick up James G. O'T▓▓▓▓ at ▓▓▓▓▓▓▓▓▓▓▓▓▓▓▓▓▓▓▓▓▓▓▓▓▓▓ M/W, DOB: ▓▓▓▓▓▓▓▓ for the purpose of interviewing him as to the reason why his driver's license was located at the residence of John Gacy. Detective Sommerschield conducted the interview of D'Toole and will forward a report on this.

R.D. # 78-35203

C.I.D. CONTINUATION REPORT ☐

C.I.D. SUPPLEMENTARY REPORT / DES PLAINES POLICE

16 Dec 78   2120 Hours

Original Offense: Missing Person

Victim: Piest, Robert J.

NARRATIVE:

On 15 December 1978 at approximately 2315 hours Detectives Adams and Pickell went to Northwest Hospital, at Central and Addison Streets, Chicago, and interviewed Margaret DeNeo, ███████████. Mrs. DeNeo is a nurse at Northwest Hospital and was working the 4th Floor Nurses Station in the west section of the building on the 11th of December 1978. At approximately 2300 hours on that date Mrs. DeNeo advised that a male/white person, described as being possibly 5'11", heavy set, chunky, with possible light brown hair and possibly wearing a cloth jacket, came to the nurses station and asked for Mr. Scow. This person looked puzzled, because the Scow family had been there and left. He did not identify himself. He asked about Mr. Scow and Mrs. DeNeo seemed to think that he did not know that Mr. Scow had expired. He looked very puzzled. Mrs. DeNeo does not know how he got up to the 4th Floor at that hour, since all the hospital doors are locked and security guards are on duty. Mrs. DeNeo advised that this person did not look like the kind of person who would associate with the Scows, since she thought that the Scows were a little higher class than this person. Mrs. DeNeo advised that she was familiar with Mrs. Scow and Mr. Scow and she does not recall this person visiting Mr. Scow in the past. She did add, however, that she is only a part-time employee and only works three days a week. Mrs. DeNeo did not see this person leave the area. She stated that she may be able to recognize this person again if she saw a picture of him. She does not know if any other nurses saw or spoke with this person and she was under the impression that he was called by the family, although he seemed uninformed. Mrs. DeNeo believed that Mr. Scow expired sometime around 2210 hours on the 11th of December 1978. Mrs. DeNeo advised that this person's age was approximately the early 40's. She was shown a series of photographs in an effort to identify the person who was at the nurses station at the above date and time mentioned. Mrs. DeNeo observed photographs #71-142, #69-138, #71-22, #74-301, #69-60, and #69-249, and a photograph of Mr. John Gacy that was a mug shot from the Chicago Police Department reference CB5289230-IR273632, dated 15 July 1978. Mrs. DeNeo looked at each photograph individually and she picked out photograph #69-138 as being that person most closely resembling the person who was at the nurses station on the 11th of December 1978. Mrs. DeNeo did say, however, that the person only resembles the person who was at the desk and was not definitely the person who was in the hospital on that date and time. Mrs. DeNeo went on to say that the Unit's Secretary may have also seen this person. The Unit Secretary was available and at approximately 2334 hours on 15 December 1978 Reporting Officers interviewed Patricia Ax, ███████████.

Miss Ax advised that she was working at the 4th Floor Nurses Station on the 11th of December 1978 at approximately 2300 hours. She stated she did remember that a person had come up to that nurses station inquiring about Mr. Scow. Miss Ax thinks that the Scow family had just left the hospital. She recalled that he identified himself as a nephew and she described him as being chunky with a nylon jacket and possibly wearing glasses. Mrs. Ax was sitting at the desk and she did overhear the conversation with this person and Mrs. DeNeo. Miss Ax was shown the same photographs that were shown to Mrs. DeNeo and after looking closely at all the photographs, she picked out photograph #74-301 as being the one that most closely resembled the person who was at the 4th Floor Nurses Station on the 11th of December. She stated, however, that she could in no way be

Date/Time Report Completed: 16 Dec 78

Reporting Officer: Det. J. Pickell   229

sure that this was the person that was at the nurses station. Both Mrs. DeNeo and Miss Ax agreed again to be interviewed should the need arise in the future.

DAVID CRAM INTERVIEW

C.I.D. SUPPLEMENTARY REPORT / DES PLAINES POLICE

Original Offense: Missing Person

Victim: Piest, Robert J.

NARRATIVE:

The following is a recording of an interview of David Cram in reference to R.D.#: 78-35203. This interview is taking place at the Des Plaines Police Station the Second Floor Conference Room. Present for the interview are Detectives Pickell and Adams of the Des Plaines Police Department and David Cram. The starting time is 1411 hours on 16 December 1978.

David, do you understand that this interview is going to be taped?

David: Yes.

Do you have any objection to this interview being taped?

David: No

Do you understand that you are not under arrest?

David: Yes

Okay David, let me start out by asking you your address please.

David:

Your Phone number.

David:

And your Date of Birth.

David:

How long have you lived at your present address?

David: About a year.

What high school did you attend?

David: Schurz and Sullivan.

When did you attend Schurz?

David: Around '73.

And you were there for how long?

David: A full semester.

Would that be a half of a year?

David: A full year.

And what year of high school was that?

David: Freshman

After that, you transferred to another school?

David: Yes, Sullivan.

And you attended Sullivan for how long?

David: A half of term.

What happened after that half of a term at Sullivan?

David: I quit school after that and went to work for McDonalds.

Are you a high school graduate?

David: No, I'm not.

The McDonalds that you worked at where is that located?

David: Rogers Park on Clark Street.

And after McDonalds where did you work, Dave?

David: I was working at a Clark Gas Station on and off.

Okay, how long did you work at the Clark Station?

David: About 3 full years.

And, did you also work at the Jewel Food Store?

David: Yes, I did.

And you entered the Army on about February of 1975?

David: February 7, 1975.

And you were discharged on about February of 1976, is that correct?

David: Yes.

You also worked. Where did you work besides there?

David: I worked at Cassidy Tire.

And how long did you work there?

David: Approximately two months before meeting John.

Did you recall when it was that you first met this person, John? Who is John?

David: John was my previous employer.

What's his last name?

David: Gacy.

And do you recall when you first met him?

David: Um.

Would it have been the summer of '76.

David: Yes, the summer of '76 approximately the end of August or the beginning of August.

Under what circumstances or how did you meet John?

David: I was hitchhiking home and he picked me up in an Oldsmobile Station Wagon which was new at the time. I seen the P.D.M. Contractors sign in the window. We got in a discussion of construction, which I wanted to get into for a long time and he asked me what qualifications I had, and I explained them to him. And then he asked me if I could do any painting and I said I was pretty fair at it. With that he told me that he could use me on a job. He doesn't

CID CONTINUATION REPORT

C.I.D. CONTINUATION REPORT / DES PLAINES POLICE — PAGE 3

know how steady it would be, but that he could use me.

Who were you living with at the time that you met John?

David: I was living with my grandmother I believe.

And what is her name?

David: Violet Duchon. She is deceased now.

Are your parents alive?

David: Yes

Are they living together?

David: No they're not. They are divorced. My mother remarried.

And you indicated that you are now living with who?

David: My mother and my stepfather.

Okay, and her name is what?

David: Diane Weber.

Have you ever been arrested?

David: Yes, I have.

For what?

David: For Theft.

Okay, and how old were you when you were arrested?

David: 19

What was the disposition of that arrest?

David: A year's probation.

Okay, Have you ever at any time had occasion to live at the home of the employer, John Gacy?

David: Yes I have.

Can you recall when it was that you first lived there?

David: About a month or two after I started working for him.

That would bring us to approximately what month and year?

David: September, no about October or November, somewhere in there, of '76.

During the time that you lived with him, was there anything unusual regarding his behavior that you observed?

David: He ah, On occasion he asked me. We were carrying a discussion and he advised me. He came right out and stated that he was open minded and I advised him I am too. figuring that he was talking about females and it turned out to be just the opposite.

Did he ever approach you in a sexual manner to ask to participate in any type of sexual act?

David: Well he tried to bring up the discussion with me.

C.I.D. CONTINUATION REPORT / DES PLAINES POLICE　　PAGE 4

Can you tell us what you mean by that?

David: Yes Well, what it boils down to is I told him my outlook on Bi-sexualty and he he told me his and they were completely the opposite.

What was his opinion of this thing that you call bisexualty?

David: He sees nothing wrong with it. That if God didn't intend for one male to have sex with another male he wouldn't have put the organs, or something like that.

During this conversation, did he indicate what he meant by bi-sexualty?

David: When two males engage in sexual activities.

Has he indicated to you in any fashion that he has engaged in this type of sexual activity?

David: Just by the question asked.

Do you know of any time or do you know of any person that he has ever engaged in a sexual act with. This would be a person of the same sex as him?

David: No I do not.

During the time you were living with him, did you pay rent or room and board?

David: Yes, I did $25 a week.

Was that room and board?

David: No, that was just room. Intentionally I was free to use the food facilities that were on hand, but not very often.

Tell me what is your personal opinion of the type of person that this John Gacy is?

David: He is a hard working. Okay, he's devoted to his job and he lives, eats, breaths P.D.M. Contractors. But that's one side of him. The other side okay can be happy go lucky. Sometimes he's short tempered. Sometimes he's the most easiest going person in the world. Sometimes he patient. Sometimes he's not.

Has John ever been married?

David: Once that I know of.

Do you know who his first wife was?

David: No, Not off hand.

How about his second wife?

David: Carol, and I don't know her last name.

Were they married when you began working for Mr. Gacy?

David: No, they were just recently divorced to the best of my knowledge.

Does he have any children?

David: I believe he has a son, but he has never said.

Were there any other children

David: Michael

Named Michael.

Were there any other children in the marriage between he and Carol.

David: Okay, by them two no, but Carol by a previous marriage or a previous you know association with anybody she had two girls.

C I D CONTINUATION REPORT

C.I.D. CONTINUATION REPORT / DES PLAINES POLICE

During the time you were living with him has John brought home any male guests?

David: Oh yeah, there used to be male guests all the time.

Did any of them ever spend the night there?

David: No, not that I know of.

Do you know if John Gacy has ever during the time you were living with him or since you've known him gone out with young ladies or women?

David: Yes

How do you know that?

David: Well, I fixed him up with one girl. I know that. And a I went over there recent. The most recent one that I believe is another woman named Carol. There was a woman named Evelyn and there's been a few, you know, no lasting relationships.

Has John ever told you that he had a sexual relationship with any of these women?

David: Oh yeah, the same way guys talk you know a guys natural conversation.

You said that you fixed him up. Can you tell us about that?

David: Okay, we were down in Missouri and on a trip to Missouri to visit a previous girlfriend of mine and ah I fixed him up with one of her girlfriends. That I figured that he would have an enjoyable evening with. We left them at the motel and from there is heresay.

Where in Missouri were you?

David: St. Joseph.

When was that?

David: that was approximately '76 or '77. Later part of '76 or the early part of '77.

Was it over the winter months here in Illinois?

David: Yeah, I think it was around Spring maybe. Yeah, it was Spring.

What was the name of your girlfriend?

David: Sue Morris.

Do you know the name of the girl that you fixed him up with?

David: Also Sue, but the last name I'm not sure of.

Did you ever go out socially with John?

David: On occasion we go, I would meet him at bars or something like that and we go out and have a few drinks stuff like that. Sometimes we go to the Good Luck Lounge where Edward Hefner tends bar.

Do you know where that Good Luck Lounge is?

David: Yes, on Montrose and Elston.

And who is Ed Hefner?

David: Ed Hefner is an employee of his, and a friend of the family I believe.

Are there any other places that you frequented with John on more than one occasion I mean regular hang outs.

David: Ah, there's none really regulars, because we don't associate socially that often, but on occasion I've been to Vickie's Lounge, which he was going to purchase, I went to the Good Luck Lounge for about half an hour because he was going to purchase that also.

Where's Vickie's?

David: Vickie's I believe is approximately around Central, Central and right off of Irving, or maybe yeah going south from Irving.

Now you said you have been working for John for how long?

David: On and off for about 2, 2½ years. Somewhere in there.

Has he had other employees during this period of time?

David: Several

Do you recall any of their names?

David: Randy, Mike Ferraro, Ron Smith, Michael Rossi, which is working... 'm now, still. Ah and then there's more, but I really don't recall their names.

Were there several employees that have worked with him since you have been working with him?

David: Yes, most of them come in when I quit.

I see.

David: Most of them replace me or to pick up the work left.

Why do these employees

David: John, Well they just, 1) they don't like the aggravation that they have to put up with, cause John is so much of a perfectionist when it comes to the work, He wants everything, he wants it to be perfect and it gets down right to the point where he's nitpicking.

Okay, do you know how long Ed Heftner has been working for Mr. Gacy?

David: Approximately 4 months.

And you mentioned another employee. What is his name?

David: Michael Rossi?

Do you know how long he's been working for Mr. Gacy?

David: Six months before I started.

Okay, Now I'd like to ask you if you know anything about his ex wife, Carol. Do you know where she lives?

David: Well, she lived with him when he got married. So i'm not sure if she's still living at her mother's. Taking care of her mother, because from previous conversations with John the two are almost inseparable, but her mother lives on Lawrence approximately 5 blocks north of Irving, no east of Irving on the east of Cumberland.

Okay, do you know her last name?

David: No I don't.

C.I.D. CONTINUATION REPORT / DES PLAINES POLICE

Do you know Carol's last name?

David: No I don't.

Okay, I'd like to have you think about last Monday, Monday of this week, December 11th. Can you recall what you did that day?

David: Monday, the 11th. I think I stayed in all day.

Did you work

David: No, I think I slept cause I was working Sunday. I believe I slept up until my girl came over. So I could be wrong about that.

Okay, do you recall Tuesday of this week, December the 12th.

David: Yes I do.

Can you tell me what you remember about that day?

David: Tuesday I received a phone call in the morning approximately between 9 and 11 from John telling me that it would be okey to pick up the c.. .. .. . You go pick up the dry wall for a job that I'm doing on the side, cause he's got the truck available. He came and picked me up and then I found out we ended up going around to jobs and then we did get the dry wall, but I picked up another job from him, which is the Democratic Precinct Headquarters and we ran around t: a few stores Quality, which is on Elston and Wagner, Bel-Ray or Belmar Pharmacy, which is on Laramie, Belmont and Laramie, or Diversey and Laramie, one or the other. We stopped by the Les-On Drugs, which is on North Avenue. John wanted to see what kind of progress was being made. There we met Mike Rossi and Eddie Heftner, who was working on the job at the time and stopped to chat about how they were and just before he dropped me off to pick up materials, painting materials for the Demorcratic Precinct Headquarters. Then he dropped me off at approximately 5, 5:30, 4:30 somewhere in there, around Belmont and Sacremento.

During all this time you spent with John on Tuesday, did he discuss anything about the previous day, Monday.

David: If he did, it was just about the jobs.

Okay,

David: Which he's always talking about.

Did you get paid for Tuesday?

David: Cash no, but I did pick up a job for him, so I'll probably get paid. So I guess you consider it paid plus I gained knowledge from talking to the customers and finding out how to run down jobs, so on and so forth.

Can you tell me anything about Tuesday evening. Did you speak with John after he dropped you off.

David: No I didn't.

Can you recall anything about Wednesday.

David: Wednesday morning he called me up and, in the morning, woke me up and told me that I should come over and pick up. It was either I called him or he called me. The night before he told me I was to be at his house fairly early in the morning to pick up truck and materials for this painting job at the Democratic Precinct Headquarters, which is still, the materials are still on the job and the job's still not finished. And ah I did that. I

CID CONTINUATION REPORT XXX

went out there and he was not there. I picked up the keys for everything from Gordon, his office manager, and proceeded with the job. Later on that day he talked, I talked with him. Later on in the morning I talked with him and he said he would be around to check the job, but he didn't show up. The next time I heard anything about him is when I came to the house to drop off the keys after I was through with half of the job and as I walked in to work there was an investigation. I was approached by the Lt with a search warrant and badge and he explained to me what was going on.

And this was where?

David: This was at 8213 West Summerdale, his house.

Were you free to leave that location?

David: Yes.

Where did you go when you left?

David: I went to my girl's first and picked her up. Then we went over to my house, ate dinner, watched a little tv. I took her home, Oh, No, before I took her home we stopped off at a girlfriend's of her's house to see if her boyfriend had a battery for Mike Rossi for his car. Then I went and found out he didn't and went to her house, my girl's, and sat there and tried to get in contact with Michael by calling his house. Cathy, his wife, told me that he was out at John's house. So I figured that seeing as Michael had a key, he was just checking the on the premises or making sure the house was secure. I called for Michael at John's house. John answered the phone. I asked John, you know when did you get out, and so on and so forth, and he asked me where I could meet him.

Can I interrupt you now? What time was this when you spoke with John?

David: Approximately 11

At night?

David: yes.

Okay, and then what else did you say?

David: I asked him what was going on, and he said well I'd rather not talk over the phone, why don't I come and pick you up. Then I said okay and he came and picked me up, it was approximately quarter to twelve, 10 to twelve when he arrived at my girl's house. He didn't knock he beeped the horn. I went outside. From there we went to Golden Bear Restaurant on Forest Preserve Drive and Harlem, had two cheeseburgers, coffee. Left there, went to his house. At his house he felt insecure about staying there alone, not knowing whether the police were there or they would come back or not, so I stayed there for about 45 minutes to an hour. We went over his house. We tried to straighten up a few things and more or less just listen to him complain about how things were wrecked and the carpeting was torn up.

Did he specify anything that was wrecked to you?

David: Carpeting, his drawers. He said that one Officer put the stuff in his front hall closet back neatly. Then he went into his bedroom and found there was everything was all turned upside down. Not laying all over the place, still in the drawer, but not like it was.

C.I.D. CONTINUATION REPORT / DES PLAINES POLICE   PAGE 9

Did he indicate to you anything that he found to be missing?

David: Yeah, he said handcuffs, some pills, books, stuff like that.

Did he say what the handcuffs were for?

David: Well he didn't say it at that time, but I seen them before cause he does charity benefits, clowning for hospitals and stuff and that's what he uses them for.

You mentioned he said some pills were missing. Did he say what kind?

David: Preludins

What was that?

David: Preludins

Preludins?

David: Yeah

Were they prescription pills.

David: I don't know if they were prescribed for him or not cause he ____ ___e a weight problem, and I don't know if they were prescribed or not.

Did he indicate anything else that seemed to be missing?

David: No, he said he couldn't really think of anything. He'd have to go through things you know, just as he stumbled across them.

Did he walk through the house?

David: Yes he did.

Where did he go?

David: Crawl space.

Down under the house?

David: Yes

Did you see him go down there?

David: Yes I did.

When he went down there, what did he do while he was down there?

David: Okay, he seen the mud on the floor. Complained about that. Went into the crawl space with a flashlight and the lights were on also. Went down in there walked about, didn't even take a full step. He just went around in a complete circle and came back out.

Did he walk around at all down there?

David: No, he went down into the crawl space, crouched down, cause there's not much clearance to stand up under there. He went in a complete circle. All he did was check it out and then came back up into the house.

Did he go anywhere else in the house?

David: Attic, bedrooms, bathroom, laundry room, kitchen, back room, every space in the house.

And did he indicate that he found anything else to be missing?

David: Just what I said and he'd have to stumble over it. You know, if there's anything else.

C.D. CONTINUATION REPORT SXX

C.I.D. CONTINUATION REPORT / DES PLAINES POLICE

Okay, what time did you leave John's house?

David: Oh, about I'd say 1:30 quarter to two. 1:30 quarter to 2 somewhere in there.

Would that be in the morning or.

David: Ah, yeah that would be morning, early.

On which date?

David: Ah, Wednesday.

So are we talking now about the early morning hours. Would that be Wednesday or Thursday?

David: The early morning would be on Thursday.

Thursday morning.

Did he ask you anything about what happened while you were in his house and the police officers were there?

David: Yes he did. He said what were they looking for. What did they take? And also they had a few bags. There were probably other bags, because they were like mailing envelopes of some sort, brown, and he said no those were the books. He said were there about five of them and I said yeah and he goes what have they done with the book and I said they might have taken them with.

Did he say what kind of books they were?

David: He said dirty books.

Dirty Books?

David: Like that would be Playboy, all the way down the line, who knows?

Okay, do you recall what time you left John's house?

David: Approximately quarter to two.

Okay, where did you go?

David: We took a ride past the police station to see if his truck was, his car was left in the lot.

Did he tell you what his intention ...?

David: Yeah, if they were there, that he wanted to pick them up, the truck up, because he needed transportation on the jobs. If the car was there, he was going to take that, so that either a truck or a van would be supplied for the men to haul materials, so on and so forth.

Do you recall what time you got to Des Plaines?

David: I wasn't paying attention to the watch, but I arrived home at around 2:30. Give or take a few, 10 - 15 minutes anyway, and it had to be between the time I left John's house and the time I arrived home and I live in Chicago and it's approximately a 20 minute drive.

And you said you left John's house at what time?

David: It was approximately quarter to two.

Okay, you said earlier I believe that you left about 2:30, or am I mistaken.

David: No, I arrived home at 2:30 or so.

Did you have any more conversation with John after you got home?

David: After he dropped me off, the next time I talked to him was on the phone the next morning.

That would have been Thursday morning?

David: Yes, Thursday morning.

What time did you have a conversation with him?

David: Must have been around 10 o'clock, 9 o'clock somewhere in there. I talked to him on a job site. He was at a job site. He carried a radio beeper with him and I had him return the call, requesting another job.

Okay, where were you working on Thursday morning?

David: Democratic Precinct Headquarters which is on Montrose.

Do you recall what time you finished working at the Democratic Police Headquarters? Or the Democratic Precinct Headquarters?

David: Yeah about 5:25. I called in on his radio, or his telephone answering service. Left a message. Time out 4:35 and went back in the office. Knocked over paint. Had to clean that up, so it was about 5:25 when I left, so I called a cab from there. I arrived at his house at 6 o'clock, cause I stopped off at the Hunger Dog on Cumberland for a hot dog or Italian Beef and I arrived at the house at at approximately 6 o'clock. From there I met the Lieutenant and other police officers.

And what date was that?

David: That was on Thursday.

Did you work for John on Thursday?

David: Yes I did. Wednesday is when the investigation was right?

Wednesday is when the police officers were at his house.

David: That's when it was, Wednesday, not Thursday, it was Wednesday when I worked for him. Thursday I worked for the Fox Valley Shopping Center with Rich and Raphael.

Did you have any conversation with Mr. Gacy at that time?

David: Once in the morning when he picked me up so I could drop him off at his house. He originally wanted me to get a rent car with him and go pick up his vehicles at the police station and he said he couldn't get his vehicles back, so he'd have to do it himself. That Richard would meet me out at Fox Valley Shopping Center.

And what happened, how did you get out there?

David: I took the van.

And how did you get the van?

David: From John Gacy.

And how did you get to his house?

David: John Gacy picked me up at my house.

C.I.D. CONTINUATION REPORT / DES PLAINES POLICE PAGE 12

Do you recall what time you finished working at Fox Valley?

David: Yeah, 11 o'clock at night.

And what night was that?

David: Thursday.

Did you have any conversation with Mr. Gacy after that?

David: No I didn't.

Did you take the truck home?

David: Yeah, from Fox Valley Shopping Center at 11 o'clock I rolled into his house to pick up a wheelbarrow and unload headboards. I picked up the wheelbarrow and proceeded home.

Did you work Friday morning?

David: Yes I did. 7:30 in the morning I picked up Michael Rossi at his house. Followed him. Met Michael Rossi at his house, followed him, he drove his own vehicle. Followed him to North Avenue job. He parked his car at the North Avenue job, which is at North Avenue and Pulaski. Both of us drove over to a lumber yard, Southernland Lumber, which is about 4 or 5 blocks from the North Avenue job. Picked up material on the job, went back to the job with those materials. I picked up extra material that was on the job site. That I dropped off at John's garage for storage. Stopped off before going back to the North Avenue job for the second load. Stopped off and got gasoline, delivered the material from Century Tile and what material was in his garage I delivered that also. Brought it back to the North Avenue job. Made one more stop at Southernland Lumber to pick up something. From there I left the city to go to Fox Valley Shopping Center.

Did you have any conversation with Mr. Gacy when you met with him?

David: I ran into him. He pulled up in the driveway on the first trip out to his house before I stopped and got gas and I was loading up materials from his house.

And did he say anything.

David: Well, he just asked me you know, has the police got in contact with you and stuff like that.

Did he discuss anything at all about the police being at his home or related to his activites.

David: No, he said that he spent the night at his sister's house.

Where is that?

David: Approximately in Carpentersville. Somewhere around Carpentersville.

Can I ask you about your personal feeling about Mr. Gacy?

David: Well, It's hard to explain him. Sometimes he's the nicest guy in the world and sometimes he's evasive.

Has he ever indicated to you that he was arrested?

David: Yeah, he said he was arrested as odomy, I believe the word is. It's something to do with dirty films and stuff like that. Yeah, dirty films I believe it was. And prostitution. I think it was prostitution.

C I D CONTINUATION REPORT

Did he say where the arrest took place?

David: I believe it was Ohio or Oregon. Or one of the southern states down south.

Have you ever known Mr. Gacy to have an argument with anybody.

David: Oh, I argued with him all the time.

Okay, I'm talking about physically. Did he ever fight with a person.

David: Oh, Yeah, he and Michael Rossi were at Ma's Bar in Cicero, Little Joe, and they were out bar hopping. Michael, his friend and John. John was driving his own vehicle. Now this is just the story between the two of them okay. Now one has one story and one has another.. They both coincide pretty well, but you know, I wasn't there so I can't say. But the story that I got was from Michael. John wanted to shoot pool and he felt like he was being teamed up on. They were exchanging words, goofing around and like guys do and John took it personal and said "Hell with ya," and walked out of the bar. He walked out into the street. John's version, he walked out into the street, drove around the block once, came back in. He double parked out in front of the bar, which was across the street from Ma's Bar, was going to walk back in supposealy give Mike a ride back to his car, cause his car was parked on the north side. Michael was made because he stranded in Cicero, Illinois, and they also previously exchanged words earlier that day, had an argument. John pushed Michael earlier that day at a restaurant and they went outside and had a discussion and came back in, you know, buddy, buddy. Well anyway Michael had a few drinks and walked across the street. Met John halfway in the middle of the street. Knocked away two guys, one knocked his mother and went at John, where he proceeded to fight with John. John didn't strike no blows. He tried to hold Michael back. Michael swung at him and John said the other guy, Michael's friend, hit him three times. And with that John went to the hospital for a couple of days.

Do you know the name of Michael's friends?

David: No, I don't.

Do you know what hospital John went to?

David: That I don't know neither, but it should be on the police report.

Well, what police department was called?

David: Cicero Police. And the court was being held at First Avenue and Highway 65, right there at that court building. And they gave Michael a year's probation.

Mr. Gacy signed a complaint against Michael?

David: Signed a complaint against Michael, and was going to have Ma charged with Dram Shot act for serving, you know, for having that on and so forth, but after Michael This went on for about two months, I guess, Michael didn't work for him. Just before his court date John called Michael up asked him if he would like his job back. John's reason for this is no matter whether there is personal conflict or not. There should be no reason why should penalize myself because of the job, because of my job, cause Mike knows the system, Mike knows the carpentry So Michael accepted a position with John at $10 an hour. His salary and so on and so forth would be recorded at his job.

Do you know anything about the investigation that we are working on? Do you know what it's about.

David: Ah, Yeah I from what I think it's about some guy from Les-On Drugs or something like that, isn't it?

Okay. Now is there any reason for you to think that perhaps Mr. Gacy could be involved this?

David: Well, like I say John is a funny person you know, I mean in my past history from associating with people that don't put nothing past nobody.

Is there anything in your knowledge about Mr. Gacy that would cause you to believe that something similar to this might have happened before?

David: Well he is a bit of a bragger, so on and so forth and he lives in a fantasy world. I believe. Now how much is fact and how much is fiction that's left up to the individual to decide. But, he claims that he does work for syndicate and so on and so forth you know. But that's neither here nor there. I don't have actual proof of the individuals, You know actual proof that I could come right out and stake my life on it.

Has he ever told you that he has been involved in something like this before.

David: Ah, Yeah he said he was, you know.

What does he say?

David: Well, he said he, well let's see if I can get this right. He's said he set people up before and he's just a few different things, just basically like that.

Did John have any statement to make to you about whether or not he was involved in this?

David: Ah, yeah he said I did not have nothing to do, I Swear to you that I had nothing to do with this one, with this guy.

Did he lead you to believe that perhaps he was involved with somebody else?

David: Ah, Yeah you could come to that assumption.

Can you talk about that a little more.

David: Well, just by the way. I don't know. I imagine an innocent man would conduct, I mean he would get a little pissed off at the whole matter. Rather than to be shaken by it. Okay, I realize that it is a serious charge and everything, but why would he be upset as far as nervous and drawn out and you know go spend the night at his sister's house and be afraid of his own shadow more or less. Like I said it's personal opinion.

Have you ever found anything suspicious around his home or property?

David: Well, okay he's had a couple of wallets in the garage you known with identification in it. The identification was a driver's license, library card, military I.D. from maybe the Army Reserve or something like that. That was a little while back. school I.D., college I.D. I believe it was from De Vry Tech, De Vry Tech. I believe that's where it was from, De Vry Tech School I.D.

Do you recall any names on this identification?

David: I can't think of the names, no.

Now, how many wallets did you find?

David: About three.

Where were they?

David: They were in the cabinet, garage and the storage. Where he keeps his ah, nails and keeps his office supplies and just little junk more or less.

How long ago did you see these wallets?

David: About six months after I was working with him.

Did you mention finding these wallets to Mr. Gacy?

David: Yeah, I asked him if I could use the I.D. He said I was underage, so on and forth, and ah to go out with a couple of my older partners. To do drinking. He said, no you don't want those.

Did he say why?

David: He said cause they were some people that were deceased.

Would you repeat that?

David: Deceased. No longer living.

Did you ask him how he knew that?

David: No, because by the way he lives in that mysterious way. See I can't know if he was trying to put up an impression, because I grew up on the rough side of the street and I think he was more or less putting up an impression and he could be putting up an impression towards me. But then again he does it with just about everybody that I know of, so I just took it for granted. I just went by, you know didn't even ask a question, didn't have to.

Did Mr. Gacy ever mention anything about a trip to Wisconsin?

David: Ah, yeah he said he had to use a van one night for a trip to Wisconsin.

Okay, do you recall why he wanted to use the van?

David: He said he had to deliver a package. He said he had to deliver a package for "Let me quote his exact words" for something like Mr. Big or something like that you know.

Was there anything unusual about this particular trip?

David: Yeah, it was to late at night to be taking a trip to Wisconsin and coming back that morning.

What time was it about?

David: Well, he said he had to leave late.

And what time would you consider late?

David: We got done at 9 o'clock. We got done with the polls at 9 o'clock.

And what polls are you referring to?

David: Regular polls, Voting.

Do you recall which election it would have been?

David: The last one. The last election '78.

Presidential? Aldermanic

David: No, what was the last election that was just held,

Dunne?

David: Ah, the school superintendent.

C.I.D. CONTINUATION REPORT / DES PLAINES POLICE PAGE 16

Gubernatorial?

David: Yeah

Okay the gubernatorial election of '78?

David: Yes.

Was about the time he made the trip to Wisconsin? That would have been on/or about November 6, is that right?

David: Yeah

Okay, did anyone else have knowledge of that trip?

David: No they didn't. As a matter of fact it was the day before the voting.

And was there anything unusual about the van at that time? As best you can recollect.

David: Yes, it was on empty when I left and it was on empty when I brought it back and I did get chewed out, because I left the truck empty. Rule being that anybody using the vehicle is to fill it up. But seeing as it was so late at night and I was using it for the polls and I didn't take it anyway. I didn't think about filling it up.

Do you know where he went in Wisconsin?

David: No, I don't.

Do you know for a fact that he did make the trip?

David: I don't know for a fact, no.

Did you see him leave in the van?

David: No I didn't I went home I took the pickup truck home.

Has Mr. Gacy ever shown you any articles of jewelry?

David: Yeah, he gave me a couple of watches.

Okay, and where were the watches kept? And where did he obtain them?

David: Well he got the watches out of his dresser drawer.

Were they in a jewelry box or were they just laying loose?

David: Cigar box I believe.

Cigar Box. Did you question him about the watches?

David: I said thank you for the watch. I said why are giving this to me. Or no he goes. Previous to the conversation I was late and that week I was late about three four times and previous to the conversation after the ass chewing that I got everything calmed down a little bit and he walked into his room and said C'mere. I went in there and he said, he was digging through his box. He said here. Now there's no excuse for you to be late, and he handed me the watch. I said thanks a lot. At the time the watch was in fairly good condition and ah I said, where'd you get this one from and he goes from a dead person.

Did you question him any further about that comment?

David: no

Could you describe that watch?

David: Ah, Yeah it's a leather band with three smaller leather bands going around it. It was like a wrist band with a watch on it.

And do you recall the type of watch mechanism?

David: It was an off brand make. It was not a Seiko, but no, I'll take that back it I really didn't care very much. I think it was Lafayette or something like that.

And where is that watch now?

David: I have the band at home and I have a few watches laying around. I believe I might have them at home.

Did he ever give you any other or subsequent pieces of jewelry other than that particular watch?

David: He gave me another watch after I buried the one. Well, I was working on cement and the mechanism didn't keep time, so it lost 10 minutes everyday.

So the first watch was ruined? You retained the band.

David: Oh I kept the band, the band was beautiful. I mean i was in beautiful condition.

Did he then give you a second watch mechanism?

David: Yes he did.

Did you question him as to where he obtained the second mechanism?

David: No, the second one I didn't. I didn't question him the second time.

Have you ever seen any other articles of jewelry that he owns or has in his house?

David: Oh yeah, there was a lot of it in his box.

Do you recall any specific items?

David: Yeah, there's rings and stuff like that.

Had Mr. Gacy ever told you where he gotten any of the jewelry?

David: Not the jewelry itself, except for that watch in particular.

Have you ever seen any wedding bands, engagement rings, class rings, anything of that nature?

David: I couldn't tell you yes, because I'd be lying to you, cause I don't know for sure, I couldn't really place it right now.

Is there anything else that you can relate to us that you might consider importation to this investigation were working on?

David: Well, as far as violence goes with John, alright we wrestled around a few times He's a strong guy, but for someone wanting to, alright just an assumption you know If this guy that is missing, if he had a struggle with John. I think it could have been a fairly good fight if he was a halfway decent guy. But John's physical appearance, he's not as strong as he looks.

I'd like to ask you one more thing about the wallet in the garage. You mentioned that you wanted to use the identification perhaps to purchase alcohol.

David: Right, to go out drinking in bars.

Okay, as far as the driver's license is concerned?

David: It was still valid.

It was still valid.

David: I think it had a year left on it.

C.I.D. CONTINUATION REPORT

Would the description on that license be fairly similar to your physical stature and build at that time?

David: Ah, yeah I would say about at the time I was around 155 or 160. I was about 5'8" - 5'7", no about 5'8", 5'8 ½" and a brown hair, brown eyes.

Had you ever seen any other items of identification that may have belonged to anyone else in Mr. Gacy's home or his garage?

David: Well there was another wallet in there, but it doesn't flashback in my memory because I guess it didn't compare to me.

Are we talking about two wallets now or three.

David: No, there's two wallets.

Two wallets. Do you recall the color of those wallets?

David: One was brown and one was black.

Were there any other identifying features about the wallet?

David: one was a triple, okay you folded it twice and that was the wallet with it my description, and that was black. And the other one was just a regular fold wallet.

The brown was a regular billfold.

David: Yes billfold.

Do you recall any particular piece of identification in the brown wallet. The billfold?

David: No, I can't. No, maybe a couple of pictures, but that was about it.

Has Mr. Gacy ever been known to retain pieces of identification such as driver's license social security cards or school I.D. cards or things of that nature that other youths might be able to use.

David: Well, not really Okay like say when I was living there okay I get a tendency to misplace things at times. Like one time my wallet was missing and I don't know where it was with all my identification, all my pictures, so on and so forth. Now whether it would be it wants to create a psychological effect or something I don't know.

Does Mr. Gacy own any real estate in Wisconsin, or does he have any relatives that would own any property.

David: Yes he has a relative that just moved out of Wisconsin back to Elgin. And ah they had a hot dog stand.

And do you recall the location of that hot dog stand.

David: No, but it's on his job files. The hot dog stand is now closed down because they were, there pending an investigation, his relatives, and

What would the investigation involve?

David: He was caught stealing money from a bank?

Embezzlement?

David: Yeah.

Do you recall the names of those relatives?

David: Not off hand, Kuzman I think.

Kuzman?

David: Yeah

And that was near any particular town that you can recall, or city?

David: No, like I said it should be on his job file. Okay, the investigation that's pending is Odebt Kuzmas. The FBI I guess is going through it. She's now back in Belgium.

Is there anything else that you can tell us that you feel we should know in reference to to this investigation?

David: Not off hand.

Did we have a conversation at the Friendly Restaurant at the Fox Valley Shopping Center today, 16 December 1978 at approximately 1145 a.m.?

David: Yes we did.

This interview was terminated at 1712 hours on 16 December 1978.

SURVEILLANCE AND MORE EVIDENCE

SUPPLEMENTARY REPORT / DES PLAINES POLICE

Date/Time Report: 16 Dec 78 - 2019 Hours

Address: 2722 Craig

On December 16, 1978 at approximately 1027 hours Detectives Pickell and Adams interviewed Richard Raphael, DOB: [redacted] in The Friendly Restaurant at the Fox Valley Shopping Center in Aurora, Illinois. Richard Raphael, a general contractor, entered the contracting business approximately 10 years ago and, as indicated by Mr. Raphael, he is responsible for building stores. Raphco Incorporated is only a few months old and was started by Mr. Raphael in August of 1978. Prior to being involved with Raphco, Mr. Raphael was involved in with a company known as Henber. Mr. Raphael said he is presently associated with Mr. Gacy, as Gacy is considered a superintendent in the Raphco Company, although he emphasized that Mr. Gacy is not considered a partner. The P.D.M. Company is solely owned by Mr. Gacy. Mr. Raphael met John Gacy approximately 3 years ago, in which case John and Richard started on a subcontractor basis. While affiliated, John Gacy provided general building services such as painting and carpentry. Mr. Raphael indicated that he has never had any problems with Mr. Gacy. Approximately 2½ years ago Richard Raphael entered into a new partnership, at which time John Gacy did not get along with Mr. Raphael's partner, therefore Richard Raphael sold his interest in the company. At approximately the same time John Gacy quit a company which was referred to as P.E. Systems and Gacy came to work for Richard Raphael. As a superintendent, John Gacy is paid $675 weekly, plus labor and material, in which case Gacy receives his money from Richard Raphael and in turn John Gacy pays his employees from the money he receives from Mr. Raphael. Mr. Raphael indicated that his association with Gacy began in September of 1978 and had not seen Gacy in 1977 or 1978 prior to September of 1978. Mr. Raphael indicated that John Gacy did have access to the Raphael residence. Mr. Raphael was then questioned regarding the personal relationship between him and John Gacy, at which time Mr. Raphael replied that he did not consider himself to be on the same social level as John Gacy. When asked to elaborate on that statement, Mr. Raphael said "Most of my associates are more professional, such as doctors or lawyers," and that he never socialized with Gacy. Mr. Raphael went on to say that he has only been married two years and that his relationship with John Gacy is 100 per cent business. Mr. Raphael indicated that he had never observed any odd behavior on John Gacy's part and a couple of weeks ago Gacy had mentioned to his wife that he was married or had been married. Gacy had further stated that approximately 2½ years ago a female with a couple of kids had been living with him, although it is unknown if the female he was referring to was, in fact, Gacy's wife.

Upon being questioned about Mr. Gacy's employees, Mr. Raphael replied that John used to pick up guys to work for him, although he does not recall the names of the employees, because there were to many names to remember. Mr. Raphael used Mr. Gacy and Mr. Gacy's employees whenever necessary and was certain that the following individuals are presently employed by John Gacy. #1: Michael Rossi, #2: Ed Heftner and #3: David Cram. Mr. Raphael was then asked if he had any information regarding Ed Heftner, at which time he replied he believes Heftner is 23 or 24 years old, is married, has 2 children and appears to be a nice guy. We then asked Mr. Raphael if he was familiar with an individual named Gordon, at which time he replied that he believes Gordon is a relative of John Gacy's and that Gordon does the book work for John Gacy and works about a half a day.

We then questioned Mr. Raphael regarding Max Gussis, the plumber, at which time he replied Max is very strange, not worth talking to, a nut, unreliable, can't be trusted, must be watched very closely and in addition not a very good plumber. When asked if Mr. Raphael had any additional information regarding John, he stated that John is not known to take vacations and would be considered a workaholic, that he talks a big time and is the commissioner of streets in Norwood Park. We then requested any information regarding any telephone conversations between Richard Raphael and the Nisson Pharmacy on Tuesday, December 12, 1978.

As best as Mr. Raphael can recall, he stated that he had called the drug store and spoken with a pharmacist and believed that call was placed sometime during the day. When asked about the business relationship, Mr. Raphael indicated that John Gacy is responsible for making estimates and if it involved something worthwhile, he would become involved. Mr. Raphael feels that John Gacy is not up on complex matters, although he could be trained. Mr. Raphael said on Monday, December 11, 1978, he had a phone conversation with John Gacy, in which case he believed that John Gacy was to spend a portion of his day on a job site on North Avenue and had a subsequent appointment at 1700 hours at Nisson Pharmacy. Mr. Raphael stated that the last time he spoke with John Gacy on Monday, December 11, 1978, was sometime between 1730 and 1830 hours, although he does not recall if he called John Gacy or John Gacy called him. Although he does remember that he was at his residence, although he does not know the whereabouts of John Gacy. On Monday, December 11, 1978, at approximately 2230 hours Richard Raphael attempted to contact John Gacy to inquire why John did not attend an important meeting which had been scheduled for 1900 hours that date. Mr. Raphael stated that when he attempted to contact Gacy at 2230 hours, he found that Gacy's phone was busy. Richard Raphael advised these Officers that at approximately 2235 hours he received a call from John Gacy, at which time Gacy advised him that, although he was home, he did not answer his phone. Mr. Gacy further advised Mr. Raphael that he had a flat tire and was concerned because his uncle was sick or had died and that he did not want to talk and did not want to do business. Mr. Raphael then informed Mr. Gacy that he would speak with him at 0700 hours on Tuesday, December 12th. On December 12, 1978 Mr. Raphael met with Mr. Gacy, at which time Mr. Gacy stated to Mr. Raphael that he did not want to talk on the phone and he did not have a flat tire. During the conversation between Mr. Gacy and Mr. Raphael, both individuals were at their respective homes. The 0700 hours conversation involved the fact that John Gacy missed the important meeting which had been scheduled for 1900 hours on 11 December 1978. Mr. Raphael stated that he went to John Gacy's home on Tuesday, December 12, 1978, at approximately 0745 hours, as the two had planned to have breakfast and while at the Gacy residence, Mr. Gacy was on the phone with someone from the police department, at which time he was advised by Gacy that the police department wished to speak with him, as he had been a character witness. Mr. Raphael indicated on Tuesday morning John Gacy and Richard Raphael met for breakfast and, after breakfast, went to give an estimate and ultimately went to the Gacy residence. While at the Gacy residence, Mr. Raphael observed that Gordon was in the office. Mr. Raphael advised us that Mr. Gacy had placed a few calls and subsequently went to the police station. John Gacy had indicated to Mr. Raphael that he had an appointment at Nisson Pharmacy for 1700 hours and is certain of that time because he had scheduled an appointment for 1730 hours that date. Mr. Raphael advised us that John Gacy had stated that while at Nisson Pharmacy, he had forgotten his book. Richard Raphael stated that he did not notice anything odd about Gacy's behavior on Tuesday morning, December 12th.

When questioned regarding the activities of Mr. Gacy on Wednesday, December 13, 1978, Mr. Raphael was unable to provide us with any information regarding that date.

Mr. Raphael stated that he went to the Gacy residence at approximately 2330 hours the same date Gacy was released from the police station. Mr. Gacy then advised Mr. Raphael that the police had taken some magazines, some speed, some marijuana and

had stated there and had plasma attacks. Mr. Raphael has never known John Gacy to smoke grass and did make reference to some stag films. Mr. Gacy further advised Mr. Raphael that the police had taken a portion of his carpeting, which contained blood stains and that the blood on the carpet was from a cut when the carpet had been installed when someone cut himself. Mr. Raphael was asked if he was aware of any employees presently living with John Gacy, in which case he replied negatively. Mr. Raphael was familiar with the fact that at one time Michael Rossi and David Cram did stay at the Gacy residence and that other young kids had also been staying there. Mr. Raphael was then questioned regarding the important meeting which had been scheduled for Monday, December 11, 1978.

Mr. Raphael advised us that sometime between 1700 and 1800 hours on December 11, 1978 he had received a phone call from John Gacy, although John did not give his location, at which time John advised him that he would attend that meeting which had been scheduled for sometime between 1900 and 1930 hours. Mr. Raphael further indicated that he was under the distinct impression that John and another individual would attend that meeting and he had further stated to John that he had ordered a pizza for him. Mr. Raphael stated that the four individuals that were to attend the meeting to discuss some fixtures were the superintendent of the Bruce/Ken Pharmacy, himself, Richard Raphael, a Les-On representative and John Gacy. Mr. Raphael stated that when he determined that John Gacy did not attend the meeting, which had been scheduled for 1900 hours, he attempted to reach Gacy and ultimately Gacy contacted him at 2235 hours. Mr. Raphael was then questioned regarding the Tuesday meeting he had with John Gacy, which was held at the Bruce and Ken Pharmacy at which time we were advised that the Tuesday meeting was not scheduled until after John Gacy had missed the important meeting on Monday evening.

Richard Raphael said that on Wednesday John Gacy was to be running the North Avenue job and a few other errands, although when he spoke with him, Gacy appeared to be somewhat incoherent. In Mr. Raphael's opinion, John Gacy did not know he was going into the police station. Mr. Raphael stated that he first knew John Gacy was at the police station at approximately 1430 hours when he received a call from Gacy, at which time Gacy requested that Mr. Raphael get him an attorney, as he was aware of the fact that Mr. Raphael's father is an attorney. Prior to concluding our interview, Mr. Raphael was asked how well he knew John Gacy, to which he replied "I never took the time to know him that well." John has been acting irrational or scared since Wednesday. We then asked Mr. Raphael if John Gacy was aware of the fact that we were going to interview him today, to which he replied yes, John is aware of our meeting and that he made no request regarding any coaching. John advised Mr. Raphael to tell the police everything they know. We then requested any pertinent information Mr. Raphael might have regarding the youths employed by Mr. Gacy, at which time we were advised that he has only known the kids for a couple of months, therefore did not have to much information. Prior to terminating the interview, Mr. Raphael was advised that it may be necessary to speak with him again, at which time he advised us that he would cooperate in any way possible. The interview was terminated at 1140 hours on 16 December 1978.

DES PLAINES POLICE DEPARTMENT 78-35203

CONSENT TO SEARCH WAIVER

RB # _____

I, ███████████████, hereby give my consent to the search of my Boss's {JOHN GACY}, ~~home~~, VAN TRUCK ~~_____,_____,_____~~) upon the request of Officer J. PICKELL. I understand that I have a constitutional right to refuse to allow this search ~~████████████████████████████~~. However, I agree to allow this search of my own free will, without any force, promises or threats. (In the case of a joint tenant, wife, mistress or other party [Company] include: "This (house, apartment, room, automobile, etc.) as above described is used jointly by ███████████████ and myself, but it is also my WORK VEHICLE (home or automobile) and as such you may search the WORK VEHICLE, (house, apartment, room, automobile)."

Dated this Dec. 16 day of 6 , 19 78 at 3:06 (p.m)/a.m.).

Signed: ████████████████

Witnesses:
████████████████

SUPPLEMENTARY REPORT / DES PLAINES POLICE

16 DEC 78

MISSING PERSON

ROBERT J. PIEST

Off. Mukahiru + Off. O'Connell were assigned to assist the Illini Search and Rescue Team (equipped with dogs) in a search of the wooded areas from East River Rd west to River Rd and Lawrence north to Higgins Rd. The search began at 07:45 hrs. and ended at 16:15 hrs. due to darkness. All results proved negative at the termination of the search.

Date/Time Report Completed: 16 DEC 78 16:45

VEHICLE TOW REPORT - DES PLAINES POLICE

Offense Code: 1050
Date/Time Occurred: 16 Dec 78
Beat Assigned: 100
Date of Occurrence: 16 Dec 78

8. REASON FOR TOW:

1. ☐ ABANDONED — CITY CODE 10-14-2, 7-DAY NOTICE ISSUED _____ DATE _____ TIME _____
2. ☐ ILLEGAL PARKING - PRIVATE PROPERTY — CITY CODE 10-13-1, CITATION NO. _____
3. ☐ RECOVERED STOLEN VEHICLE — LOCAL ☐ FOREIGN ☐
4. ☒ HOLD FOR INVESTIGATION - EXPLAIN IN NARRATIVE
5. ☐ TRAFFIC HAZARD — OBSTRUCTING TRAFFIC - CITATION NO. _____ EXPLAIN IN NARRATIVE
6. ☐ UNDER ARREST - VEHICLE CONTROLLED BY ARRESTEE

10. Towed by: DNA

13. Color	14. Year	15. Make	16. Body	18. Year	19. State	20. Appears Driveable
Black	1978	Chev.	Van	1979	Ill	Yes ☒ No ☐

21. VIN: CGL258J118817

25. Vehicle Searched By: CCSPD
28. Evidence Tech Processed: Yes ☒ No ☐

29. Name Owner: Gacy, John W.
30. Address: 8213 W. Summerdale, Norwood
31. Home Phone: 457-1614
32. Business Phone: 457-1614

33. Name Driver: Cram, David

37. Personal Property in Vehicle: Yes ☒ No ☐

NARRATIVE:

Vehicle Driven T. 1420 Miner Street, Des Plaines, By David Cram, From Fox Valley Shopping Center, Aurora. Vehicle In Squad Garage. Vehicle Held For Processing And Investigation.

40. Date Report Completed: 16 Dec 78

Reporting Officer: Det. Ryan / R. Adams #162

SUPPLEMENTARY REPORT / DES PLAINES POLICE — 16 Dec 78 2260 hours

Piest, Robert J.

The following report reflects my activities in a follow up investigation of a missing person's report which was originally filed on December 10, 1978 by the victim's mother.

On December 14, 1978 I had an occasion to go to the residence of Michael A. Rossi on [redacted] to transport him to the station for questioning in regards to the missing person's case we were working on at the time. It was at this time that I observed Michael Rossi arrive at his home in a white '71 Plymouth Satellite bearing Illinois for '78 plates [redacted]. Michael Rossi was then transported to the station for questioning and subsequently released.

On December 16, 1978 I had an occasion to speak to Detective Bellmini, of Area 6/General Assignment, Chicago Police Department, reference to the John A. Szyc case and obtained a copy of the missing person's report. While at the station reviewing the report, I noticed that the vehicle in question that was listed for John Szyc was a '71 white Plymouth Satellite bearing license plate number [redacted]. It was at this time that it occurred to me that this was the same type of vehicle which was being driven by Michael Rossi. I attempted to get a 10-28 on the '76 plate [redacted] but due to the age I was unable to do so. I was advised that Officer Adams had obtained a amount of paperwork from Szyc's mother and among them was the registration for 1977 for Szyc's car. The license plate issued to him was [redacted] Illinois for 1977. I was able to obtain a 10-28 on this, which registered to John A. Szyc at [redacted] This vehicle showed that it had a serial number of RH23G16239297 on a 1971 Plymouth Satellite 2 door. I then went to the Soundex System and looked up Michael A. Rossi Jr. and found that he had a 1971 white Plymouth Satellite bearing Illinois '78 plates [redacted] This plate, when run through the computer, indicated that it had a registration of RH23G16739297. It was here that it was determined that this was very probably the same car. The only number difference would have been the number following the second 6. On Szyc's registration it shows as a 2 and on Rossi's it shows as a 7. A registration check was immediately sent and it was later determined that this was one in the same vehicle after one of the officers went down to the house of Rossi and also viewed the vehicle and saw the serial number to be, in fact, a 2 and not a 7 as indicated on his registration and title form. It was now positively determined that this was the vehicle that belonged to John A. Szyc at one time. Further action to follow.

16 Dec 78

Det. R. Tovar 222

PROPERTY INVENTORY

DES PLAINES POLICE DEPARTMENT

1. **Offense:** Missing Person
2. **Date and time property recovered:** 16 Dec. 1978 1400 Hrs.
3. **Complaint Number:** 78-35203
4. **Location:** Police Garage - 1420 Miner, Des Plaines, Ill. 60014
5. **Check One:** Recovered X Evidence X
6. **Owner Name:** Unknown
7. **Recovered From:** 1979 Oldsmobile - Black - 1978 - [REDACTED] - VIN: 3N69R9X105706

Item	Quantity	Description	Value	Rel./Sed To (Signature) Date
1.	1	Hair Like Fiber		
2.				
3.				
4.				
5.				
6.				
7.				
8.				
9.				
10.				
11.				
12.				

14. **Reporting Officer:** Lt. Joseph Kozenzak 12-16-78
15. **Supervisor Approving:**
16. **Date:** [REDACTED] 566 16 Dec 78 1615
17. **Returned to Custodian:**

FINAL DISPOSITION OF PROPERTY

PROPERTY CUSTODIAN

PLAINES POLICE DEPARTMENT — PROPERTY INVENTORY

Offense: Missing Youth
Date and Time Property Recovered: 16 Dec. 78 1827
Complaint Number: 78-3520B

Check One: □ Found [ ] Recovered [X] Evidence

Recovered From Name: CRAM, David

Quantity	Description	Value	Released to (Signature)	Date
1	Paisley Print Multi Color S.S. Shirt Traditional 15-15½		▇	1/2/79
1	Lausanne Men's Watch, ½ the Band Missing		▇	1/2/79
1	Black Leather Watch Band		▇	1/2/79
	X X X			
	Voluntarily T.O.T. R/O For Investigation			
	X X X			

Reporting Officers and Star No.: ▇367

form #51

Offense: Missing Youth

Date and Time Property Recovered: 18 Dec 78 1700

Check One: Evidence ☒

Recovered From: Szyc

Item	Quantity	Description	Value	Released To (Signature)
1.	1	Brown Bag Containing A Various Assortment Of Papers		
2.	1	Motorola Guarantee And Service Book Serial T3167 9894, Model No. BP3050KN, Factory Code 24M73.		
3.	1	Sears Radio Brochure Listing Model Number 800-20140400, 57 2014.		
4.	1	1977 Veh. Reg.		

Reporting Officers and Star Nos.: Det. Ronald F. Adams #467

NAME	ERSON	DATE AND TIME PROPERTY RECOVERED 19 DEC, 1978 1618 HRS	
LOCATION 1920 TOUHY AVE, DES PLAINES, ILL		CHECK ONE: FOUND ☐ RECOVERED ☐ EVIDENCE ☒	

RECOVERED FROM: LINDA MERTES

ITEM	QUANTITY	DESCRIPTION	VALUE	RELEASED TO (SIGNATURE)
1.	1	8½" X 11" SHEET OF PAPER TITLED "DAILY LOG OF ORDERS" SUNDANCE PHOTO, INC INDUSTRIAL DRIVE JACKSON, WIS. 53037 PHONE (414) 677-2233		
7.				
8.		ENVELOPE NUMBERS #36090, RECEIVED 12/2 & RETURNED THROUGH #36120, RECEIVED 12/2 & RETURNED 12/14		

REPORTING OFFICERS AND STAR NOS.
R. ADAMS #167 & J. PICKELL #229

Missing Young ▓ 19 Dec 78   1521

☐ FOUND ☐ RECOVERED ☐ EVIDENCE

RECOVERED FROM: D.P.P.D.   ADDRESS: 1420 Miner Street

ITEM	QUANTITY	DESCRIPTION	VALUE	RELEASED TO / SIGNAT
1	4	IBM Disk Packs		
2		L7X9143-52		
3		L7X8873-53		
4		L7X8877-04		
5		L7X9144-05		

#167

C.I.D. SUPPLEMENTARY REPORT / DES PLAINES POLICE	1. DATE/TIME THIS REPORT 17 Dec 78 1430 Hours
2. ORIGINAL OFFENSE: Surveillance	3. OFFENSE CHANGED TO
4. VICTIM	5. ADDRESS

NARRATIVE:

At about 0010 hours R/O and Officer Albrecht started our surveillance of John Gacy. We relieved the other units and began to follow Gacy westbound on the Kennedy Expressway at Lawrence. At 0030 hours Gacy drove to the Moose Lodge in Des Plaines. While in the Moose Lodge, Gacy spent most of the time speaking with a Ed Hefner. At 0130 hours Gacy left the Moose Lodge and went to the Pot & Pan Restaurant in Des Plaines and stayed at that location until 0200 hours. Gacy then drove south on River Road to Algonquin, east on Algonquin to Talcott, Talcott to Cumberland and he entered the Kennedy Expressway towards Chicago. At approximately 0215 hours Gacy arrived at the Good Luck Bar in Chicago located on Elston and Pulaski. Parked right by the door was a brown van, license number 127-603RV. Gacy got in the van, spoke with the occupants for a few minutes and then entered the Good Luck Bar by himself. He left the bar at approximately 0315 hours and went to another bar located at 3535 West Irving Park in Chicago. The name of that bar was PJ's. He stayed at that location from approximately 0315 hours to about 0430 hours and most of that time sat and spoke with a female by the name of Pam Sokolowski. At 0430 hours he went to a bar called the Unforgetable at 4200 West Irving Park Road in Chicago. He left that location at 0500 hours. The subject then drove to Franklin Park looking for an open bar with negative results. The subject then proceeded to Cumberland Avenue where he went in the Golden Bear Restaurant in Norridge. After eating breakfast, he drove back to his home and arrived there at 0615 hours. At 0910 hours a black Lincoln Continental with license plate number AF-7426 driven by a Ed Frey stopped by the house and he entered the house. A short time later both subjects left the house in their own vehicles. They were en route to Pulaski and North at their construction site. On the way to that location, Gacy stopped on Tripp Avenue in Chicago, where Ed Hefner lives. He stayed there for a few minutes and then went on to the construction site by himself to Pulaski and North. At about 1230 hours Ed Hefner then showed up at the construction site at Pulaski and North and went inside. We were then relieved by the on-coming shift.

6. CASE STATUS: ☐ CLEARED/ARREST ☐ CLEARED/EXCEPTIONAL ☐ UNFOUNDED ☐ INACTIVE FILE ☒ FURTHER ACTION REQUIRED	7. DATE/TIME REPORT COMPLETED 17 Dec 78
8. PROPERTY/EVIDENCE RECOVERED YES ☐ NO ☐	9. LEADS MSG. REQUESTED YES ☐ NO ☐	10. CONTINUED ON C.I.D. CONTINUATION REPORT ☐
11. REPORTING OFFICER-PRINT: Off. D. Hachmeister STAR 231	12. REPORTING OFFICER SIGNATURE	13. SUPERVISOR: Joseph Kozenczak

R.D. # 78-35203
DPPD FORM # 211

VEHICLE TOW

EAST RIVER RD. N. SOUTH OF		17 DEC 78	13:30
OUT OF TOWN	A-12		SUN.
R/O			

NARRATIVE: A MEMBER OF THE ILLINI SEARCH AND RESCUE TEAM WHILE SEARCHING THE ABOVE AREA GOT HIS VEHICLE STUCK ON THE EAST SIDE OF THE STREET. THE TEAM WAS WORKING WITH DES PLAINES POLICE IN CONNECTION WITH A MISSING PERSON. R/O CALLED SCHIMKA FOR THE TOW. THE BILL WILL BE SENT TO THE CITY.

VEHICLE: 1976 INTERNATIONAL SCOUT
YELLOW
IL 78,

MISSING PERSON

PIEST, ROBERT J.

R/O AND THE JCLIUI SEARCH AND RESCUE TEAM MADE A SEARCH OF THE AREAS FROM HIGGONS NORTH TO TOUHY AVE, AND FROM RIVER RD. EAST TO DEE RD. THE TEAM ALSO COVERED AN AREA FROM RIVER RD EAST TO THE DES PLAINES RIVER AND FROM TOUHY NORTH ABOUT A MILE AND A HALF.

THE SEARCH TEAM DISCOVERED CAR TIRE TRACKS STARTING ON TOUHY AVE 1/4 MILE EAST OF RIVER RD. HEADING NORTH INTO THE WOODS. R/O AND THE TEAM FOLLOWED THE TRACKS (DOWN AN OLD WORK TRAIL) 3/4 OF A MILE INTO THE WOODS ALONG THE RIVER. (THERE ARE MARKS WERE THE CAR WAS STUCK TWICE 50 FT APART) A SHORT DISTANCE LATER THE CAR TRACKS STOP IN AN AREA CLOSE TO THE RIVER. THERE ARE SEVERAL FOOT PRINTS FROM THE ROAD DOWN TO THE RIVER. THE TRACKS THEN LEFT THERE STILL HEADING NORTH ABOUT 50 FT TO A TURN AROUND SPOT. THE CAR THEN FOLLOWED THE SAME PATH BACK TO TOUHY AVE, GOING OFF THE TRAIL NEAR THE END ALMOST HITTING A FENCE. THE CAR THEN BACKED INTO THE PATH AGAIN AND LEFT THE AREA.

17 DEC 78 1615

| C.I.D. SUPPLEMENTARY REPORT / DES PLAINES POLICE | 1. DATE/TIME THIS REPORT 18 Dec 78 · 0130 Hours |

| 2. ORIGINAL OFFENSE: Surveillance | 3. OFFENSE CHANGED TO |
| 4. VICTIM | 5. ADDRESS |

NARRATIVE:

On 17 December 78 at 2345 hours R/O and Officer Albrecht began a surveillance of John Gacy. This subject entered the Marriott Hotel in Chicago on Michigan Avenue. He checked on a job site at that location and left the hotel at 0005 hours on the 18th of December 78. He then drove to another job site, a shopping center under construction called The Brick Yard, which is located at Diversey and Nina in Chicago. He arrived there at 0035 hours and left that area at 0050 hours. He then proceeded to the Golden Bear Restaurant at 0100 hours, had breakfast and left that area at 0220 hours. He then proceeded to his home. He arrived there at 0235 hours and that is at 8213 Summerdale. He stayed at that location until 0845 hours. At 0900 hours he arrived at 222 Prospect in Park Ridge and spoke with his attorney until 1055 hours. He went back to his home at 1100 hours. While at his home, two subjects arrived, one driving a black over yellow '68 Oldsmobile Cutlass license number US-2154. The second subject arrived at 1125 hours driving a black over blue Olds 98 license number AD-1517. At 1230 hours Reporting Officers were relieved by the on-coming shift.

R.D. #78-35203

6. CASE STATUS: ☐ CLEARED/ARREST ☐ UNFOUNDED X FURTHER ACTION REQUIRED ☐ CLEARED/EXCEPTIONAL ☐ INACTIVE FILE	7. DATE/TIME REPORT COMPLETED 18 Dec 78
8. PROPERTY/EVIDENCE RECOVERED YES ☐ NO ☐	9. LEADS MSG. REQUESTED YES ☐ NO ☐	10. CONTINUED ON C.I.D. CONTINUATION REPORT ☐
11. REPORTING OFFICER-PRINT: Off. D. Hachmeister STAR 231	12. REPORTING OFFICER SIGNATURE	13. SUPERVISOR APPROVAL: Lt. Joseph Kozenczak

DPPD FORM # 211

C.I.D. SUPPLEMENTARY REPORT / DES PLAINES POLICE

Date/Time This Report: 18 Dec 78 1500 Hours

Original Offense: Missing Person

Victim: Piest, Robert

NARRATIVE:

At 1355 hours on 17 December 1978 Detective Pickell and Cook County Sheriff's Police Investigator Bedoe interviewed Michael A. Rossi, ▓▓▓▓▓▓▓▓ DOB: ▓▓▓▓▓▓▓▓ The interview took place in the second floor conference room of the Des Plaines Police Department. Also present for portions of the interview was Lt. Kozenczak.

In summary, Michael said that he was born in Arkansas and his parents moved to Chicagoland when he was about two months old. He lived periodically in Cicero and in Berwyn. At present his mother lives in an apartment attached to a tavern she runs called "Little Joe's" at ▓▓▓▓▓▓▓▓ He is presently living at ▓▓▓▓▓▓▓▓ a building that is owned by his father-in-law. Michael attended Morton East High School for two years, '74/'75, and '75/'76. After high school, he went to work for Max Gussis, who ran Hock Plumbing. He stated that he worked for Hock Plumbing for a couple of months, but the pay was no good, so he quit and went to work for P.D.M. Construction Company. The owner of P.D.M. Construction Company was John Gacy. Mr. Gacy was a friend of Max Gussis. Michael started at P.D.M. Construction in approximately June of 1976. At present Michael is a carpenter for P.D.M. Construction making $10 per hour. He is happy with the work and he has no interest in becoming a union carpenter. He advised that during the winter of 1977/1978, he lived with his employer, John Gacy, for two to three months to save money. He was paying Mr. Gacy $25 per month, which did not include meals. He was single at the time and after living with Mr. Gacy for that two to three month period, he then got his own apartment at ▓▓▓▓▓▓▓▓ Michael got married in the spring of 1978. His wife's name is Kathleen and her Date of Birth is ▓▓▓▓▓▓▓▓ He has a son, ▓▓▓▓▓▓▓▓ age 9 weeks. Michael advised that approximately 1000 hours on 12-17-78 Mr. Gacy called him at home from the North Avenue job. He wanted to know if Mike had called David to work that day at the North Avenue store. Mike told Mr. Gacy that he had not called David and that Mr. Gacy should call him himself. At approximately 1030 hours on 17 December 1978 David Cram called Mike Rossi and at that time Mike Rossi told David to call Mr. Gacy. Cram told Mike that his car had been vandalized on 16 June 1978 in the area of the International Amphitheater in Chicago where Cram was attending a concert. Rossi further advised that Mr. Gacy had asked him about his interview with the Des Plaines Police Department on the 14th of December 1978. Rossi advised that on 12-16-78 he worked with Gacy. He said that Mr. Gacy had called him and directed Rossi to pick Gacy up at his home. After picking Gacy up, he went to the Shell Gas Station on Higgins between Canfield and Cumberland to gas up and then both parties went to Tannenbaum Hardware on Belmont. Rossi advised that worked until 1800 hours and after quitting working he had a couple of beers at the tavern next door to the North Avenue job and he then went home. He was asked if he took Mr. Gacy home, and he stated that Mr. Gacy had left the job with an electrician named Ed Fry in Mr. Fry's 1971 black Continental. Rossi stated that Mr. Gacy told him that he had paid his attorney $10,000 and he advised that he was upset. He also asked Rossi if the police had questioned him in regards to sex and dope, and Mr. Rossi stated that he answered in a round about way. Rossi advised that Mr. Gacy is a work horse, that business comes first and social life comes second. He also advised that Mr. Gacy likes to brag about things, such as money. Mr. Rossi was asked about present employees with P.D.M. Construction and he advised that at present in addition to Mr. Gacy and himself were employees David Cram, ▓▓▓▓▓▓▓▓ and an office man Gordon Nel▓▓ ▓▓ was asked about

Date/Time Report Completed: 18 Dec 78 1645 Hours

former employees and he stated that Mike Carrao, of [REDACTED] presently with L & M Construction, had worked at P.D.M. until last summer. He mentioned another former employee, Teddy, last name unknown, who was from Colorado. Teddy presently works at Belra Material in Chicago. Rossi next mentioned a Harry Shaft. Mr. Shaft was hired by P.D.M. in August and he left P.D.M. in November. He further advised that Mr. Shaft never came back for his paycheck. Rossi next mentioned a youth named Jeff, last name unknown, age about 19. Jeff worked for P.D.M. the summer of 1976 and attended high school, possibly Taft. Rossi next mentioned Randy Stewart, age 19 to 20, who lives in the area of Foster and Higgins. He is presently working at a print shop as of the summer of 1976. Rossi next mentioned a Ron Smith, age late 30's or early 40's, who is a carpenter, and Rossi advised that he thought Smith might be "AC/DC," meaning that he like boys as well as girls. Rossi next mentioned Dominick, last name unknown, who was a carpenter. He was fired on the first day that he worked last summer by Mike Carrao. Rossi next mentioned Charlie Itulla or Hitula, mid 20's, blond hair, 6'1", medium build, divorced. Charlie had a child, whereabouts unknown. Charlie also lived with his brother in the city. Rossi advised that last summer Charlie drowned. He had previously told Rossi that his wife's brothers hated him. The family of Charlie came for his last paycheck, according to what Mr. Gacy had told Rossi. Charlie was reportedly found dead in a river 60 miles south or west of Chicago. He was reportedly found in a river in the same town that his divorced wife lived in. Rossi next mentioned Bruce Borc, age 21 or 22. He stated that Bruce was well known to the Stone Park Police, because he got in various mischievous problems in that area. Borc is about 6' tall, skinny with dark brown hair and drives a Ford or a Chevy pickup truck black in color. He also reportedly has a cyclops tattoo on his left shoulder. He lives on [REDACTED] south of Grand Avenue and his father, Robert Borc, is a tile setter. Rossi next mentioned a former employee named Donny Bingham, early 20's, who presently works with the People's Gas Company. He advised that Donny Bingham knew Bruce Borc. Rossi next mentioned two friends of David Cram, Chris Cottles, who lives in the area of Belmont and Kedzie. Chris worked for P.D.M. last summer and another friend of David Cram's named Buddy, last name unknown. No other information about Buddy. Rossi next mentioned Bill, last name unknown, who was a friend of Ron Smith. Bill is in his late 30's, approximately 5'8", and 250 pounds. Rossi next mentioned Gregory, last name unknown, in his mid 20's, 6', medium build. Rossi last saw Gregory last year and he was a carpenter with P.D.M. Rossi next mentioned Greg Godzik, age 19 to 20. He stated that Greg started work about a year or so ago in the summer of '77. He worked two days and then left. He was on drugs and he advised that Godzik told a weird story about having a fight with another young man over his girlfriend. He stated this person kicked him in the forehead. Godzik had a pierced right ear and lived in the area of Norridge. He advised that the police and his parents were looking for him at this time. Michael Rossi was asked about his activities on Monday, 11 December 1978.

He advised that on that date he had worked on the North Avenue job until approximately 1330 hours, at which time he went to the unemployment office. He stated in the late morning, sometime around 1100 hours, he gave his time cards to Mr. Gacy who came to the job site. He thought that Mr. Gacy stayed at the North Avenue job site until approximately 1400 hours. At approximately 1650 hours Mr. Gacy called Mike Rossi at his home and they had discussed something about the business, but Rossi does not remember what it was. Rossi was asked if he knew if Mr. Gacy had an appointment to go to Nisson Pharmacy on Monday, 11 December 1978, and Rossi stated that he did not know. Mike Rossi was questioned about his activities on Tuesday, 12 December 1978, and he stated that on that date he was working at the North Avenue job. He stated that he saw John Gacy sometime around 1430 hours. Mr. Gacy was with David Cram, and he said they stopped by the job site for a short time and left. He does not know where they went. Sometime around 2100 to 2130 hours on 12-12-78 Mike Rossi took the P.D.M. van from his home to Mr. Gacy's home. When he arrived at Mr. Gacy's, there were some police officers there talking to him. He stated that the police officers were asking Mr. Gacy to come into the station to give a written statement and Mr. Gacy advised that he would be in later that night, perhaps around 2300 hours. After the police left Mr. Gacy's home, Mr. Gacy made a phone call to Chester Colletti and had some conversation in reference to having some checks signed. Michael advises that Mr. Colletti is associated with the Norridge Park Lighting Commission. Mr. Gacy then advised Michael that he wanted to pick up a Christmas Tree. Gacy told Rossi to go to Ron Rohde's Christmas Tree Lot at approximately 5000 Cumberland and Mr. Gacy would meet him there after running an errand. Rossi believed that Mr. Gacy may have gone to Mr. Colletti's house to have some checks signed. Rossi went outside to his van and he pulled the van up closer to the rear door of Mr. Gacy's home. He loaded up some Christmas Tree ornaments and Mr. Gacy told him to go to Ron Rohde's Christmas Tree lot and Mr. Gacy would meet him there after first running an errand. Rossi went to Mr. Rohde's Christmas Tree lot and bought a Christmas Tree for $10. He waited until approximately 2300 hours on the 12th of December 1978 and Mr. Gacy did not show up. Rossi then went back to Mr. Gacy's house and he believes that Mr. Gacy was out on the driveway, possibly having just arrived home. Mr. Gacy then got into the van with Rossi and they went to an area behind Ripoff's Hot Dog Stand at Bryn Mawr and Cumberland. Mr. Gacy was interested in cutting down a Christmas Tree, many of which grow in that area behind the hot dog stand. Rossi went on to say that last year at Christmas time he and Mr. Gacy went into that area to cut down a tree and they found seven other Christmas Trees cut and tied. He stated that it's possible that somebody may have stolen those trees from the Christmas Tree lot and hidden them in that area. Rossi advised that he and Mr. Gacy took those seven trees and, after taking their own, sold the rest. Mike Rossi said that when he and Mr. Gacy arrived at the area where the Christmas Trees were allegedly growing, Mr. Gacy stated "It looked to messy to go out and look," and he then directed Mike Rossi to drive him to Rohde's Christmas Tree Lot. Rossi stated that he and Gacy never got out of the truck while they were in the area where the Christmas Trees reportedly grew wild. Upon arriving at Rohde's Christmas Tree Lot, they found that Mr. Rohde was gone and the lot was closed. Rossi then took Mr. Gacy home, arriving at approximately 2315 to 2330 hours. Mike Rossi then went home himself, arriving sometime around 2330 to 2345 hours. On Wednesday, 13 December 1978, at approximately 0015 to 0730 hours Mike Rossi went out to Rich Raphael's house in Glenview. He stated that he did some work around Mr. Raphael's home. He chipped some ice off of the roof and he laid a heater wire on the roof. He stated that he left Mr. Raphael's house sometime around 0900 hours on that date and he went to the Shell Station on Higgins between Canfield and Cumberland to gas up. He then went to the North Avenue job and arrived at approximately 1000 hours, at which time he spoke with Mr. Gacy.

Mike Rossi was asked if Mr. Gacy had ever given him gifts, and he stated that from time to time he did give him small gifts, such as perfume for his wife and other small articles. He was asked if he had ever given Rossi any jewelry, and Michael stated that he had not.

Mike Rossi began to talk about his automobile and he was asked where he had gotten the automobile. He said that he bought his '71 Plymouth Satellite from a friend of John Gacy's, who was named Szyc. Mr. Rossi spelled Mr. Szyc's name. In summary Rossi said that Mr. Gacy had told him that a friend was selling his car and that if Rossi was interested in it, he could purchase this vehicle. On one morning Rossi advised that Mr. Gacy called him to say that he had gotten the car keys from the owner and together Rossi and Gacy went to the area of Clark Street and Ohio Street, where they found the vehicle parked on the street. Mr. Gacy gave the keys to Mr. Rossi and

C.I.D. CONTINUATION REPORT / DES PLAINES POLICE PAGE 4

Mr. Rossi drove the vehicle around to test it. Gacy told Mr. Rossi that if he was not interested in purchasing that vehicle he, Gacy, would sell it to somebody else. After driving the vehicle, Rossi decided to buy it for $300. Rossi advised that Mr. Gacy informed him that he had paid the owner $300, therefore he, Rossi, owed $300 to Gacy. Rossi advised that he paid Mr. Gacy back at the rate of approximately $50 per week. Rossi went on to say that Mr. Gacy first got the title in both Gacy's name and Rossi's name. When the car was paid off, Mr. Gacy gave the title to Mr. Rossi. Rossi stated that after purchasing the vehicle, Gacy would not let him drive it until $200 of the $300 was paid to Mr. Gacy. The truck was parked in Mr. Gacy's driveway near the rear garage. After Rossi got the title, he then purchased his own plates. Mr. Rossi was asked if Mr. Gacy ever told him why the owner was selling the vehicle and Rossi stated that Mr. Gacy told him the former owner was moving to California, and he didn't want the car.

Michael Rossi was asked if he had ever been arrested, and he stated that he had been arrested for a traffic offense. He stated that he was involved in an incident where he tried to run away from the police. He was caught and placed on probation. He further advised that he was involved in a theft of gasoline in the winter of 1977 - 1978. He stated that he pulled into a gas station with his Plymouth Satellite and he g...... up. He left the station without paying for the gasoline. He stated that prior to pulling into the station, he had put on the license plates, which were owned by the former owner of the car and which were on the car when he purchased it. He stated that he had his own plates, but he put these other plates on the vehicle so that his could not be traced. He stated, however, that he was not smart enough. That the police officers traced the plates to the Szyc family and the Szyc family told the police that the vehicle was missing. They apparently then checked the title and traced the title to Mr. Gacy, who informed the police that Mr. Rossi had the vehicle. Mr. Gacy picked up Mr. Rossi and transported him to the police station, where this matter was resolved. The police officer told Rossi to get rid of the former owner's plates, which Mr. Rossi said that he did do.

Rossi was asked if he had learned anything about Mr. Gacy during that period of time that he lived with him. Rossi advised that he found that John Gacy is a lonely person, that he works very hard, that he likes to clown and that he enjoys going to Moose. When Rossi first moved in with Mr. Gacy, Mr. Gacy asked him if he was liberal minded. Reporting Officer asked Mr. Rossi what he meant by that and Mr. Rossi stated Mr. Gacy meant did he like boys as well as girls. Rossi told him that he was not interested in guys and he was not bothered by Mr. Gacy after that. Rossi was asked if he knew if Gacy had ever been arrested, and he stated that Mr. Gacy had spent some time in jail for gambling and prostitution. He went on to say that Mr. Gacy's father had died while John Gacy was in prison and John Gacy apparently did not find out until a month after his father had passed away. He appeared to be quite angry about that.

On 17 December 1978 at approximately 1900 hours Reporting Officer Pickell had some additional conversation with Mr. Rossi. Mr. Rossi advised that he remembered another former employee of P.D.M. Construction named Don Bacon, age/mid 20's, He worked for P.D.M. in the summer of 1977 and at present he was with Pharmaceutical Environments, a company that Mr. Gacy does work for. He also remembered two other friends of his that had worked for P.D.M, #1: Chris LaCore, age 20. Rossi advised that his friend Chris LaCore told him that John Gacy offered $100 to Chris LaCore if Chris would let Mr. Gacy b... .... Rossi was referring to oral copulation. LaCore worked at P.D.M. Construction during the summer of 1977. A second friend of Mr. Rossi's, Jerry Caldwell, age 20, also worked at P.D.M. during the summer of 1977. Mr. Rossi further advised Reporting Officer Pickell that during the summer of 1978 shortly after he began working for P.D.M. Construction, he had found a wallet in Mr. Gacy's

R.D. #78-35203

C.I.D CONTINUATION REPORT EX

garage in some cabinets in the smaller part of the garage. One of the wallets contained a California driver's license, as well as other California I.D.'s. It also contained pictures of girls. He believed that the age on the California driver's license of the registered driver was 24. He stated that he found another wallet in the same area. The second wallet was brown in color and it too contained some pieces of identification. He thought that it might have contained an Illinois driver's license with possibly the age of the registered driver being under 21, because the license was similar to those issued to drivers under 21. Mike Rossi finally advised that these wallets had also been found David Cram.

C.I.D. SUPPLEMENTARY REPORT / DES PLAINES POLICE

DATE/TIME THIS REPORT: 18 Dec 78 1555 Hours

ORIGINAL OFFENSE: Missing Person

VICTIM: Piest, Robert J.

NARRATIVE:

The following report reflects my activities in a follow-up investigation of the missing person report of the above mentioned subject.

On 17 December 1978 at approximately 1000 hours I was advised by Lt. Kozenczak that the name of another individual who might possibly be missing had been brought up by the ex wife of John Gacy. This individual was allegedly to have had ties with Gacy by having been friends with him and having worked for the corporation P.D.M. The name given was one John Bukavitch, who was approximately 17 years of age in 1972, that would make him approximately 23 years of age at the present time. I took the telephone directory from Chicago and attempted to find someone by that name, however the only one I came up with was one Joseph Bukovich, of [REDACTED]. I contacted these people and they indicated they do not have any missing people in their family, nor was there anyone by the name of John in their family.

I then called 744-6222, the Missing Person Bureau, City of Chicago, Officer Frazier. Officer Frazier checked and advised that he had a negative for a missing person in 1972 by that name. At approximately 1130 hours Missing Person's Bureau called back and Officer Frazier indicated that in 1975 they had one by the name of John Butkovich, who had been missing since July 21, 1975, who was a M/W, 18 years of age, Last Known Address: [REDACTED]

I attempted to get information on this subject via telephone and located through the Haines Book that there are three phone numbers listed for that building, one is [REDACTED] to a Ronni DeMay, another phone number is [REDACTED] to a Jerald Hoskinson and [REDACTED] to a Jarvis Richards. It was later ascertained that none of these phone numbers or people had anything to do with John Butkovich. I also learned that the date of birth for Butkovich is [REDACTED]. Although LEADS and NCIC do not show a hit on him as missing, Chicago does confirm him as still active for missing. Missing Persons also provided the name of Officer Burkart as having been the one who handled the case from Area 6/Missing Persons, and I had a conversation with him at phone number 744-8266. Officer Burkart related to me that according to the information he had the youth had been at [REDACTED] with friends the night before he was found missing and, while there, he had been involved in some kind of disturbance, but nothing drastic. He indicated that he was to be moved in to an apartment the following day, but never did make it to the apartment. His 1969 gold and black Dodge was found approximately one block from his residence and in the car were found the items that he had left behind, which included his wallet and jacket. Approximately four months later he indicated they received, his family, a phone call from a girl calling from Puerto Rico, who indicated that John was alright, he was with them and hung up. The officer was able to trace the call, since it was a collect call, and called a business establishment in Puerto Rico where the owner, one Juan Perez, indicated that the phone was a business phone and was used by a lot of people and could not provide any further information. The officer indicated that the only thing odd about it was that all friends who used to come by the house all of a sudden stopped coming and never were heard from again. He indicated that the youth did hang around with Puerto Ricans and that he had worked for P.D.M. Construction Company, 8213 West Summerdale, Norwood Park Township. The officer

DATE/TIME REPORT COMPLETED: 18 Dec 78

REPORTING OFFICER: Det. R. Tovar 222

R.D. #78-35203

indicated that he also contacted those people, but they advised him he had been terminated and that as a matter of fact the subject never removed his money out of the Ravenswood Bank that he had left. He indicated that he had heard some rumors that the subject had been going to Puerto Rico and had been running dope. Subsequent to this, Detective Ryan and myself went to the Chicago Police Department, Area 6/Youth, and obtained a copy of the original report and one supplement, which pretty much gave us the same information that Officer Burkart had given us with the exception that the call had come at approximately one year after the subject had been shown missing. This subject did have in his possession a card from P.D.M. Construction Company. The father listed under the missing person's report is one Marco Butkovich, of ███████ with a phone number of ███████. I determined that this phone number was not a good phone number and did, through the Soundex Machine, locate a license plate number for a Mark Butkovich. That was ███████. This registered to Marco Butkovich at ███████ ███████ We went to that location, however there was no Marco Butkovich living there at that time. This report is all filed under Report Number T300203.

Two other phone numbers were shown for the subject, one being ███████ for the father. Illinois Bell indicates there is no listing for that number and ███████ which is one of the many phone numbers for Amtrak Service.

The report of this missing is part of the Robert J. Piest file at this time. Also part of this file will be a Secretary of State's Office reply on a 10-27 on John Butkovich of ███████ M/W, DOB: ███████, which shows his corrected driver's license expired on ███████ and had not been renewed and the printout from the 10-28 of KF-7996 shows Marco Butkovich at ███████ on a '74 Dodge Station Wagon.

C.I.D. SUPPLEMENTARY REPORT / DES PLAINES POLICE

Date/Time This Report: 18 Dec 78 1115 Hours

Original Offense: Missing Person

Victim: Piest, Robert J.

NARRATIVE:

On 12-15-78 Reporting Officer contacted the University of Illinois, Agricultural School Extension in DuPage County, tx 682-7486, and spoke to Wally Schmidt, who is the Advisor. At this time Reporting Officer informed him as to why I was calling in reference to dirt samples that were taken off of a vehicle belonging to Gacy. At this time he was requested by Reporting Officer to see if they might possibly be able to do a test on the dirt sample and other findings from the vehicle, to determine if possible what area they might have come from in our general location in regards to a possible forest preserve area. At this time he related that the only tests they might possibly be able to do, which would not help us very much, would be on potash or phosphate P.H. content and that they would have to have actually an exact area and a sample from that area to test along with our sample. He related that even a sample from a possible location could vary very much in that the soil itself might not even be the same in different locations from the test site. He then related that it would still be difficult to even tell what area it might come from. He related that another subject at the University of Illinois in Champaign, a Doctor Ted Peck, who is the head of the Soil Chemistry Testing Lab, might be able to give Reporting Officer better information and they might also be able to do better tests. His phone number is Area Code 217-333-4256. Reporting Officer then contacted Doctor Peck and informed him as to why I was calling and he related that yes some tests could be made, but they would really need an area where possibly this suspect dirt and other samples came from. He could possibly give a general area, but he stated he was not sure. They would run tests on the organic matter, PH, acidity and phosphate. He further related that they could not definitely pin down any particular park or forest preserve where this sample would have come from, and that the best idea would be to have a possible suspect site and then checks could be run to see if the suspect site and our test samples were related, but then they still could not definitely tell whether or not our sample came from the suspect site. He related that should we need to send samples down to them, we could send it down in care of Ted Peck/Agronomy Department, University of Illinois, Urbana, Illinois, 61801.

Reporting Officer on 12-15-78 was able to get a hold of a John A. Schimmel, DOB: address of in reference to his initials being the same as on the ring located in the Gacy residence. At this time Reporting Officer spoke to him and he related that he was not sure exactly where he left his class ring. That he felt that it might have possibly been left on a picnic bench in Grasslake or one of the Fox Lakes, or possibly at an unknown location in Wisconsin. He related he was not sure, due to the fact that it was quite a long time ago and that it does not come to clear to his memory right now. In describing the ring, he stated that the ring had a light blue stone in it and that it had some type of an emblem or design in the middle of the stone. He requested that, since he was not to far from the station, he might be able to come down and look at the ring to see if definitely it was his. Reporting Officer requested that yes he should come down and look at the ring. Upon his coming down and looking at the ring, John Schimmel related that that definitely was not his ring, that it was the bigger one of two rings you could buy similar to that. That the stone in his was ?????? and that he purchased his ring definitely at Maine West High School, and did not purchase it through Herf Jones on Miner Street in Des Plaines.

Date/Time Report Completed: 18 Dec 78 1145 Hours

Det. J. Kautz 217

On 12-15-78 Reporting Officer spoke to Mrs. Szyc whose son, John A., DOB: ▮▮▮▮ who used to live with her at ▮▮▮▮▮▮▮▮▮▮▮▮▮▮▮▮▮▮▮▮ also has the same initials J.A.S., as found on the Maine West Class Ring at the Gacy residence. The class ring was for 1975. At this time she related that her son apparently purchased the ring from Herf Jones in Des Plaines when he had transferred to Maine West in his junior year. She related that he had been last seen on the 20th of January 1977 when he left work after working overtime at approximately 1930 hours. He worked at a Sargent & Lundy Engineers at 55 East Monroe Street in Chicago. Apparently at this time he was living at ▮▮▮▮▮▮▮▮▮▮▮▮▮▮▮▮▮▮▮▮▮▮▮▮▮▮▮▮▮▮▮▮ Apparently a missing person's report had been filed in Chicago. Reporting Officer was able to determine on the 26th of January 1977 the report was filed and their R.D. Number is Y027095. According to Chicago, upon who Reporting Officer had contacted, it had been cleared on 09-10-77. According to the mother at the time her son was reported missing his hair would have been short and that it is red, but being short it looks like a darker color. He would have also had a mustache and, according to her, she did not believe he was wearing glasses, but that his eyes were getting bad and there was a possibility that he could have purchased them. She further related that apparently his apartment was left virtually untouched, there was not anything out of order except that the following items were noticed missing, a 12 inch Motorola black and white tv, which would have had a muddy to dirty color beige cabinet, purchased at Polk Brothers, a digital clock radio, which was possibly bought at Sears, which was dark in color, and not small but sort of standard size; an electric hair dryer and an electric iron. Apparently most of the electrical appliances in his apartment had been taken, except for his electric toothbrush. None of his clothes from the apartment were missing and apparently none of his winter clothes. According to her when she viewed the apartment, his winter coat was on the bed, the bed was unmade, there were tax forms on the kitchen table and it also appeared that he might have possibly eaten because some of the dishes were done. She related that he had approximately $1.71 left in his checking account. He also had $30 left in his savings account and that he had also left a check still at the place where he worked. His Driver's License Number would be ▮▮▮▮▮▮▮▮▮▮▮▮▮▮▮▮▮▮▮▮▮▮ His bank account would have been at the First Pacific Bank of Chicago, Chicago, Illinois 60603, and his account number would have been ▮▮▮▮▮▮▮▮ According to her, he apparently also left his place of business and the last time he was seen he was in good spirits. She further related that apparently his car, as far as she could determine, had been located on August of 1977 and that another youth had, according to her, used it in an armed robbery of a gas station, but she was not sure. Apparently this youth said he had purchased it from her son in February of 1977. This was the information she related she had gotten through Chicago and an Officer Geary, who was handling the case, tx 744-8365, out of the Shakespeare Station in Chicago, had related this information to her. She related also that the dentist that did extensive dental work on her son would be a Doctor Vivirito, who has a office on Oakton Street. Reporting Officer checked the phone book for a Doctor Vivirito and the Des Plaines Phone Book shows that there is a Vincent C. Vivirito, D.D.S. at 1475 Oakton Street, tx 296-5166. Mrs. Szyc further showed Reporting Officers other items of her son's, including an address book and several pictures of him, whereupon two pictures and the address book were recovered along with other items of her son's for possible follow up investigation. Reporting Officer was also able to find that he had an Illinois for 1976 plate of KJ-963 and a possible '77 plate of ▮▮▮▮▮▮▮▮ Apparently also located in an address book was a note from Investigator Harry Belluomini, Area 5/General Assignments, 2138 North California, tx 744-8364 or 489-4905, in which he related to Mr. & Mrs. Szyc that he was unable to locate their son, but he did learn that apparently their son sold his auto in February of 1977 and told the buyer that he needed money leave town. That was all the note said and this has also been recovered.

C.I.D. CONTINUATION REPORT

C.I.D. SUPPLEMENTARY REPORT / DES PLAINES POLICE	1 DATE TIME THIS REPORT 19 Dec 78 1400
2 ORIGINAL OFFENSE: Missing Person	3 OFFENSE CHANGED TO: dna
4 VICTIM: Piest Robert	5 ADDRESS: 2722 Craig

NARRATIVE:

Arrived at 8213 Summerdale on surveilance.
At 0840 Gordon Nebel arrived at Gacy's in his yellow 63 Olds Cutlas s.
0845 Michael Rossi arrived in his white plymouth.
0930 Gacy left his home to be in route to Waukegan.
Stopped at service station that Gacy has an account at Higgins and Washington (Shell.)
1030 arrived at a Les-On Drug store on the 700 block of Glen Flora in Waukegan
1125 Gacy went to the Waukegan Rent-All to rent a power tool one block west of drug store.
1130 Gacy stopped across street for sweet rolls and returned to the drug store.

Rossi was also at the Drug store working with Gacy.

1245 Relieved from surveillance.

CASE STATUS: ☒ FURTHER ACTION REQUIRED
7. DATE/TIME REPORT COMPLETED: 19 Dec 78 1420
11 REPORTING OFFICER PRINT: Hachmeister/Albrecht 209

C.I.D. SUPPLEMENTARY REPORT / DES PLAINES POLICE

1. DATE/TIME THIS REPORT: 19 Dec 78 2000 Hours

Missing Person

Piest, Robert

NARRATIVE:

At 1618 hours on 19 December 1978 Detectives Adams and Pickell went to Nisson Pharmacy at 1920 Touhy Avenue. Reporting Officers spoke with Linda Mertes, the Store Manager. Reporting Officers asked Linda Mertes if she had a log book of the names of persons who brought film in to be developed, and she stated that they did have such a log book. Reporting Officers requested to see that log book and Linda Mertes produced the book. During this examination of the film log book, Reporting Officers observed that envelope number 36119 had been used by Kim Byers for film processing. That film was apparently placed in the envelope on 11 December 1978. Reporting Officers asked Linda Mertes if they could bring that sheet into the station, and she stated that it was alright with her, but the only thing is is that she would like to have a copy back for her book. Reporting Officers recovered that log sheet and made a copy and at approximately 1704 hours Detective Pickell returned a copy of that log sheet to the pharmacy to be placed in the film log book.

Det. J. Pickell 229

19 Dec 78

C.I.D. SUPPLEMENTARY REPORT / DES PLAINES POLICE

Date: 19 Dec 78 **Time:** 2030 Hours

Original Offense: Missing Person

Victim: Piest, Robert

NARRATIVE:

At 1900 hours on 12-19-78 Mr. John A. Lucas, came into the Des Plaines Police Station to offer some information relative to the above incident. In summary, Mr. Lucas advised that he is the owner of the Higgins and Washington Shell Station, 300 Higgins Road, Park Ridge, Ill 698-2360. Mr. Lucas advised that he has run that gas station at that location for the last 12 years, and he went on to say that he is presently doing business with Mr. John Gacy. He advised that last week Mr. Gacy came into his station and said to him that he was suspected of murdering Robert Piest, the missing boy from Des Plaines. Mr. Gacy further went on to say that he had nothing to do with it, namely the disappearance of the Piest boy and he could account for all but 20 minutes of his time on the date of the Piest boy's disappearance. Mr. Lucas advised that he first started doing business with Mr. Gacy sometime around April of 1978. Prior to doing business with his Shell Station, he advised that Mr. Gacy did business with the E-Z Go Station on Higgins approximately two blocks east of Cumberland. Mr. Lucas was asked if he remembered what vehicles the defendant used, and he stated that he had a four door black Oldsmobile with a spotlight and he further thought that he had three pickup trucks and one van all black in color with P.D.M. markings on them. He was asked if he had seen any other vehicles driven by Mr. Gacy and he said that Friday of last week he came in with a gray or silver AMC product that Mr. Gacy said was a rented car. Mr. Lucas was asked if he had ever seen Mr. Gacy or any of his employees come in with white or red pickup trucks, and he stated that he has not seen any such trucks. He further went on to say that Mr. Gacy told him that he was with the F.B.I., implying that he was working for them. He specifically stated that he worked for the F.B.I. when Lillian Carter, the United States President's mother came into town. The defendant also told Mr. Lucas that he works all over the United States. Mr. Lucas stated that Mr. Gacy appears to be a very nervous and ornery person and that he appears to have a dual personality. He feels that Mr. Gacy is not the kind of guy to mess with. Mr. Lucas advised that the van with the P.D.M. markings on it only gets gas on Wednesdays. He stated this was an arrangement with Mr. Gacy, because the driver of the van takes that vehicle home and uses it for his own purpose; therefore that driver buys his own gasoline and Mr. Gacy only fills the tank once a week.

Mr. Lucas was asked for the names of his present employees and he stated that working with him now are Lance Jacobson (Lance Jacobson accompanied Mr. Lucas into the Des Plaines Police Department), Ronald Thorn, Rod Zimmerman, Rich Harley, and a person nicknamed Harley. Mr. Lucas does not know Harley's name, but Harley works at Flying Tiger Airlines at O'Hare Field full-time and he only works for Mr. Lucas on a part-time basis. This person Harley formerly worked at the E-Z Go Gas Station, mentioned earlier in this report, and apparently knew Mr. Gacy from when Mr. Gacy did business at that gas station. Mr. Lucas stated that sometime ago his employee, Lance Jacobson, told him about a youth who had been working for Mr. Gacy. Apparently this youth quit working for Mr. Gacy without giving notice, and a short time later Mr. Gacy invited the youth to go out drinking with him. He proceeded to get this youth intoxicated and they then went back to Mr. Gacy's home where Mr. Gacy and the youth went into the garage. He advised that the story he heard was that Mr. Gacy tied this subject up and beat him up. Mr. Lucas advised that the story had first been related by the person named Harley to Lance Jacobson and Lance Jacobson then related the story to Mr. Lucas. After hearing the

Date this report completed: 19 Dec 78

Reporting Officer: Det. J. Pickell **Star:** 229

R.D. #78-35203

story first from Jacobson, Mr. Lucas advised that the person called Harley also related the same story to him and there were no differences between the story told by Jacobson and the story told by Harley.

Mr. Lucas also related that Mr. Gacy told him that he has his own body guard. Mr. Lucas said that he believes Mr. Gacy to be a person who likes to exaggerate and brag about things and he does not know what is truth and what isn't.

At 1735 hours on 19 December 1978 Detectives Adams and Pickell interviewed Lance P. Jacobson, ▓▓▓▓▓▓▓▓▓▓▓▓▓▓▓▓▓▓▓▓▓▓▓▓▓▓▓▓▓▓▓▓▓▓▓▓▓▓ Mr. Jacobson stated that he had worked for John Lucas at the Higgins and Washington Shell for the last 8 years. He is the mechanic and manager of the station. Mr. Jacobson stated that he has been told that Mr. Gacy has sold marijuana to another gas station employee, Rich Henley, a student at Maine South. Mr. Gacy has reportedly said that he can get anything, meaning any type of drug. Sometime back, Mr. Jacobson stated that he saw four to five plastic freezer bags containing marijuana in Mr. Gacy's briefcase. Also present in the briefcase were bottles of pills. Mr. Jacobson said that he has seen Mr. Gacy give pills to his, Mr. Gacy's, employees. Mr. Jacobson said that he had been ▓▓▓ to Mr. Gacy's home for a party, but that he never went. He said, however, that three other gas station employees did go to that party. The youths are Robert Zimmerman, Rich Henley and Steve Hoyle. He advised that these three youths went to a party at Mr. Gacy's home in August. He advised that it was a big party and the youths that attended said that there was a lot of dope there. Mr. Jacobson was asked if he knew if any of these youths regularly visited Mr. Gacy, and he stated that Rich Henley may go to Mr. Gacy's house to visit him from time to time. Mr. Jacobson further went on to say that another employee of the gas station, a subject nicknamed Harley, was, in fact, Bill Cygon. Mr. Cygon works daily at the gas station from 1100 to 1400 hours. Bill Cygon told Mr. Jacobson to stay away from Mr. Gacy, because he's trouble. Mr. Cygon went on to relate a story to Mr. Jacobson. A friend of Cygon's worked for Mr. Gacy for about a month and a half, perhaps six or so months ago. He advised Mr. Jacobson that his friend quit working for Mr. Gacy's P.D.M. Company without giving notice. A few days later Mr. Gacy invited this former employee to go out drinking with him. Mr. Gacy reportedly got the former employee drunk and then took him back to his house where he tied this former employee up and beat him up. Jacobson said that Cygon had told him that the former employee had been beaten up quit severely. Mr. Jacobson was asked if he could recall the vehicles that Mr. Gacy brings into the station for gas. He advised that there is a '77 Chevrolet Van, black in color, with P.D.M. markings on it. He advised that there is a '78 Chevrolet Pickup Truck, black in color, with P.D.M. markings on it and with a red "Western" plow on the front. He also advised that Mr. Gacy comes in in a '78 black Olds license ▓▓▓. Mr. Jacobson was asked if he knew of any other vehicles that Mr. Gacy brought into the station for gas and he stated that he could not recall any other vehicles. He was asked if he recalled any red or white pickup trucks that Mr. Gacy brought in for service, and he stated that he could not remember any such vehicles. He did recall, however, that one of his employees, a male/white, age about 26, 6', tall, brown hair, and presently employed by Mr. Gacy, did come into the station with a red pickup truck, no markings, and a cap on the back, back in July of 1978. He stated that he has not seen this vehicle since that time. Mr. Jacobson further said that Mr. Gacy had told Bob Zimmerman that he got busted for dope at his house recently, and Mr. Jacobson went on to say that Mr. Gacy is a boisterous type person who trys to impress people by exaggerating. Mr. Gacy apparently told Mr. Jacobson that he wants to retire by age 45.

G.I.D. SUPPLEMENTARY REPORT / DES PLAINES POLICE   19 Dec 78, 2100 Hours

Missing Person

Piest, Robert J.

NARRATIVE:

The following report reflects my activities in a follow up investigation of a missing person's report on the above mentioned subject and my events for today's date, the 19th of December 1978.

On today's date I went to the Cook County Sheriff's Police Facilities at Maybrook Center in Maywood at approximately 1030 hours where I obtained a colored photograph of an enlargement of an overview of the bedroom of John Gacy. This photograph was taken by the evidence technician on the date of the search warrant, which shows a beigeish brown or tan black and white Motorola Television Set. The television set is on a jewelry box, black in color, between the two mirrors of the dresser in the master bedroom of John Gacy's house at 8213 West Summerdale, Norwood Park Township. The reason for obtaining this enlargement is to compare it against the information we have as to the possibility of this being the television set that used to belong to John A. Szyc, formerly of Des Plaines, and listed as a missing person out of Chicago.

We then proceeded to the Cicero Police Department, located at 4932 West 25th Place in Cicero, and obtained a copy of the arrest card and the Bureau of Identification information sheet on one Michael Rossi, M/W, DOB: ███████. This would be covering the arrest of Michael Rossi of December 4, 1977 for the charges of disobeying a stop sign, eluding the police and reckless driving. On the arrest sheet, they show that the disobeying of the stop sign was SOL'd (Stricken On Leave To Reinstate) and the charges of eluding police and reckless driving said he pled guilty, was found guilty, received a 2 year suspension plus a $50 fine and no fine on the other charge. The copy of the transcript from the Illinois Bureau of Identification shows only that arrest from Cicero. These are now part of the original file of the missing person's report on Robert J. Piest. The above mentioned activities were conducted while in the presence of Detective David Sommerschield.

Upon my return to the station, I then proceeded to the Motorola Corporate Headquarters at Meacham and Algonquin Roads in Schaumburg, Illinois, where I was advised that they no longer have anything to do with television sets and that I should contact the Quasar Center in Franklin Park reference any information that I might want reference the televisions. The purpose of going here was to ascertain if we could get a photograph or a copy of the pamphlet on the television set which matched the papers and serial numbers that Mrs. Szyc had given us, as having been the papers that belonged to the television set that belonged to her son. This television set is missing and was in the possession of her son at the time that he turned up missing, however when she went to check the residence, the television as well as other electrical appliances were all missing. This is indicated in Detective Kautz's report of December 18, 1978 indicating he spoke to Mrs. Szyc and she described it as a 12 inch black and white Motorola television. She indicated the color was muddy to a dirty color beige. I then subsequently spoke to Mr. George Tatulio, of Customer Service at Motorola in Franklin Park, at 9401 West Grand Avenue, who advised me that the television set in question that I am referring to is a M-N? BP-3050KN. This is the same model number that is indicated on the guarantee that Mrs. Szyc provided us. He told me that he did have a pamphlet for it and it was a 1974 issue television set and that he would give me a copy of it.

Det. R. Tovar   222

R.D. # 78-35203

CID CONTINUATION REPORT / DES PLAINES POLICE   PAGE 2

Mr. Tatullo subsequently brought it by the station and attached in the file you will find one 12 inch diagonal black and white Motorola television set, Model BP3050KN. This is a high impact plastic cabinet in a two tone beige color. It should be noted that this tv is identical to the one in the blow up photograph, and is identical to the one myself and Detective Kautz observed in the bedroom of John Gacy.

Subsequent to this, I was ordered to ascertain from the family if a cross type of the victim's blood had ever been obtained and I subsequently telephoned the victim's parents, who advised me that Robert Piest had been at the doctor several times and he had had his tonsils out back in 1970. I subsequently contacted his family doctor, Howard Bresler, at 1585 Ellinwood Street, who indicated that he did not have it on his files, however that one Doctor Dale, who is on staff at Holy Family Hospital, could possibly have it, since he had done the tonsillectomy. I contacted Doctor Dale's Office at 825-2428 and they indicated that the only people that would probably have it would be the lab at Lutheran General Hospital, where the operation had taken place. I subsequently contacted Medical Records at 696-6150 at Lutheran General and ascertained from them that the blood was not typed and they did not have it on file.

On today's date I continued to attempt to find the correct spelling and/or any information on the other victim, who allegedly is missing, and was an ex employee of John Gacy, one Charles Hattula. On yesterday's date, the 18th of December 1978, I sent a message to the State of Texas asking the Department of Public Safety Office in Texas to search their records for any vehicle registration or any driver's license information on a Charles Hattula, spelled in various ways including Hattalla and Hutallo, indicating he was a male subject approximately 27 or 28 years of age and last known to have resided in Houston, Texas. On today's date, the 19th, I contacted the Chicago Police Department, Missing Persons, at 744-6222, and ascertained that there is no missing person's active on him in Chicago. I checked the telephone directory for Houston, Texas, and ascertained that there is a party listed for the Houston area under the name of Hattula with a non listed phone number. This was in reference to an answer that I received from the driver's license division of the Department of Public Safety in Texas indicating that they do have a Charles Antonio Hattula at ▉▉▉▉▉▉▉▉▉▉▉▉▉▉▉▉ with a Texas Operator's license ▉▉▉▉▉▉ which was issued on February 10, 1978 and due to expire on ▉▉▉▉▉▉. They described him as a male/white, blond hair, blue eyes, 6', 170 pounds, Date of Birth of ▉▉▉▉▉▉ After having failed to get a telephone number, the Harris County Police Department in Texas, of which Houston is a part of, was notified to see if they could obtain the number and they indicated they could not, however I had a conversation with one Sgt. Cooper at Area code 713-221-6020, who was with the Harris County Sheriff's Police Department, and they indicated they would go to the residence and ascertain any information they could. Subsequent to that I did receive messages from Houston Police Department indicating that they had no missing person's report on that subject, nor was there any criminal history in the State of Texas and also received information that there was no vehicles listed for him under that name that could be obtained with the information provided.

I did finally run a 10-27 in the State of Illinois and received word that he is revoked under the name of Charles A. Hattula, with an address of ▉▉▉▉▉▉▉▉▉▉▉▉ ▉▉▉▉▉▉ license number ▉▉▉▉▉▉▉▉ This license did expire on ▉▉▉▉▉▉. I then went to the Chicago Police Department and obtained an I.R. number for Charles Hattula. That number being 4674222. Under CB number 4681007, I found a report under RD number 1706673, which shows that he was arrested for possession of controlled substance and marijuana at his home on April 20, 1976 as a result of a search warrant. In his arrest report he does indicate that he is employed by P.D.M. Contractors as a carpenter. Also on his rap sheet they show an arrest for Charles Antonio Hattula in Freeport, Illinois on March 12, 1971 for curfew and possession of marijuana.

R.D. #78-35203

A photograph of the subject was also obtained from Chicago Police Department records and subsequent to this I was advised by Detective Kautz that Sgt. Cooper from the Harris County Police Department did call and indicated that they had spoken to someone at that residence and they in turn called here. The subject is the aunt of the subject Hattula, who indicated that Hattula had drowned in Freeport, Illinois on Mother's Day, 1977. Detective Kautz will make a further supplement to this conversation after we receive the information from the Freeport Police Department. Further reports to follow.

Des Plaines Police — Supplementary Report
19 Dec 78   2130 Hours

Missing Person
Piest, Robert J.

NARRATIVE:

At approximately 1800 hours this date I contacted Mrs. Byers to determine if her daughter, Kimberly, was at home. I was then advised that Kimberly was at a swim meet at Maine North High School, but was expected home at approximately 2000 hours. I then requested that Mrs. Byers contact this Department in reference to Kim providing us with a statement regarding photo receipt number 36119.

At approximately 2023 hours Kim Byers came to the police station with her father. Kim indicated that at approximately 1930 hours on December 11, 1978 she was turning in some film and the pictures were to be used as Christmas presents. The youth informed this Officer that she wished to have some enlargements made and, because of the fact the envelope would not be filled out in the usual manner, she had made a mistake on envelopes numbered 36117 and 36118 and subsequently envelopes 36117 and 36118 were torn up and thrown away. The youth stated that after completing envelope number 36119, she placed the receipt in the right front pocket of Rob Piest's jacket and subsequently the missing youth left the store wearing the blue jacket with the receipt in the right front pocket. The Byers provided this Officer with a written statement regarding the photo receipt. Kimberly Byers was advised that it may be necessary to recover the envelope and photos which she had sent for processing and those items would become a part of this investigation.

R.D. #78-36203

19 Dec 78

FIELD SUPPLEMENTARY REPORT / DES PLAINES POLICE — 19 Dec 78 1600

MISSING YOUTH

PIEST, ROBERT J

NARRATIVE

ON THE ABOVE DATE MEMBERS OF THE ILLINI SEARCH & RESCUE TEAM SEARCHED THE FOREST PRESERVE AREA SURROUNDED BY RIVER RD, LAWRENCE AVE, IRVING PARK RD AND EAST RIVER RD. ALSO VACANT FIELDS ON BOTH SIDES OF CUMBERLAND AVE AT BRYN MAWR AVE. ONE ITEM FOUND AND RETURNED TO THE REPORTING OFFICER WAS A LICENSE PLATE ▓▓▓▓ ILL 79. SEE R.D. # 78 35939. NAME WAS NOT ON FILE AT THE TIME OF THIS REPORT.

Des Plaines Police Department
WITNESS STATEMENT

78-35203

12/14/78 Time 7:29 PM Place Des Plaines Police Station

Kimberly [REDACTED], am 17 years of age

my address is [REDACTED]

On the night of December 11th, 1978 – I worked from about 5:20 – 10:00. I brought in with me an envelope of pictures and negatives from Homecoming 1978. My sister wanted copies of some of these pictures. I decided it would make a nice Christmas present. (They were pictures of me and my boyfriend) So I would have to have them done soon. So about 7:30, The store was kind of quiet, it would be a good time to put my order in for the pictures. I went to my bag and got the envelope out. I walked over to the counter, took an envelope, – and began to fill it out. The order I wanted was confusing (1 of #3+1 + 5x7 of #3). Normally you put the order in different envelopes – But I couldn't cut the negative – Anyhow – I ended up throwing out 2 envelopes because of explanatory mistakes. I finally was satisfied with the way I wrote it up (corrected*) then recorded it into the log-Book. Took the tab off + put the envelope into the bag on the side of the counter. I stood there for a second dumb founded – not knowing what to do with the stub. I would normally either throw it out – or put it

Des Plaines Police Department
WITNESS STATEMENT

Date 12/19/78 Time 8:29 Place Des Plaines Police Station R.D. #_____

I, Kimberly Byers, am 17 years of age and my address is ███████

it on a hook behind the counter. But these pictures meant alot to me + for some reason I thought I shouldn't throw it out. I started to stick on the hook, I hesitated, then stuck it in Rob's pocket of his jacket (the rt. one) (I was wearing his jacket because I had a short sleeved shirt + was very cold). — I Really don't know why I did — Maybe I meant it as kind of a joke — bc maybe just to put a responsibility on him — not to lose the ticket — I think the most probable reason I put it in his pocket — was that I intended him to find it, ask me about it + I would remember to take it home. Anyway — I had second thoughts about putting it into his pocket — thinking he would say something like — "Kim — what did you put this in my pocket for" — But for some reason — I decided to leave it there. Awhile later — Rob came to the front and asked for his jacket to take the garbage out — I gave it to him. Then the next time I saw the jacket off of him was when he was working the front. It was on top of the cases of cigarettes. Then of course when he left he grabbed it and walked out.

I have read the 2nd page of this statement and the facts c████████

─169─   (Signature of witness)

page 2 of 2 pages

C.I.D. SUPPLEMENTARY REPORT / DES PLAINES POLICE	1. DATE/TIME THIS REPORT 12-20-78 1500 Hours
2. ORIGINAL OFFENSE: Surveillance	3. OFFENSE CHANGED TO
4. VICTIM	5. ADDRESS

NARRATIVE:

We arrived on the surveillance at Mr. K's Restaurant, Harlem and Higgins. Left that location at 1 a.m. From the restaurant we proceeded to his home at 8213 West Summerdale. We stayed at that location until 8:30 a.m. and proceeded to 831 Lake Street, unincorporated Glenview, arriving at that location at around 9 a.m. At 9:20 a.m. left with Rayfield for breakfast. The restaurant was on Waukegan just north of Lake Avenue. At 10:20 a.m. we left the restaurant and stopped at an Ace Hardware Store at Waukegan and Lake. He dropped off Rayfield back at his house at 831 Lake Street and proceeded from Glenview to the Sportmart at Dempster and Harlem in Niles. We left that location at 11:10 a.m. At 11:40 arrived back at home on Summerdale. Just prior to arriving home, he stopped at the Shell Gas Station at Washington and Higgins in Park Ridge. At 12:45 hours left Summerdale and went to 7535 Montrose, the Norwood Park Regular Democratic Organization. Left that location at 1300 hours and proceeded to 4819 Irving Park, where he went to lunch with David Cram and girlfriend. At 1400 hours left the restaurant and procceded 2659 Milwaukee Avenue, Action Sales Company. David Cram was still with him. We were relived at 1430 hours.

R.D. # 78-35203

6. CASE STATUS: ☐ CLEARED/ARREST ☐ UNFOUNDED ☒ FURTHER ACTION REQUIRED ☐ CLEARED EXCEPTIONAL ☐ INACTIVE FILE	7. DATE/TIME REPORT COMPLETED 12-20-78
8. PROPERTY/EVIDENCE RECOVERED YES ☐ NO ☐	9. LEADS MSG. REQUESTED YES ☐ NO ☐	10. CONTINUED ON C.I.D. CONTINUATION REPORT ☐
11. REPORTING OFFICER-PRINT: Off. M. Albrecht STAR 209	12. REPORTING OFFICER SIGNATURE	13. SUPERVISOR APPROVING

CASE SUPPLEMENTARY REPORT — DES PLAINES POLICE

DATE/TIME THIS REPORT: 20 Dec 78 1950 Hours

Offense: Missing Youth

Piest, Robert J.

NARRATIVE:

On the above time and date Robert L. Zimmerman, DOB: ███ of ███████ was interviewed by Detectives Tovar and Adams. Zimmerman indicated that he works at the Shell Station which is owned by John Lucas, located at 300 Higgins in Park Ridge, approximately 20 to 23 hours per week. He stated that he was familiar with John Gacy, as Gacy uses his credit card to obtain gas for his black vehicles. Zimmerman stated that he first became acquainted with John Gacy during the summer months of 1977, at which time he met Gacy at a party, in which case he felt the party consisted of approximately 10 per cent young people. Bob recalls that he remained at the party from approximately 2:00 until 0000 hours, was not familiar with any other individuals that attended the party and sat at the far end of the table. Once before Zimmerman had visited the Gacy residence, in which case a youth was already present at the Gacy home and he recalls that that youth was Rich Henley. Upon arriving at the Gacy residence for the second time, Zimmerman observed that Gacy and Henley had already been engaged in a pool game and allegedly Henley had been waiting for the Zimmerman youth and subsequently the three individuals became engaged in a game of pool. Zimmerman advised us that at approximately the same time they became engaged in a pool game, Gacy wanted to make a bet that if the individual won the pool game, he would give him a blow job or any unspecified amount of money. Gacy then asked Zimmerman and Henley if they wanted to bet, at which time Zimmerman advised Gacy " I don't get turned on by that." Zimmerman indicated that he then left the party, although Henley remained at the Gacy residence. The following day Zimmerman engaged Henley in a conversation and asked if he had stayed to play pool, at which time Henley advised Zimmerman that he had left shortly after Zimmerman. Zimmerman stated that the last time he was at the Gacy residence was approximately two months ago, at which time he played bumper pool. When asked about personal opinions of Gacy, Zimmerman replied that Gacy does construction work and sells dope and on one occasion had mentioned something about pharmaceutical drugs. Zimmerman advised us that he had observed some black pills on one occasion, although he did not pay to much attention, as he is not involved in drugs. Prior to the termination of the interview, Zimmerman advised us that a female from the Edison Home in Park Ridge had purchased drugs from Gacy on two occasions, although he had no additional information regarding that incident.

C.I.D. SUPPLEMENTARY REPORT / DES PLAINES POLICE	1. DATE/TIME THIS REPORT 12-21-78 1300 Hours
2. ORIGINAL OFFENSE: Surveillance	3. OFFENSE CHANGED TO
4. VICTIM	5. ADDRESS

NARRATIVE:

Arrived at the surveillance at 2400 hours at 222 Prospect Avenue in Park Ridge. This location is the office of Attorney Sam Amerenti. Also at this office when we arrived was Leroy Stevens another attorney. We stayed at this location until 8:30 in the morning, at which time he proceeded to the gas station at Washington and Higgins in Park Ridge. He left that location at around 9:30 in the morning and proceeded to his home at 8213 West Summerdale. At 1005 hours he left the Summerdale address in route to the Roehde residence at Higgins and Washington. We left that location at about 1055 hours and went to 3300 West Belle Plaine in Chicago. At that location was Michael Rossi and David Cram. We left that location at 1145 hours in route to Di Leo's Restaurant on Elston Avenue. At this time David Cram was with him and David Cram was doing the driving.

R.D. # 78-35203

6. CASE STATUS: ☐ CLEARED/ARREST ☐ UNFOUNDED ☒ FURTHER ACTION REQUIRED ☐ CLEARED/EXCEPTIONAL ☐ INACTIVE FILE	7. DATE/TIME REPORT COMPLETED 12-21-78
8. PROPERTY/EVIDENCE RECOVERED YES ☐ NO ☐	9. LEADS MSG. REQUESTED YES ☐ NO ☐	10. CONTINUED ON C.I.D. CONTINUATION REPORT ☐
11. REPORTING OFFICER-PRINT Off. M. Albrecht STAR 209	12. REPORTING OFFICER SIGNATURE	13. SUPERVISOR APPROVING

DPPD FORM # 211

SUPPLEMENTARY REPORT / DES PLAINES POLICE

Date: 21 Dec 78

Missing Youth

Piest, Robert

NARRATIVE

On the above time and date a conference was held with William Cygan, DOB: [redacted] of [redacted]. Previously we had received information from John Lucas, the owner of the Shell Station at 300 Higgins, Park Ridge, in which case Mr. Lucas had advised us that Mr. Cygan might be able to provide us with information regarding this case. During my interview with Mr. Cygan, Mr. Cygan indicated that he presently works at both the Shell Station and at the Flying Tigers Airlines, O'Hare Field, and his supervisors are Frank Cich and Julian Bellin, and he can be contacted at the Flying Tigers Airlines at 686-7105. Upon speaking with Mr. Cygan, it was determined that he has known John Gacy for approximately four years, in which case Mr. Cygan has been an employee of the Shell Station at 300 Higgins Road in Park Ridge. Mr. Cygan was then questioned if he had any personal knowledge of Mr. Gacy, to which he replied that he felt Mr. Gacy tried to be a high roller, a big shot in front of a crowd, had two daughters and was divorced for approximately two years. Mr. Cygan further described Mr. Gacy as being high strung. I then advised Mr. Cygan that we had received information regarding a specific incident which may have involved Mr. Gacy and he was aware of the incident to which I made reference. Mr. Cygan indicated that the incident would involve a David Edgecombe of [redacted] and he believes the incident occurred approximately two years ago. Mr. Cygan advised this Officer that to the best of his knowledge he had informed Mr. Edgecombe that Mr. Gacy was seeking employees for construction work and the incident may have been precipitated when, as indicated by Mr. Cygan, John Gacy became pissed off when David terminated his employment with Mr. Gacy. Mr. Cygan advised this Officer that as best as he can recollect the incident occurred around Halloween about two years ago after he had driven David Edgecombe home to his residence. The following morning Cygan questioned Edgecombe, as he had observed that David Edgecombe had been beaten up, at which time Edgecombe indicated to him that after he had arrived home; he heard someone knocking on his window. When Edgecombe looked out the window, he encountered Gacy, at which time Gacy asked him to go out drinking. Mr. Cygan advised this Officer that David Edgecombe allegedly consumed an entire bottle of alcohol and during the time they were drinking, he had his pet Husky named Ivan with him and apparently the alcohol was consumed at the residence of John Gacy. Mr. Cygan stated that he had been advised by Mr. Edgecombe that the beating had taken place in the garage of John Gacy while David Edgecombe was handcuffed and Ivan was allegedly locked outside the garage. Mr. Cygan advised this Officer that in the event it should be necessary to speak with him again, he can be contacted either at home or at his place of employment through Mr. Cich or Mr. Bellin.

C.I.D. SUPPLEMENTARY REPORT / DES PLAINES POLICE

Date/Time This Report: 21 Dec 79 1108 Hours

Original Offense: Missing Youth

Victim: Plest, Robert

NARRATIVE:

On the above time and date Detectives Adams and Sommerschield went to the Nisson Pharmacy to determine if photo envelope #36119 had been returned from the processor. I then spoke with Linda Mertes and advised her that during a previous conversation with Kim Byers, Miss Byers gave this Officer permission to retrieve the envelope when it was returned from the processor. Miss Mertes then checked with Larry Torf, in which case I again advised Mr. Torf of my conversation with Miss Byers, at which time the photo envelope was turned over to this Officer.

Detectives Adams and Sommerschield then returned to the police station, at which time we picked up a brown bottle containing an unknown substance and both the photo processing envelope and the bottle were transported to the Crime Lab, 1401 South Maybrook Drive in Maywood, and were turned over to Chemist George Dabdoub, at which time we advised Mr. Dabdoub that we would like to have him examine both the receipt #3619 and the photo processing envelope #36119 to determine if they at one time had been joined and to make an attempt to determine the contents of the brown bottle. Mr. Dabdoub advised Detectives Adams and Sommerschield that he would perform the necessary tests and he felt the items would be ready by 22 December 1978.

Date/Time Report Completed: 21 Dec 78

Reporting Officers: Dets. Adams & Sommerschield

R.D. # 78-36203

DEPARTMENT OF LAW ENFORCEMENT
DIVISION OF SUPPORT SERVICES
JOHN G. LANDERS - DEPUTY DIRECTOR

Bureau of Scientific Services
1401 South Maybrook Drive
Maywood, Illinois 60153
(312) 344-5425

Date: December 21, 1978

SUBMITTING AGENCY:

Des Plaines Police Department
1420 Miner Street
Des Plaines, IL 60016
ATTN: Lt. J. Kozenczak

Received: December 21, 1978

From: Det. Ronald P. Adams #167

Section: Trace

Case Name: Robert Piest

Agency Case No.: 78-35203

Laboratory Case No.: M78-6123

EXHIBIT	ITEM SUBMITTED	FINDINGS
11a	Piece of red paper with black print "Customer Receipt"	Items #11a and #11b were examined to determine if they were at one time joined together. It is this examiner's opinion that items #11a and #11b were at one time physically joined.
11b	Red and white envelope with various printing	
12	Sealed brown glass bottle	Due to the absence of a sample in the bottle, analysis was not possible. However the inside of the bottle emitted a chloroform like odor.

Respectfully submitted,

George Dabdoub
Forensic Scientist

GD/mh

DLE6-180 (REV.10/78)

107 ARMORY BUILDING • SPRINGFIELD, ILLINOIS • 62706

The photo receipt found in the garbage can in Gacy's house which placed Rob Piest in Gacy's house.

DES PLAINES POLICE DEPARTMENT

OFFENSE: Missing Youth

DATE AND TIME PROPERTY RECOVERED: 21 Dec. 78 1108

EVIDENCE: X

OWNER'S NAME: Byers, Kim

RECOVERED FROM: Mertes, Linda

ITEM	QUANTITY	DESCRIPTION	VALUE	RELEASED TO
1.	1	Photo Processing Envelope No. 36119, Processing Number CH21-1-3220, In The Name Of Kim Byers, Dated 12/11/78.		

167

Des Plaines Police Department
WITNESS STATEMENT

Date 12-21-78 Time 1:00 Place Des Plaines Police Dep. I.D.# and 78-36160 / 78-35203

I, LANCE P. JACOBSON 9/27/55, am 23 years of age

and my address is ███████

JOHN GACY CAME INTO HIGGINS & WASHINGTON SHELL WHERE I WORK, GOT GAS AND CHARGE IT. ON HIS WAY OUT, JOHN GACY SAID "I HAVE SOMETHING FOR YOU." AND SHOWS ME A BAG WITH ABOUT THREE "JOINTS" IN IT. JOHN SAID TAKE THEM. I SAID I DON'T WANT THEM, YOU ARE CRAZY. THEN I WALKED INTO THE STATION TO GET CHANGE FOR THE OTHER CUSTOMER I WAS TAKING CARE OF. AS I WAS MAKING THE CHANGE, JOHN GACY SLIPPED THE BAG INTO MY LEFT JACKET POCKET, AND SAID HE CAN'T AFFORD TO GET CAUGHT WITH THE MARIJUANA (GRASS) ON HIM. I DIDN'T WANT HIM TO GET MAD AT ME SO I JUST LEFT IT IN MY POCKET, AND THEN JOHN GACY LEFT AND THE DETECTIVE WAS STILL IN THE OFFICE, SO I GAVE THE BAG TO MY BOSS, JOHN LUCAS AND HE GAVE IT TO THE DETECTIVE. WHILE JOHN GACY WAS IN THE STATION HE SAID THE END WAS COMING, THEY ARE GOING TO KILL ME. HE MENT. BY THEY THE 2 GUYS HE CALLED HIS TO BODY GUARDS, THAT HAD ALWAYS BEEN FOLLOWING HIM.

Criminal Offense Report / Park Ridge Police

Offense: Possession of Marijuana
Date: 21 DEC 78
Time: 0900
District: DELTA-2
Location: Higgins & Washington, Park Ridge, Ill. — Gas Station

Reporting Officer: Det. Hachmeister #231, D.P.P.D.
Witness: S/A #26
Witness: S/A #26

Offender: Gacy, John Wayne
- Sex: M Race: W Age: 36 Height: 5'8" Weight: 218 Eyes: Blue Hair: Salt/Pepper Build: Heavy
- Address: #13 Summerdale, Norridge, Ill.

Vehicle: Silver, 1978 Plymouth, 4 dr, Ill 78

Supervisor at Scene: See Narrative

NARRATIVE:

ON THE ABOVE DATE AND TIME THE REPORTING OFFICER OBSERVED THE FOLLOWING: WHILE AT THE SHELL GAS STATION AT HIGGINS & WASHINGTON (PARK RIDGE, ILL) I OBSERVED THE ABOVE OFFENDER TAKE FROM HIS POCKET A PLASTIC BAGGIE CONTAINING WHAT APPEARED TO BE ROLLED MARIJUANA CIGARETTES. THE OFFENDER SHOWED THE CONTENTS TO AN EMPLOYEE OF THE SHELL GAS STATION (LANCE P. JACOBSON 7514 W. ARDMORE AVE. CHICAGO, ILL D.O.B. 09-27-55) AND THEN PLACED IT BACK INTO HIS POCKET. THIS OCCURRED IN THE AREA OF THE

(OVER)

12-21-78   1330 HRS

Det. Hachmeister #231

Gacy phase a short time later the suspect went inside the gas station with the employee. While Det. Bachmeister and Albrecht were standing outside of the front glass door, we observed Gacy take the plastic baggie from his pocket (containing what appeared to be marijuana cigarettes) and place it in the employees pocket. After Gacy and Albrecht left the area, Det. Bachmeister spoke with the employee and recovered the suspected marijuana.

Because of the magnitude of our original case (R.D. # 78-35203), the officers did not make an arrest at the above time and place. Surveillance continued. The suspect was arrested at 1215 hrs. in the area of Milwaukee Rd. and Oakton St. upon the approval of Sgt. Lane.

CLERK OF THE CIRCUIT COURT OF COOK COUNTY

FELONY

IN THE CIRCUIT COURT OF COOK COUNTY, ILLINOIS

The People of the State of Illinois
Plaintiff

COMPLAINT FOR PRELIMINARY EXAMINATION

v.

No. _____

JOHN WAYNE GACY JR.
(Defendant)

OFF. RONALD ROBINSON #212
(Complainant's Name Printed or Typed)

complainant, now appears before The Circuit Court of Cook County and states that

JOHN WAYNE GACY
(defendant)

has on or about

DECEMBER 21, 1978
(date)

at GARDEN & MILWAUKEE NILES, ILLINOIS
(Place of Offense)

committed the offense of **POSSESSION OF A CONTROLLED SUBSTANCE** in that he

KNOWINGLY AND UNLAWFULLY POSSESSED VALIUM

in violation of Chapter ____ 56½ ____ Section ____ 1402(b) ____

ILLINOIS REVISED STATUTES

1420 MINER ST., DES PLAINES, ILL 67118
(Complainant's Address)

STATE OF ILLINOIS)
COUNTY OF COOK   ) ss.

OFF. RONALD ROBINSON #212
(Complainant's Name Printed or Typed)

being first duly sworn, on HIS oath, deposes and says that he has read the foregoing complaint by him subscribed and that the same is true.

Subscribed and sworn to before me ____ 21 DECEMBER ____, 19 78

I have examined the above complaint and the person presenting the same and have heard evidence thereon and am satisfied that there is probable cause for filing same. Leave is given to file said complaint.

JOHN WAYNE GACY (defendant) has, on or about

DECEMBER 21, 1978 at OAKTON & MILWAUKEE NILES, ILLINOIS
(date) (place of oc...)

committed the offense of POSSESSION OF A CONTROLLED SUBSTANCE in that he

KNOWINGLY AND UNLAWFULLY POSSESSED VALIUM

In violation of Chapter **56**, Section **1402(b)**
ILLINOIS REVISED STATUTES

STATE OF ILLINOIS)
COUNTY OF COOK) ss.

OFF. RONALD T. ADSON #717

being first duly sworn, on **HIS** oath, deposes and says that he has read the foregoing complaint by him subscribed and that the same is true.

Subscribed and sworn to before me **21 DECEMBER**, 19 **78**

I have examined the above complaint and the person presenting the same and have heard evidence thereon and am satisfied that there is probable cause for filing same. Leave is given to file said complaint.

Summons issued, Judge
or
Warrant issued, Bail set at
Judge
or
Bail set at

3-12 DES PLAINES ILL   26 JANUARY 79 AT 1:30 PM AT 1420 MINER ST DES PLAINES, ILL ROOM 102
(Court Branch)   (Court Date)

MORGAN M. FINLEY, CLERK OF THE CIRCUIT COURT OF COOK COUNTY

CCMC1-235   MISDEMEANOR

IN THE CIRCUIT COURT OF COOK COUNTY, ILLINOIS

The People of the State of Illinois
Plaintiff   COMPLAINT

v.   No. _____

JOHN WAYNE GACY, JR.
(Defendant)

OFF. DAVID HACHMEISTER _____ complainant, now appears before
(Complainant's Name Printed or Typed)

The Circuit Court of Cook County and states that

JOHN WAYNE GACY, JR. _____ has, on or about
(defendant)

21 DECEMBER 1978 _____ at 300 W. HIGGINS ROAD PARK RIDGE, COUNTY OF COOK
(date)   (place of offense)

committed the offense of _____ POSSESSION OF CANNABIS _____ in that he

KNOWINGLY AND UNLAWFULLY POSSESSED (3) Three GRAMS OF A SUBSTANCE CONTAINING CANNABIS

_____

_____

_____

_____

_____

in violation of Chapter ____56½____ Section __704 (b)__

ILLINOIS REVISED STATUTES

███████████████████████████
(Complainant's Signature)

1420 MINER ST DES PLAINES ILL 297-2171
(Complainant's Address)   (Telephone No.)

STATE OF ILLINOIS)
) ss.   OFF. DAVID HACHMEISTER #231
COUNTY OF COOK   )   (Complainant's Name Printed or Typed)

being first duly sworn, on _____HIS_____ oath, deposes and says that he has read the foregoing complaint by him subscribed and that the same is true.

███████████████████████████
(Complainant's Signature)

Subscribed and sworn to before me _____, 19__

███████████████████████████

I have examined the above complaint and the person presenting the same and have heard evidence thereon, and am satisfied that there is probable cause for filing same. Leave is given to file said complaint.

21 DECEMBER 1978 at 300 W. HIGGINS ROAD PARK RIDGE, COUNTY OF COOK
(date) (place of offense)

committed the offense of __POSSESSION OF CANNABIS__ in that he

KNOWINGLY AND UNLAWFULLY POSSESSED (3) Three GRAMS OF A SUBSTANCE CONTAINING CANNABIS

in violation of Chapter __56½__ Section __704 (A)__

ILLINOIS REVISED STATUTES

(Complainant's Signature)

1420 MINER ST DES PLAINES ILL
(Complainant's Address)

STATE OF ILLINOIS) ss.
COUNTY OF COOK)

OFF. DAVID HACKMEISTER #491
(Complainant's Name Printed or Typed)

being first duly sworn, on __NJR__ deposes and says that he has read the foregoing complaint by him subscribed and that the same is true.

Subscribed and sworn to before me _____, 1978

I have examined the above complaint and the person presenting the same and have heard evidence thereon, and am satisfied that there is probable cause for filing same. Leave is given to file said complaint.

Summons issued, Judge _____
or
Warrant Issued. Bail set at _____
Judge _____

or
Bail set at $1,000 = 10%
Judge RULE OF COURT

December 27, 1978

Cook County Sheriff's Police Department
1401 South Maybrook Drive
Maywood, IL 60153
ATTN: Criminalistics Section

December 26, 1978   JOHN WAYNE GACY

Pat Jones   803640/12555

Serology   M78-6219

1   A. Section of green carpet   Red and blue fibers removed, will be held upon submission of comparable evidence.

       Human blood grouping results inconclusive.

    B. Section of blue carpet padding   Group O human blood.

                                         Respectfully submitted,

                                         Michael Podlecki
                                         Forensic Scientist

MP/e

cc: Lt. Joseph Kozenzak
    Des Plaines Police Department
    1420 Miner St.
    Des Plaines, IL 60016

THE CONFESSION

DES PLAINES POLICE DEPARTMENT

MIRANDA WAIVER: PERSON UNDER ARREST

RB # 78-35203

I, John Gacy, hereby state that I have been informed that I have a right to remain silent and that I do not have to talk with the officer(s) unless I want to do so.

_____ (initial)

I know that if I do say anything, such statements can and will be used as evidence against me in court.

_____ (initial)

I know that I have a right to consult with a lawyer and have a lawyer present while I am being questioned. I understand that if I am unable to pay for the lawyer, I can have a lawyer appointed for me without any cost to me. _____ (initial)

Knowing and understanding these rights, I waive them at this time and agree to talk with the officer(s); knowing and understanding also that if I desire to stop talking to the officer(s) at any time, I am free to do so. _____ (initial)

I make this waiver freely and voluntarily without any force, promises or threats.

Dated this 21 day of Dec, 1978 at 10 PM (p.m./a.m.).

Signed: _____

Witnesses:

_____

_____

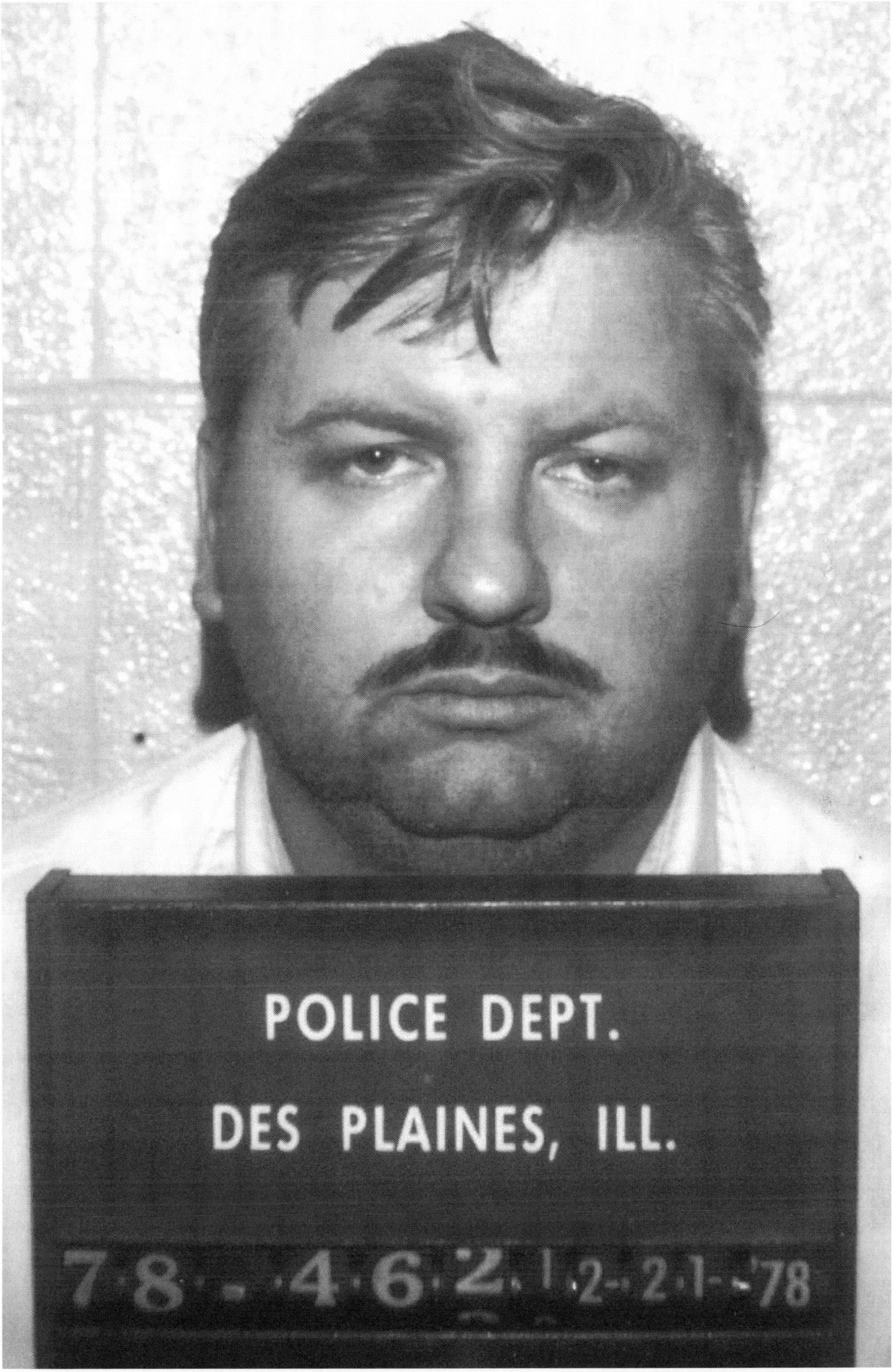
POLICE DEPT.
DES PLAINES, ILL.
78-462 12-21-78

CONFIDENTIAL

Gacy was brought back to the Des Plaines Police Station from Holy Family Hospital at 1725 hours on 21 December 1978. Upon arriving at the station, Gacy was escorted to the security area by Officers Albrecht and Hachmeister. In the security room, Gacy was searched by Reporting Officer. Gacy was then read his rights under Miranda and asked if he understood those rights. Gacy indicated he understood his rights. Gacy was then given a copy of the Miranda Waiver and asked to orally read each statement on the waiver and place his initials after each statement. Gacy complied and signed the Miranda Waiver, also indicating the date and time and then giving it back to the Reporting Officer. This was witnessed by Officers Hachmeister and Albrecht. Officer Hachmeister was then momentarily called out of the security room. The following is a summary of the statement and interview with John Gacy at the above date and time.

Gacy then started speaking to Reporting Officer and stated he knew it was all going to be over since he spoke with his attorneys the night before. Gacy asked if we had been in the crawl space. Reporting Officer answered affirmatively to Gacy. Gacy then said "that was what the lime was for." Reporting Officer asked him what was the lime for? Gacy replied "The lime was for the sewage dampness." He then hesitated and said "What he found there."

Gacy then said he has four Johns and he doesn't know all of the personalities.

Reporting Officer asked Gacy how many bodies are in the crawl space. Gacy replied he wasn't sure how many bodies were in the crawl space. Reporting Officer then asked Gacy about the boy from Nisson; if he was in the crawl space. Gacy said "No he's not there." That he would have a hard time pinpointing where he is, but he could find it. Officer Hachmeister then came back into the room joining John Gacy and Reporting Officer. As Officer Hachmeister entered the room, Gacy looked at Hachmeister and said to him "David, I want to clear the air. I know the game is over. The lime was used to cover the smell. The bodies down there have been there a long time. There is more bodies off the property."

Gacy then said he is a bisexual not a homosexual. Anytime Gacy did anything in sex he did not use force. It was always by consent. Gacy said he never forced anybody, he is not that strong and is unable to fight with anyone; especially with his heart condition.

Gacy then asked "Who else do we have in the police station. There are others involved." He was asked how they were involved directly or indirectly. Gacy answered directly. They participated in it. Interviewers then asked him who was involved. Gacy answered it was his associates, several of them. He then mentioned the names Rossi and Cram. He did not mention another name. Gacy asked us if Cram was there now. Before being able to answer Gacy, he asked how we knew the bodies were in the crawl space. We answered Gacy by saying that these two Officers had not seen the search warrant. Gacy then looked directly at the Reporting Officer and said "Mike, you know I won't be in jail very long. I won't spend a day in jail for this." When asked to elaborate on what he meant by this statement, Gacy just shrugged and did not say anything further. Officer Schultz entered the room with Gacy and Officers Hachmeister and Albrecht and asked if he wanted to speak with us. Gacy answered Schultz by saying there was a lot he had to say to us.

At this time Gacy indicated that he was a little chilly and all parties immediately went into a warmer room. Officer Schultz asked Gacy if the Piest boy was in the crawl space. Momentarily Gacy had a puzzled look on his face and Officer Albrecht mentioned to him "The boy from Nisson." Gacy replied that "Oh, I didn't know his name. No he is not down there." He was asked where is he? Gacy said he didn't know. I didn't transport. Gacy was asked who did? Gacy replied that he couldn't say, but you'll find out when Leroy gets here. He knows, I told my lawyers everything last night. Officer Hachmeister then told Gacy that he didn't have to speak to us unless he wanted to. Officer Albrecht then said to Gacy "John, do you recall when your dad died?" Gacy answered yes he did remember. Officer Albrecht said to him "You weren't able to go to the funeral were you?" Gacy replied that he wasn't able to go to the funeral. That the prison officials didn't tell him about it until after his dad had been buried. He was then asked if that was around the Christmas Holidays. Gacy replied that it was and that it had bothered him a lot that he wasn't able to go to the funeral. Officer Albrecht then told Gacy "That is why we want to find the Piest body; for the family." Gacy then said "The body is at a location about an hour to an hour and a half drive from here, but we would never find it." Officer Albrecht said to Gacy "Well if you just tell me where it's at and if I can't find it, I will tell you John that I can't find it and you were right." Officer Hachmeister then asked Gacy if the body was above ground or was it buried. Gacy answered that he was above ground. Gacy was then asked how did he die. Gacy replied they were all strangled. None of them were tortured. Gacy then specifically mentioned the Piest boy saying "He had put a cord around his neck and twisted it only twice when the phone rang." When Gacy went to answer the phone, Piest was still standing in the room. When Gacy returned, Piest was on the floor and Gacy noticed he had urinated all over himself. Gacy also said he noticed that Piest was convulsing and he picked the body up, put him on the bed and at that time he said he felt Piest was dead.

Sgt. Lang came into the room where the interview was being conducted and told us to move to another room. All parties involved went to another interview room outside of the security area of the police station. Gacy told the Officers there that the conversation would cease in 15 minutes. Gacy was replied to then by the Officers that "We haven't pressured you at all John, have we?" Gacy answer no, everything that I have said has been voluntary. Gacy then mentioned Jack and said that Jack didn't like homosexuality. Officer Schultz then asked Gacy "But why death?" Gacy replied "Because the boys sold their bodies for $20. They killed themselves." Officer Schultz asked Gacy how could they strangle themselves. Gacy replied because of what they did. They put the cords around their neck. They killed themselves.

Officer Schultz asked Gacy "Why didn't you bury them all in the house? You had a great plan." Gacy replied "Because of his heart condition, he can't dig a grave anymore and also because the basement crawl space area is full." Officer Schultz then asked Gacy what did he do to the boys. At this time Sgt. Lang entered the room and asked if we would stop this interview at the time, that he wanted to speak with the Officers. Gacy was left in the room and this interview was concluded.

CONFIDENTIAL

C.I.D. CONTINUATION REPORT

C.I.D. SUPPLEMENTARY REPORT / DES PLAINES POLICE

Date: 22 Dec 78 **Time:** 2000 Hours

2. ORIGINAL OFFENSE: Missing Person

4. VICTIM: Piest, Robert J.

Rough Draft

NARRATIVE:

At approximately 5:15 p.m. on December 22, 1978 I had occasion to take John Gacy to his cell in the Des Plaines Lockup, Cell C-1. At that time, as John Gacy was being put in the cell, he indicated that he wanted to speak with Larry and myself. He indicated Larry meaning the Assistant State's Attorney Larry Finder to whom he had been speaking with earlier in the day. I indicated to him that I would get Mr. Finder and return to the cell area to speak with John Gacy. When Mr. Finder and myself returned to the cell block area, Mr. Finder indicated to Gacy that he did not have to speak with us and, in fact, if he did speak with us, anything that he did say could be used against him. Gacy replied that he understood his Miranda Rights and it was his business if he wanted to speak with us and it was his decision. He also said that he knew what his Miranda Rights were and subsequently began to recite the Miranda Rights from memory. Gacy initially started speaking of the events of December 11, 1978 and the murder of Robert Piest. In summary, John Gacy related the following to Mr. Finder and the Reporting Officer on the events of December 11, 1978.

Gacy had been at the Nisson Drugstore on Touhy Avenue completing a remodeling job. He left the store for the evening and returning home determined that he had left his appointment book at the store. This being very important to him, Gacy returned to the store around 8 or 8:30. He stayed in the store for a short time and then left through the front to his vehicle, which was parked in the front of the store. As Gacy started to leave the area, he noticed Robert Piest come out of the store and start coming towards his vehicle. Gacy motioned to Piest to come around to the other side of the car and get in. Piest indicated to Gacy that he was interested in working and making money. Gacy then asked him how much time he had and Piest said he had 30 minutes to one hour. Gacy asked Piest if they could take a ride and talk about the job. Gacy immediately went to his home in Norwood Park. During the trip to his home, there was small talk about how liberal Piest was and Piest also indicated how important it was for him to make money. At the house Gacy and Piest went inside. Gacy asked Piest if he would have sex with a man, and Piest answered him that he would not have sex with a man; to which Gacy asked him "What if it involved a lot of money," and Piest indicated to him that he would think about it. At this time Gacy interjected into the conversation that he hated people who had sex for money and that he was not a homosexual. He considered himself a homosexual and that he never forced sex upon anybody, and that only homosexuals have sex for money and would be forceful with their sex acts. Gacy then talked about Piest again saying that he told Piest he was a clown and had a few tricks that he could show him. Gacy told Piest that he had an interesting trick to show Piest with handcuffs. He told Piest to put the handcuffs on behind his back loosely not making them to tight. Gacy put the second cuff on Piest behind his back. Gacy then indicated to Piest how restricted a person would be when they had handcuffs on them in this position. Gacy said at this time it appeared that Piest began getting noticeably scared and wanted to go home. Reporting Officer then asked Gacy how he took the clothes off Piest. Initially he said that Piest took his clothes off. I replied to him "How could he take his clothes off with handcuffs on behind his back." He answered by saying that Piest did not try to stop him when he started to take his pants off. Gacy took off Piest's pants and then performed oral sex on Piest. After that Piest became very scared and wanted to leave; Piest being in tears. Gacy told him that he only had one more trick to show him and that was the rope trick. Gacy indicated he put the rope around Piest's neck, tied a loose knot at the neck, then another knot a few inches from his neck and a third knot

R.D. # 78-35203

about 2 inches from the second knot. Gacy inserted a stick between the second and third knots and twisted. By the third twist the cord became tight on his neck and Piest started choking. Gacy indicated shortly thereafter then the victim would pass out and convulse; sometimes for very long periods of time. Reporting Officer then asked Gacy if he had anal sex with Piest. Gacy replied that he didn't, but Jack may have. I asked him if Jack usually had anal sex with his victims, and Gacy answered affirmatively; indicating that he couldn't get hard any other way. That was the only way that he could do it. Mr. Finder then asked Gacy if he could explain how he did the rope trick. Gacy asked if he could have a rope and this Officer told him that wasn't possible and Gacy answered "Shit, I'm not going to kill you." Gacy then reached into his pants and took out a rosary and asked Mr. Finder to put his arm through the cell doors. He had the rosary in his hand and he indicated to us that Mr. Finder's fist would be the head and his wrist the neck. He put the rosary around Mr. Finder's wrist, tying a loose knot right at the wrist and then two knots further from that point put a pencil between the second and third knots and then twisted. He indicated it would just take three or four quick turns and the victims would be strangled. He took the rosary off Mr. Finder's wrist and put it back in his pocket. Gacy then said that after the Piest boy was strangled, he took the body off the floor and put it on the bed and slept with it during the night. The following morning when he got up for work, he put the body into the attic right at the top of the stairs. Gacy demonstrated that he would put the body over his shoulder and walk up the attic stairs. After placing the body in the attic, Gacy proceeded through a normal work day.

Gacy then mentioned while the body was in the attic at the end of his work day in the early evening, Lt. Kozenczak, of the Des Plaines Police Department, came to his residence. Gacy referred to Lt. Kozenczak as an asshole. Immediately after Lt. Kozenczak left his home, Gacy went up, retrieved the body and placed it down at the bottom of the attick stairs. He put the body down on the floor and his back door bell rang, he answered it and found it to be Mike Rossi. Gacy had previously made arrangements with Rossi to go to a Mr. Rohde's christmas tree lot to look at christmas trees. Gacy made an excuse to Rossi and told him that he wouldn't be able to go with Rossi at this time. After Rossi left, Gacy returned to the body, put the body in an orange blanket and put it in the trunk of his car. Gacy went southbound on I-294 to I-55. Gacy came upon the bridge that goes over the Des Plaines River and stopped on that bridge. He had intentions of throwing the body over the bridge. He was unable to immediately do it because of traffic, and he heard CB traffic on his CB radio of a Smokey being on the bridge, that being an unmarked Smokey apparently talking about his vehicle. Gacy then proceeded on made a few passes back and forth on the bridge until he felt it was a good time to throw the body over the side. He stopped on the inside lanes of southbound I-294 and threw the body into the river. From that point he proceeded back towards Chicago on I-294. In the vicinity of Old Chicago he threw out the Piest's identification and shortly thereafter, he threw out the orange blanket in which he had had the Piest's body wrapped. Gacy ended up speaking of the Piest incident by saying that if he didn't forget his appointment book at the Nisson Pharmacy, that none of this would have happened.

Reporting Officer then asked Gacy how he managed to put the rope on the victim. Gacy replied that at times he didn't have to some of the victims would put the rope around their own neck; anticipating seeing a rope trick. At other times Gacy put the rope around their necks while facing them; under again the auspices of showing them a rope trick. Mr. Finder then asked Gacy when he started killing his victims. Gacy said he thought it started about 1974 and then proceeded to tell us about his first victim. Gacy was down at the Greyhound Station in downtown Chicago when he met a young man. He began talking with the young man and the gentleman indicated to Gacy that he was horny and would like to cruise the city to see if they could find some women. Gacy drove around the city for awhile, but they could not locate any women. Gacy then began talking to the young man saying that there was more than one way for a man to have sex. Gacy said he did this in order to find out if this man maybe bi-sexual. The young man responded to Gacy saying that two men could have sex. Gacy pretended to be ignorant not knowing what he was talking about. The young man responded to Gacy saying that there was no difference for a man to get a blow job from a man or from a woman; that it was all the same thing. After this statement, Gacy asked the young man if he would like to go to his home for a few drinks, to which he accepted and they proceeded to Gacy's house. Gacy then asked the young man if he would like to spend the night, to which he replied he would. Shortly thereafter they had sexual relations and then went to bed. Gacy then related that he woke up for some unknown reason in the morning and at that time when he did wake up, he found the young man to be coming at him with a knife. He struggled with the young man, got the knife from him and then stabbed him two or three times in the chest. The victim was then dead and he took him down into the crawl space and buried him. It was at a later time that he poured concrete over the spot where he buried the victim. Reporting Officer asked John Gacy if he knew what this man's name was, and he said he wasn't sure. He gave a name of possibly Randy or even possibly David. He was not sure.

Mr. Finder asked Gacy if he kept any tokens or mementos from his first victim, and he said no he didn't. That after that he didn't kill anybody for six months, because of his marriage.

Gacy then asked us if we had Michael Rossi or David Cram under arrest at the station. We told him no and asked Gacy why and Gacy said that they were his accomplices. Reporting Officer asked Gacy if they had any part in any of the killings, Gacy did not answer that question directly, but rather started talking about having sexual relations on numerous occasions with both of these people. He also indicated that Cram was a pusher and a pimp. Gacy said that Cram would make contacts for him, because he could supply his young people with drugs. Gacy then said that David Cram's father had committed murder once, but had never been arrested for it. When asked by Reporting Officer, Gacy did not know who the victim had been. Mr. Finder then asked Gacy the specifics of how Cram and Rossi had been involved in the killings. Gacy indicated that because of his heart condition, he had Rossi and Cram dig the trenches in the crawl space. Reporting Officer then asked if one or both had ever been involved with burying a victim, or handling the bodies in any way. Gacy indicated they had not, but had only dug the trenches. Gacy was then asked if Rossi and Cram had known what was in the crawl space. Gacy replied that they never said anything to him about what was in the crawl space, but if they didn't know what was down there, they were fucking stupid. Gacy was then asked about the odor that was in the crawl space. He replied that some of the odor was not caused by the bodies, but by the dampness that was in the crawl space. Gacy indicated that he put lime in the crawl space to get rid of the dampness. He said he put a mercuric acid on the bodies to dissolve them at a faster pace.

Reporting Officer then asked Gacy if he had had bi-sexual relations with a man while he was married; to which he answered affirmatively. He also said that he met a lot of his sexual partners, some of which were victims, in an area called Bug House Square. Gacy indicated that he was able to have his relationships at his home, because his wife would often at times leave for the evening, spend the night at a friend's, or leave the home and go to an area in Minnesota.

Mr. Finder or myself then asked Gacy about the Szyc boy. Gacy said that he remembered him and also remembered that he spelled his name in a very unusual manner. Gacy said he felt that Szyc was rather strange in some of the things that he liked to do.

Gacy then rather abruptly said that Szyc was in the crawl space. I asked Gacy if he kept anything of any kind of a memento from Szyc and he answered affirmatively, saying he kept a ring.

Reporting Officer then asked Gacy if he could explain where the bodies were in the crawl space. He tried to describe it and was having a difficult time in telling us exactly where the bodies were buried and asked if he could draw us a diagram. I supplied Gacy with a pen and a pink sheet of paper. Gacy at first couldn't get the pen to work and made a comment on the lousy pen I had given him. He then drew a diagram of the house, showing where the crawl space entrance was and explaining by drawing a short line where each body was. Also making a point of showing where the first victim had been buried and put under some concrete. Gacy drew the first half of the diagram very neatly and explained to us in great detail what he was drawing. Just prior to finishing his sketch, Gacy became very tense and clenched his fists very tightly and closed his eyes. He remained in this position for about 30 seconds. After Gacy relaxed his body, he looked at us and then we told him to take it easy and get some rest. Gacy then looked at the sketch he had just drawn and said that that was a sketch of his crawl space and showed where the bodies were; that Jack must have drawn it. At this time I took the pen and paper from Gacy, told him to get some rest and that we would be back later to talk to him. Gacy then became very apologetic, asking what did he say and what did he do wrong and why we had to leave him. We replied to him to get some rest and take it easy and that we would be back to talk to him later. At this time Mr. Finder and myself left the cell block area.

Mr. Finder and myself proceeded back to the Detective Section of the police station, where we were met by Assistant State's Attorney Bill Ward. In his possession he had two pictures of victims that had been taken from the Des Plaines River in Will County. He asked us if we would show these pictures to Gacy to see if he could identify the people. We returned to the cell area and spoke to Mr. Gacy, showed him the pictures; one of the pictures being that of a Frank Landegen. Gacy looked at the Landegen picture, said that he recognized that subject knowing him from a bar in Franklin Park. I asked him if that was one of his victims, and he said no I don't think so. Gacy indicated that the other subject was not familiar to him at all.

CONFIDENTIAL

This statement was taken on December [illegible], 1978 at [illegible] a.m. Present at the interview was John Gacy, his Attorneys, Sam Amirante and Leroy Stevens, Des Plaines Police Officers Albrecht, Kachmeister, Schultz and Robinson, Cook County State's Attorney Investigator Greg Bedoe, Cook County Sheriff's Officer Earl Lundquist. At around 2 a.m. on December 22, 1978 Mr. Gacy's Attorneys in speaking with Reporting Officers indicated that Gacy wanted to take the police to the locations where the bodies were buried. This was to be done after Gacy had spoken with his sister, who was being brought to the Des Plaines Police Station at that time. At 3:30 a.m. same date Gacy, Attorneys Amirante and Stevens and several police officers gathered in the Interview Room in the Des Plaines Police Station. Gacy was going to advise the police on what locations we would be going to and how many burial sites there were. Reporting Officers sat at a table directly across from Gacy with Mr. Stevens seated at Reporting Officer's right. Reporting Officer had a note pad to take down the locations that Mr. Gacy was about to give. Mr. Amirante and Mr. Stevens in speaking to the police indicated that Gacy wanted to make a statement to the police officers. One of the attorneys asked John if he understood his Miranda Rights, and that he didn't have to say anything unless he wanted to. Gacy answered that he understood and wanted to speak with us. Mr. Stevens then told Gacy to say what he wanted to say. The following is a summary as given by John Gacy to the Reporting Officer at the above described time.

In 1974 is when the killing started. After Gacy made this statement of 1974 is when the killing started, Mr. Stevens interjected and asked John if it wasn't so that he couldn't remember what happened to him prior to 1974. Gacy nodded in agreement with the statement made by Mr. Stevens. It was observed by Reporting Officer when Gacy was speaking with his sister in another interview room, he began talking about meeting with friends that he had previously mentioned in 1971 and 1972. In continuing with Mr. Gacy's statement, there had been 25 to 30 murders all related to homosexuals or bi-sexuals. None of his victims were females. All the murders involved some proposition or talk of money. They all willingly came in car to his home. All of the victims were killed in the house. In 1978 there were five victims. All dumped in the river. Three were taken there in the van during the summer, July August and September. The last one before the Piest boy was from Elmwood Park. He was into sadism. He wanted $20 after each thing he did. He wanted more money. He started playing games. He ended up over the bridge like the rest. The Piest boy didn't know what would happen at the house as far as sex was concerned, but he wanted to make easy money too. He worked at Nisson Pharmacy. He ran up to Gacy's car to ask about a summer job. The boy said he would do almost anything for money, but he lied. Gacy put a rope around his neck. The Piest boy asked why he was putting the rope around his neck. Why did Piest ask why he was putting the rope around his neck. He was stupid. Gacy twisted the rope until he stopped breathing. Gacy then heard the phone ring and went to answer it. When he returned to the bedroom, Piest was on the floor apparently dead. Gacy then returned to his office to take phone messages off of his recorder and finish up some business that he had to tend to. Gacy indicated that he called Nisson Pharmacy to clear up something on why he didn't go somewhere. He was not real clear about that phone call. Gacy then indicated that he spoke to Max the plumber from Skokie and Ed Fry an electrician from Hoffman Estates. Rich Raphael called him to ask him why Gacy did not keep his appointment at 9 p.m. He told Raphael he didn't go because he was to tired, which was really a lie. He then let his dog out, went to the bathroom and then checked his recording device again. He learned his aunt had called and told Gacy that he should come to the hospital. Gacy went to the hospital. When Gacy arrived, his uncle had died at about 10:30. Gacy indicated he arrived at the hospital right around 11 o'clock, because it was shift change and he asked questions to a very heavy set nurse. When Gacy learned about his uncle's death, he went to his aunt's house, because she was apparently very upset. He went to his aunt's house and found that she was not home, but next door at Gacy's cousin. Gacy went to the cousin's house, consoled his aunt for a short time and then went home and spoke with his sister. Gacy spoke with his sister, asking her whether he should call his mother long distance and tell her about the uncle's death. They decided there was nothing that could be done by his mother at that time and they would call his mother in the morning. Gacy then retired for the evening. At 6:30 a.m. Gacy was to meet Richard. Gacy indicated that Richard was always in a hurry. At 6 a.m. Gacy took the boy off the bed and put him upstairs in the attic next to the stairway. He slept the night in bed with the boy and then went to work and worked a complete day. Tuesday evening Gacy went to dinner with his aunt and her daughter. At 8:30 p.m. that evening he called Mike Rossi to have him come over and they were going to look at christmas trees. After the phone call, two Des Plaines Police Officers came to his home. The asshole and Jim. They wanted to talk to him about the missing Piest boy. He said he was tied up and he had more important things to do. Gacy would try to come to the station later that night. Kozenczak kept badgering him to come into the station. He had no consideration for me. He didn't consider that I lost my uncle. Kozenczak then left and Gacy brought the body down from the attic and laid it in the hallway. After laying the body in the hallway, Rossi rang his back doorbell with the intentions of going with Gacy to Rohde's to look at the christmas trees. Gacy told Rossi he couldn't go now and Rossi then left. Gacy indicated he brought his car toward the front door to put the body in the trunk. He got stuck in the ice and decided to pull the car around to the back door. He went back in the house, put the body in an orange blanket and placed it in the trunk of his car. Gacy said he thought he was higher than a kite at that time. Gacy got on 294 south to I-55 to the bridge by the Kankakee Des Plaines River. The first time he came to the bridge, a barge was passing beneath and Gacy was not able to stop. He was to make two or three more passes on the bridge before he was able to stop. He kept on hearing on the CB Radio there was an unmarked squad "Smokey" on the bridge. He kept alternating between the north and southbound lanes. He was finally able to stop on the southbound inside lane. He flipped open the trunk, pulled the body out and threw him over the bridge into the water. After dumping the body, Gacy drove on I-55 toward Old Chicago. While on 55, he threw out the orange blanket. He knew he had to get rid of the blanket, but he wasn't sure why, because there was no bleeding by the victim; therefore there was no blood on the blanket. On 294 from 55 Gacy almost lost control of the car a few times spinning out. He finally lost control, spun out and went into a ditch. A small highway truck stopped and helped. He wasn't able to help Gacy get out of the ditch. Gacy tried putting his spare tire under the car after jacking the car up, but still couldn't get out. Gacy got back into his car and fell asleep. At around 2 a.m. a LaGrange Towing Company tow truck stopped and pulled him out without any problem. After he got out of the ditch, he remembered he had to see asshole, meaning Lt. Kozenczak. He drove to the Des Plaines Police Station and found that Lt. Kozenczak had left for the day. At 11 o'clock the next morning he called the Des Plaines Police Station and told him he had car problems and that was why he didn't show up. Gacy then spoke of the victim just before Piest. He said he was called Joe. Joe liked bondage. Gacy didn't like that stuff. Gacy wanted to get blown and that's all. Joe wanted more and each time he wanted more money. Gacy showed Joe the rope, which was only two feet long, and put it around Joe's neck. He tied the knots and twisted hard only three or four times. After the twist, Joe kept shaking and convulsing and then fell dead. Gacy put Joe in the trunk of his car and drove to the river. On the way, he picked up a hitchhiker going to Colorado. The hitchhiker said he would have sex for some easy money. Gacy was initially interested and then changed his mind and let the hitchhiker out without any advances towards sex.

Gacy said there are three others in the Des Plaines River. One of the victims he picked up around Clark and Lawrence. The other two he picked up in Washington Park, or commonly known as "Bug House Square."

All the rest of his victims were real hustlers. One victim pulled a knife and stole money from Gacy's wallet, and then said that he wasn't done with Gacy for sex. Gacy wasn't going to let him get away with that. Gacy showed him some magic with the rope and then showed the trick on victim's neck. Gacy said he didn't know his name or who he was. This victim is buried under the house. Gacy indicated that he has lost count from '74 to the present on how many bodies are under the house.

Gacy stabbed the first victim. He thought it was in December of 1974. Gacy then said matter of factly the name Jack Hanley that's me. The first victim happened while he was married and his wife was at a girlfriend's home or in Minnesota. After he had sex with the victim, they went to bed. He woke up and saw that the victim was coming at him with a knife. He stabbed at Gacy in the right forearm. They fought and Gacy got the knife from him. Gacy stabbed him, killed the victim and then buried him in the basement. Gacy said that he was married at the time, but that didn't bother him. Gacy then said that he didn't like gay men or queens. Gacy said a man is a man and he should stay that way. If a man didn't like girls, there was something wrong with him. Gacy said that he never hurt anyone while involved in any sex acts.

When Gacy was around Bug House Square, the people he came in contact with always thought he was a cop. The radio and the red spotlight made them think that. They would always do what Gacy asked. Gacy told them if they ever needed any help, they could call Jack Hanley at the Civic Center.

Sometimes he would pay the men he picked up. But he would never pay them more than $30. Gacy didn't like the ones that were greedy or would rip you off. These guys would have something done to them.

Some of the young men that Gacy picked up and took to his home he didn't have sex with. He would take them home, undress and at times just eat and talk. Some had hard luck stories and he would let them go, even giving a few of them money.

Gacy didn't like the ones that lied to him and would sell their body for $20. Gacy told them someone could kill them for that. They would answer "He could do whatever he wanted." Gacy did not like s & m. Some of the guys he picked up were really weird. One incident Gacy brought two guys home at the same time. They both wanted a good time. He showed them some magic and some handcuff tricks when the handcuffs were behind his back. Gacy asked one of the men if he could get hard with a rope around his neck. Gacy told him he would twist the rope three times and then would blow him. Gacy twisted the rope around the victim's neck until he died. Gacy went to another room where the second subject that he had brought home with him was and told him that his friend was dead. The second subject wouldn't believe him. Gacy then said that he had had both subjects previous to any involvement with him handcuffed. Gacy took the second person into the room where the body of the first was. Gacy then indicated that he strangled the second victim right in front of his friend.

Gacy said that Rossi dug some of the graves in the basement. Rossi would dig trenches two feet by four feet deep. Gacy indicated he would bury some of his victims on top of one another. Gacy indicated there is no more room in the basement for any more bodies. Gacy then began talking about another victim. One guy that was really jet. He owned a car and was real smart ass. The victim had his car title with him and Gacy asked him if he would sign the title over to him. Gacy never indicated again whether the victim signed the title, but did say that he gave this car to Michael Rossi. He met this victim in Arlington Heights apparently at the race track. The victim danced with a g string. Every time he did something he wanted $20 for this and $20 for that. The victim asked Gacy what he did and Gacy showed him some magic with cards and then the rope trick. He put the rope around his neck and then inserted the stick. Gacy twisted it two or three times and then he went into convulsions. That was the end of him. Now he's under the house.

CONFIDENTIAL

Two and a half to three years ago Gacy had a drag queen. The victim danced like a broad. He was real weird. God didn't put people on earth to do that. Gacy twisted the rope trick and then read the victim the 23rd Psalm, then turned the rope one more time and the victim died. Gacy then mentioned the 15th, 16th and 17th victims. He didn't even know who they were. Five victims were put in the river off the I-55 Bridge to be washed away by the barges. Gacy said he had doubles two or three times. He explained the phrase doubles to mean that two victims killed in the same evening at about the same time.

One was a speed freak and Gacy didn't know the victim's name.

Gacy said he didn't know the names of all his victims, but could pick pictures out of a book.

Gacy said he put lime or acid on them under a foot of dirt.

John is buried in the garage. One victim is from Round Lake. He said he met someone from Des Plaines. He met another victim on Montrose between Lincoln and Devon. One of the victims was from Michigan. That victim had appeared in the gay magazine. In Clearwater, Florida Gacy liked to get it on there. He got the clothes of some seamen.

Gacy was then shown a driver's license of Robert Hasten. Gacy said he didn't know him, but the license was in someone else's wallet that had been killed. Gacy then mentioned the card he had in his possession from Man Country, a lounge on Broadway, that had a number on it. Gacy said he had that just to show some of his victims. Gacy said he did not like to go into gay bars.

In 1975 Gacy was propositioned by a subject for $10. That was insulting to Gacy and he threw the man out of the car. Gacy said that he was always the domineering one. He would make any and all propositions. Gacy then spoke of Jeff Rignal. He indicated he can't recall the incident very clearly. He picked up Rignal around Clark and Diversey. Gacy said Rignal is familiar, but can't recall him too well. Rignal claims he was attacked in May by Gacy. Gacy was arrested until July. Then in August and September Rignal was sick with hepatitis and didn't appear in court.

Gacy said he had affairs with 150 people and they all got paid.

All individuals knew what was going on. Gacy never bothered straight people. Rossi didn't get into it with the victims. He liked to have sex. I would blow him and watch girlie flicks to get him excited. Rossi would initiate the action where ever he wanted it; a favor. Gacy had a fight with Rossi in August. Rossi wanted Gacy to

CONFIDENTIAL

him a friend. Gacy would not hire him. Rossi pressed the issue and asked why he wouldn't give his friend the job. Gacy told Rossi his friend had nothing upstairs and he would not hire an incompetent. At that time they were in Rossi's mother's tavern in Cicero. Rossi and the friend started calling Gacy a jag off and wanted to fight. Gacy said he wouldn't fight and started to leave. Outside of the establishment the two approached Gacy, called him a jag off again and then they started hitting Gacy. Gacy told them to leave him alone. They then knocked Gacy down and started kicking him in the chest. Gacy thought that he went into cardiac arrest and was hospitalized.

Gacy then spoke of his daily schedule in general time periods. He said he would work late. Many times working from 7 a.m. until 10 p.m. After work, late at night, midnight or later, he would go whoring. He would have sex between 1 and 3 a.m. and the victims died between 3 and 6 a.m. Except for the last two. Joe was killed about 1 a.m. and the young boy from Des Plaines died at 9:30.

When Joe Kozenczak and his partner came to the house, Gacy indicated that Robbie was in the attic. (Gacy used the name Robbie.) Gacy was asked if Robbie was dead at the time. Gacy answered "He might have been." Gacy further said that after victims were strangled, sometimes they would convulse for an hour or two. Gacy said he would only have oral sex with victims, unless they would consent to do other sex acts.

Gacy said he had anal sex with Rossi but Rossi lost interest after he started seeing Kathy. While they were having sex, Rossi enjoyed it. Gacy did not use any force.

David Cram would have sex when he wanted something. Gacy then said that was a weak point. But didn't clarify on whose weak point he was speaking of.

Ed Hefner does not know anything. Mike knew nothing.

Gacy then said he threw the personal effects, clothes of the victims into the garbage.

Gacy then became very adamant and said that he was not a homosexual. People are wrong if they say he is a homosexual. Gacy said he has a strong fear of being a homosexual.

Gacy then talked about the books that were taken from his house. He said he would use the books as shock treatment for some of his victims. The books were not his. Gacy said he would not spend money on those type of books.

2159 Racine was the location that he did some work. While he was working there, he found a lot of books and snapshots.

Bug House Square. Didn't have to look for homosexuals. Gacy was then asked if he stalked his victims, and Gacy nodded affirmatively. He would have a cigarette with his victims and then ask them if they would have a party. Then the discussion would go to the price; $5, $10 or $20, sometimes $50, the most common prices.

Gacy then indicated that there are no bodies buried in any cemeteries. Outside of the house, the only place he put victims was over the bridge. In fact, he thought one of the bodies landed on a passing barge.

Gacy said he can't recall much before 1974. All bodies on Summerdale we wouldn't be able to just find them. He would have to show us where they were at. During the interview, Gacy was asked only the two or three questions mentioned in this report.

The entire rest of the statement was made on the spontaneity of Gacy. Gacy choosing and describing all subject matter. At one point during the interview, shortly after Gacy mentioned Jack Hanley and continued on with his statement, Mr. Stevens attempted to ask him a question. Addressing him first as Jack and when he did not get a response, he said John; to which he got an immediate response from Gacy. At the conclusion of the interview, Gacy was taken to another interview room to speak with his sister. At that time he immediately started talking about an incident that happened in 1971 or 1972. He mentioned the name of Jack Hanley again as being a police officer on the Homicide Unit in Chicago.

CONFIDENTIAL

Gacy's drawing of the location of the bodies in his crawlspace.
Gacy drew on the back of the his Des Plaines Police Department Personal Property Receipt.

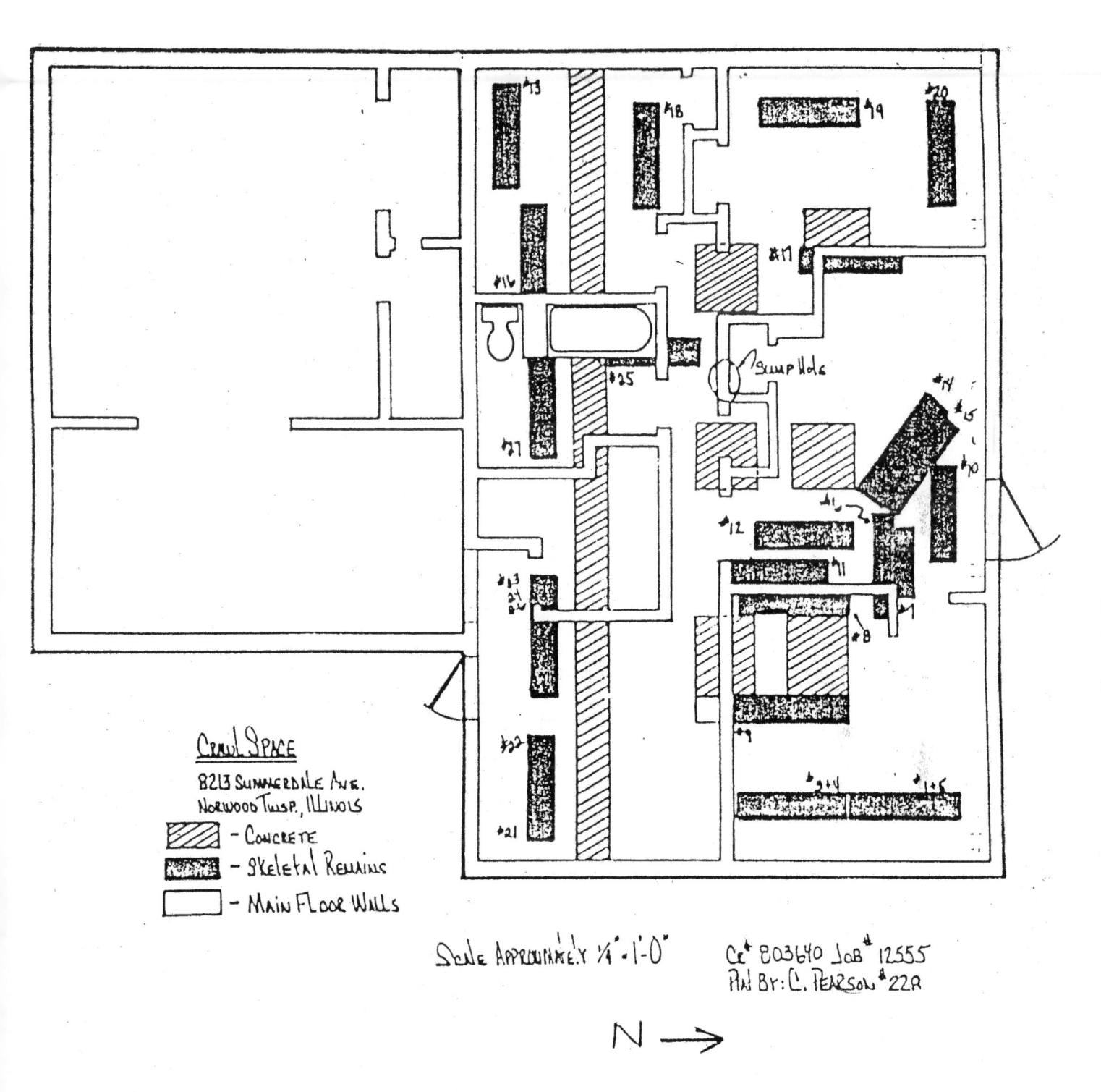

Gacy's house, 8213 W. Summerdale Avenue, floorplan of crawlspace with location of bodies.

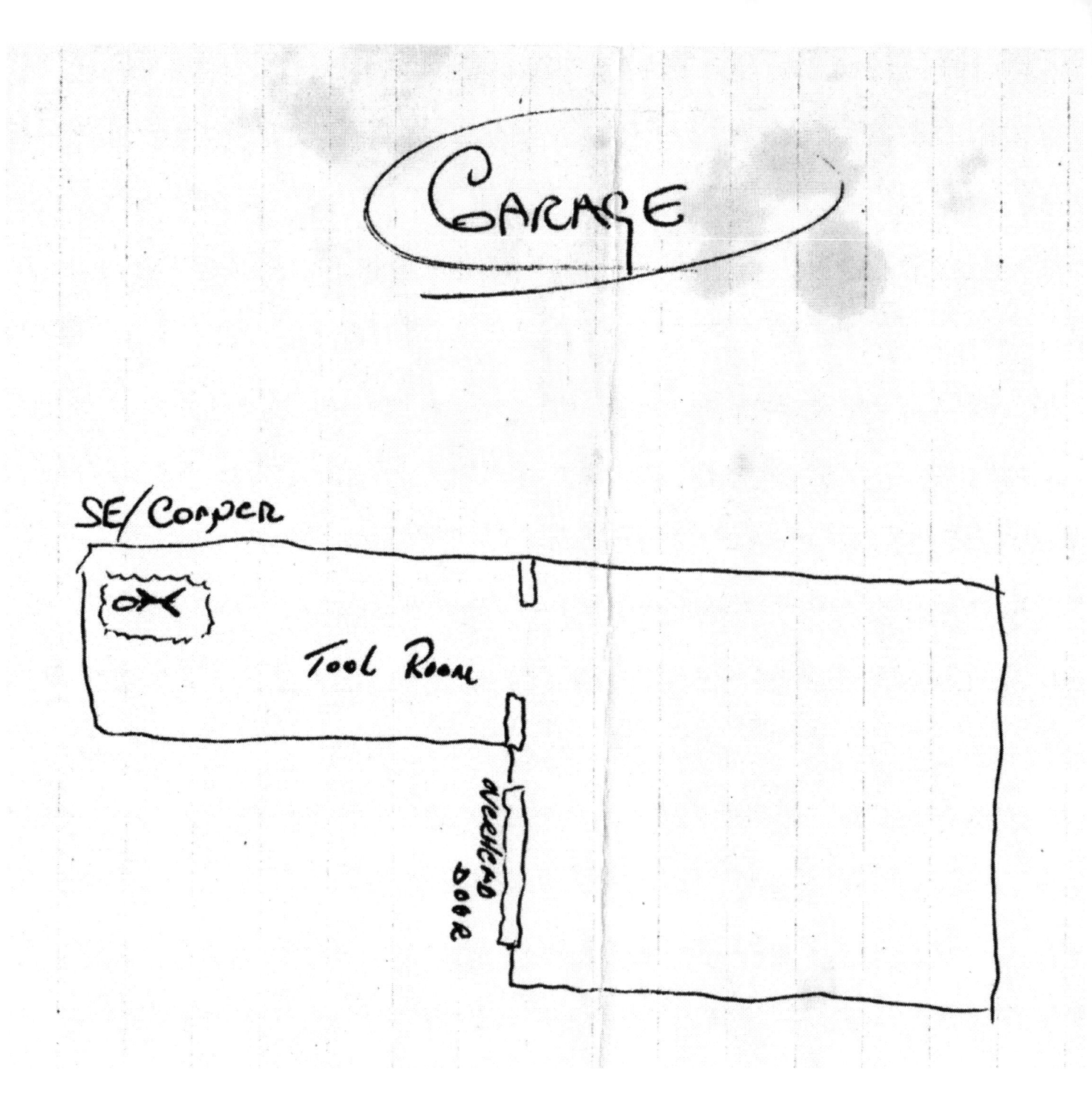

The location of John Butkovich's body, buried under the garage floor.

Gacy's garage.

Washington Square Park in Chicago, A.K.A. Bughouse Square. Gacy would search for victims at the park.

One of Gacy's victims in the crawlspace found during the excavation.

IN THE CIRCUIT COURT OF COOK COUNTY, ILLINOIS — SUB DEPT. — 3RD DIV/DISTR.

Proceedings and Judgments, before the Circuit Court of Cook County, Illinois

Held at: **1420 Miner St, Des Plaines** (Address/City), Illinois, Branch **0312** on **12/22/78**

Present: Honorable **Marvin J. Peters**, One of the Judges of the Circuit Court of Cook County, IL

File: MORGAN M. FINLEY, CLERK
BERNARD CAREY, State's Attorney
RICHARD J. ELROD, Sheriff

STATE (Plaintiff)
v.
John W. Gacy Jr. (Defendant)

Indictment or Case # **78 300 8080-01**

CHARGE: Chapter **38** Section **9A1** Paragraph _____ of the Illinois Revised Statutes.

The Offense of **MURDER**

Bail Amount $ **NO BAIL — BAIL DENIED**

BAIL (REDUCTION) (INCREASE)

New Bail Amount $ _____

Date __/__/__ By _____ Judge

FAILURE TO GIVE BAIL

THE DEFENDANT **John W. Gacy Jr.** having been held to bail in this cause and having failed to give bail, the sheriff is commanded to take him into his custody and confine him in the manner provided by law until the final judgment or order of this court, or until said defendant give bail as required by the court herein, or until the further order of this court, or until he shall be discharged by due process of law.

STATE OF ILLINOIS } ss.
COUNTY OF COOK }

I, MORGAN M. FINLEY, CLERK OF THE COURT, do hereby certify that the above and foregoing to be a complete copy of certain proceedings had and entered of record in said Court, in the case of

STATE (Plaintiff)
v.
John W. Gacy Jr. (Defendant)

Witness Morgan M. Finley, Clerk of the Court and the seal thereof,
at **Des Plaines** (City), Illinois on **12/22/78**

FILED DEC 22 1978

Morgan M. Finley, Clerk

TO THE SHERIFF OF COOK COUNTY TO EXECUTE

DEFENDANT'S NEXT COURT APPEARANCE

Court Date **12-29-78** Branch **0312** At **1420 Miner St, Des Plaines**
Time **9:30** Room **102** In The **Sub** Dept. **3rd** Div/Distr.

NOTICE OF RELEASE FROM CUSTODY BY GIVING BAIL

THE DEFENDANT _____ released from custody by giving bail in the amount of $ _____ on __/__/__ at ____ AM/PM.

EXCAVATION AND AFTERMATH

Page Two
Cr #803610
Job #12555

notified that a search warrant would be executed at the home of GACY, John W., located at 8213 W. Summerdale, Norwood Park Twsp., by members of the Des Plaines Police Department. The warrant was for the purpose of searching for further evidence in the case of a missing youth, a PIEST, Robert, refer to Job #12516. Reporting Evidence Technicians were requested to meet the Des Plaines Police officers and members of the Cook County Police North Investigations Unit at the residence at approximately 2000 hrs., for the purpose of assisting the processing of the residence.

Evidence Technician GENTY #366 arrived at the scene at approximately 1955 hrs. Evidence Technician HUMBERT #424, ZEKAS #235 and ROMITO #475 arrived at 2005 hrs. Evidence Technicians Humbert and Romito photographed the interior of the residence and garage. Items of evidence recovered from these locations, were also photographed (see Job #12510). Evidence Technician Genty entered the crawl space of the residence along with Investigator BETTIKER #210, of the North Investigations Unit. Genty crawled to the Southeast portion of the crawl space and observed that the entire dirt floor of the crawl space was uneven and covered with a chalk-like substance. In places it appeared to be several inches thick. The entrance to the crawl space was thru a trap door, located in the floor of the frontroom closet, which measured approximately 32½" X 20½". The trap door closet was located in approximately the center of the residence. Just below the opening of the entrance is located the sump hole, for water drainage. The area was flooded with water, as the electrical cord for the pump had been unplugged. Evidence Technician Genty plugged the cord in to the outlet provided, and the pump functioned normally.

The average height of the crawl space ranged from approximately 28" to 30" to the top of the floor joists. While enroute to the Southeast corner of the crawl space Genty observed what appeared to be hair-like fibers in the dirt, just east of the center support pillar. At arrival in the Southeast corner of the crawl space Genty observed two shallow depressions in the soil which appeared to be approximately 18" in width, by approximately 6' in length, running parallel to the south foundation wall. Evidence Technician Genty then crawled back to his starting point and proceeded to the northwest corner of the crawl space. There it was observed that the soil was mounded up into the corner above the level of the surrounding soil. Both, the northwest and the southeast areas appeared not to have been disturbed for some time.

Evidence Technician Genty then proceeded to the southwest corner of the crawl space, where three things were observed; first, that there was a small amount of fresh dirt placed against the base of the south foundation wall. The wall was covered by the white chalky substance, which had been liberally placed around the area. The chalky substance was observed on the foundation walls, ground and the floor rafters above. Secondly, the presence of three small pools of standing water, the two smallest of which, appeared to be clear water. The larger pool of water contained water which appeared to be a dark murky purple. Finally, the two clear pools contained a large

(continued)

(Page 1 of thsi report is missing from the master files.)

Page Three
Cr 1803640
Job 12555

number of thin red worms. These worms, when exposed to the beam of a flashlight, retreated into their burrows. Genty then elected to dig in this spot and upon sinking his shovel into the soil, found the dirt to be very loose. With the second shovel thrust, raised wet mud and rotting flesh. The third thrust uncovered what appeared to be a human arm bone and hair like fibers. Evidence Technician Genty was then joined by Investigator Bettiker and Evidence Technician Humbert who witnessed the discovery.

The location of the discovery was approximately 10' east of the west foundation wall and 2' north of the south wall. Evidence Technicians Humbert and Genty then crawled to the northeast corner of the crawl space, while the Medical Examiner's office was contacted by Lieutenant BRAUN of the North Investigations Unit. Humbert and Genty then in a depression along the east wall approximately 18" west of the east wall and 6' south of the north wall. It was in this area that Humbert discovered a cloth covered human leg bone approximately 10" below the surface of the top soil. Genty, then found hairlike fibers at the same depth approximately 4' south in the same depression. Humbert and Ganty proceeded to the southeast corner of the crawl space to the depression which had been observed earlier. Humbert dug in this depression approximately 8" down, locating two darkend long, apparent, human bones The bones were removed and placed next to the hole.

Evidence Technicians then proceeded to photograph the crawl space pending the arrival of the medical examiner. Dr. STEIN, Cook County Medical Examiner, and Chief Investigator FLANIGAN arrived at approximately 2300 hrs. Upon being briefed as to the circumstances, Dr. Stei and Flanigan entered the crawl space with Evidnece Technicians Humbert, Genty and Investigator Bettiker. Once in the crawl space Dr. Stein confirmed the bones found in the southeast corner to be human. Dr. Stein then ordered no further digging be done until an orderly exhumation be organized. The house was then secured by placing a uniformed police officer at the residence.

22 Dec 78

At approximately 1200 hrs., Evidence Technicians Genty, Zekas, Cox, Jones, and Lt. Taylor were present at the above listed residence.

The method of excavation was determined to be through the main floor. The decision was made to remove sections of the floor boards to facilitate the excavation process. Sections of the floor and subflooring were removed from the Northeast area of the residence, exposing the crawl space along the east wall. Assisted by members of the North Investigations Unit and Criminal Intelligence Unit, the non-bearing walls in the front section of the residence were also removed.

Evidence Technicians Genty and Humbert began excavation of an area
(continued)

Page Four
Cr #803640
Job #12555

in the crawl space at the northeast section, east wall. Shallow earth removal in this area yielded the skeletalized remains of a human body. The remains were completely unearthed exposing a skeleton. The skull was to the north, legs and feet extended to the south. The remains were positioned face upward and no evidence of clothing was found. The remains were located some 19" south of the north wall to the skull and approximately 24" west of the east wall. These remains were assigned body identification number 1. Dr. Stein was present at the scene, issued Morgue #1066 Dec 78 and pronounced the remains dead.

While excavation of body #1 was being conducted, members of the North Investigations Unit were searching the attached workshop area of the residence garage. The far east floor of the work shop was believed to contain the remains of another body. The section of flooring in question, was covered with approximately 4" of concrete, necessi... the use of a compressor and air hammer to remove same. The east outer wall of the workshop was removed to facilitate excavation. Investigators LUNDQUIST #243 and SCHWARTZ #130 were able to remove approximately one half of the concrete in an area measuring approximately 4' X 2'. Removal of the concrete revealed the skeletalized remains of a human body. Only the upper torso and skull were removed at this time, as Dr. Stein stopped excavation due to the possibility of noxious gases emitting from the grave. The body remains were issued body identification number 2. Dr. Stein pronounced the remains dead and issued Morgue #1065 Dec 78 at this time. Some clothing reminants and a shoe were removed from the area where the body was found. The remains of both bodies #1 and #2 were removed from the scene to the Forensic Institute and the entire scene was secured by uniformed officers of the Cook County Police Department.

23 Dec 78

Evidence Technicians Genty, Humbert, Kulovitz, Jones, Zekas, and Lt. Taylor arrived at the scene at approximately 0830 hrs.

The removal of the remainder of body #1 from the grave site was completed. During the exhumation of body #1 another skeleton was unearthed under the foot area of body #1. Also, at this time Investigators LUNDQUIST #243, BETTIKER #210, and RUSSELL #311, resumed removal of the concrete in the workshop, where the remainder of body #2 was recovered. Suspected material from the victim's pants, was also recovered from the grave.

The remains of the third body were located just south of body #1, also with the skull to the north, on its posterior. From the skull to the north wall measured, approximately 5' 6" and like body #1, 24" west of the east wall. Two shoes and some clothing fragments were also recovered from the grave. The remains were assigned body identification number 3. Morgue #1121 Dec 78 wass issued by Dr. Stein, who also pronounced the remains dead.

Page Five
Cr #803640
Job #12555

The remains of a fourth body were located under the feet of body #3, at approximately 1300 hrs. The skull was positioned to the south, with the legs and feet extended to the North, face up. A leather wallet was recovered in the area of the torso. Dark cloth pants and socks were in position on the remains. The body was assigned identification number 4 and pronounced dead by Dr. Stein, who also issued Morgue #1122 Dec 78. The location of the skull was approximately 11' South of the North wall and 24" west of the east wall. Evidence Technician Jones collected a section of green carpeting and pad from the southwest bedroom, for analysis. All remains and recovered material were transported to the Forensic Institute.

The scene was secured by uniform personnel of the Cook County Police Department.

Per a directive of Chief of Police Dobbs, work was suspended until after the Christmas holidays, which include the 24th thru the 25th Dec 78

26 Dec 78

Evidence Technicians Kulovitz, Pearson, Genty, Humbert, Hale, Zekas, and Lt. Taylor arrived at the scene at approximately 0845 hrs.

The days excavation began by probing the area beneath the grave of body #1, again, after shallow digging a fifth body was unearthed, and issued body identification #5, exhumation was begun at approximately 1010 hrs. Body #5 was pronounced by Dr. Stein at approximately 1208 hrs., at his arrival and issued Morgue #1265 Dec 78.

The position of body #5 was located as approximately 19" south of the north wall and 24" west of the east wall. The skull was to the north, with the legs and feet extended to the south. The remains were positioned face up at a depth of approximately 3' below the surface of the top soil and 5'7" to the top of the floor joist. The remains were clothed in a light colored cloth, long sleeve shirt or jacket and dark pants. What appeared to be a cloth material was found in the mouth of the skull. Reporting Evidence Technicians also recovered a folded piece of paper which was collected as physical evidence.

The recovered piece of paper was returned to the Maybrook Police Photo Laboratory where it was later photographed by Evidence Technician HALE #264, with infra-red photography as the paper was coated with mud and debris. Prints were made of the note and forwarded to the North Investigations Unit. The piece of paper was submitted to the Illinois State Crime Laboratory for analysis.

Continued examination of the crawl space revealed the remains of body #6 at approximately 1350 hrs. The remains were found resting parallel to the north foundation wall, on it's posterior. The skull was to the west with the torso and legs extended to the east. The remains were positioned approximately 5' south of the north wall and 16' 2" west of

(continued)

Page Six
Cr #803640
Job #12555

the east wall. The depth was noted as approximately 5' 4" to the top of the floor joist and 2' 5" below the surface of the top soil. No clothing was found with the remains. Morgue #1274 Dec 78 was assigned by Dr. Stein, who also pronounced the victim.

The remains of body #7 were located adjacent to body #6 at approximately 1415 hrs. The remains were positioned with the head to the east. The torso appeared to have been flexed at the lumbar area, as the forehead was resting on the knees of the remains. The lower appendages were also bent at the hip and the knees, in an easterly direction. The remains appeared to be resting on the bodys left side. Cloth material was found in the mouth of the skull. In addition, a plastic bag was removed from beneath the skull. The remains were positioned approximately 15' west of the east wall and 4' 4" south of the north wall. The depth of the remains was recorded as approximately 6' to the top of the floor joist and 2' 9" under the surface of the top soil. Morgue #1277 Dec 78 was assigned and the remains pronounced dead by Dr. Stein.

The unusual positioning of body #7 were misconstrued as an eighth body causing a morgue number and body #8 to be issued prematurely. Body #8 and the morgue number were reassigned the following day.

At 1425 hrs., body #9 was unearthed after removal of a 4" thick, piece of concrete. The concrete measured approximately 7' 6" X 2' 7" and was located at the east side of the east pillar support structure pad. Dr. Stein issued Morgue #1279 Dec 78 and pronounced the remains at 1430 hrs. The remains were observed with the skull to the south on its anterior side. The skull was positioned approximately 7' 2" west of the east wall and 12' 10" south of the north wall. Approximately 4', was noted to the top of the floor joist and approximately 1' under the support pillar pad surface. An elastic band, similar to those found on mens underwear, was observed around the waist area of the remains. A pair of dark colored socks were found in place on the remains.

The remains of body #10 were found at 1505 hrs., and pronounced dead by Dr. Stein, who issued Morgue #1289 Dec 78. Body #10 was positioned on its back with the head to the west, legs and feet extended to the east. The skull was positioned approximately 2' south of the north wall and 19' west of the east wall. Two reddish colored socks were removed from the grave, along with a pair of mens jockey type underwear. The depth below the top soil of the skull was noted as, approximately 7" and approximately 4' to the top of the floor joist.

All recovered remains were removed to the Forensic Institute and the scene was secured for the day by uniformed officers of the Cook County Police Department.

27 Dec 78

Evidence Technicians on the scene at approximately 0915 hrs., were Pearson, Humbert, Jones, Genty, Zekas, Kulovitz, and Lt. Taylor

Page Seven
Cr #803640
Job #12535

Prior to the days excavation Evidence Technician Jones recovered a folding pocket knife and a length of rope from the closet of the southwest bedroom. Both items were returned to the Maybrook Facility, where they were inventoried and submitted to the Illinois State Crime Lab for anlysis.

The discovery of the days first remains was at approximately 1002 hrs. and assigned body #8 and given Mogue #1278 Dec 78, both of which were issued the previously day. Dr. Stein pronounced the remains at his arrival, approximately 1215 hrs. The body was positioned face down with the skull to the north and the legs extended to the south. The arms were positioned under the upper torso of the remains. The remains were clothed in dark pants, bright blue jogging type athletic shoes, which had three stripes on the side and white socks with three stripes at the top. A ligature was found wrapped around the neck similar to rope. Over all length of the remains was approximately 5' 2". The remains were resting at the west side of the far east concrete pillar support pad and approximately 7' south of the north wall and 12' west of the east wall. The depth was recorded as approximately 4' 5" to the top of the floor joist and 16" below the top soil to the skull. All items found with the body were left in place for examination at the Forensic Institute.

At approximately 1025 hrs., the remains of body #11 was found, adjacent to body #8, on the west side. The skull being parallel to number eights' mid-torso. Morgue #1322 Dec 78 was issued and the remains pronounced dead by Dr. Stein at approximately 1220 hrs. These remains were further positioned with the head to the north, legs and feet to the south. The remains were face down, with the body curved slightly to the west. The body was clothed in corduroy pants, a gold colored knit type shirt and a western style belt buckle, white metal and multi-colored oval stone. The buckle was found beneath the remains. The buckle was collected by members of the North Investigations Unit as a possible means of identification. A ligature similar to rope was found around the neck. The body was positioned approximately 8' 9" south of the north wall and approximately 13' west of the east wall. The approximate over length of the remains were 5' 4". The depth of the skull was approximately 14" below the surface of the top soil and 4' 2" to the top of the floor joist.

Victim #12 was discovered at approximately 1030 hrs. Morgue #1323 Dec 78, was issued by Dr. Stein, who also pronounced the remains dead at approximately 1225 hrs. The remains were adjacent to victim #11 and #8 on the west side and also, face down, head to the north. The feet and legs were extended to the south. A rope-like ligature was found around the neck. Black cloth material pants were observed in place on the body. The remains measured approximately 6' 7" south of the north wall and 15' 6" west of the east wall. Approximately 12" was measured from the skull to the top of the soil and 4' 3" to the top of the floor joists.

Page Eight
Cr #803640
Job #12555

At 1400 hrs., date, the remains of body #13 were unearthed in the southwest corner of the crawl space. Morgue #1325 Dec 78 was issued by Dr. Stein and pronounced dead at 1410 hrs.

The remains were positioned with the head to the west, resting on the right side. The skull was approximately 7" east of the west wall and 1' 6" north of the south wall. The remains were found approximately 13" under the surface of the top soil and 4' 8" from the top of the floor joists. The overall measurement of the remains were approximately 6' 1". The remains were positioned on the south side, parallel to an apparently unused concrete footing. The concrete runs the entire width of the crawl space, (east to west). The concrete footing is approximately 4' 8" north of the south wall and is approximately 10" in width.

Body #14 was discovered at 1455 hrs., issued Morgue #1329 Dec 78 and pronounced dead at 1518 hrs. by Dr. Stein. The remains were positioned with the head to the east, legs extended to the northwest. The body was on an angle approximately 5' south of the north wall to the skull and 19" from the feet to the north wall. The remains were place face up, with the skull approximately 16' 6" west of the east wall. The upper torso, from approximately the waist upward was covered with an opaque plastic material. Closer inspection, revealed the victim was placed in a plastic bag. A pair of dark corduroy pants, high top athletic shoes and red socks were in place on the remains. The depth of the remains was noted as approximately 9" to the top of the soil and 4' 4" to the top of the floor joist. The plastic bag was left in place, as found, as per the request of Dr. Stein.

While exhuming body #14 Reporting Evidence Technicians, unearthed the remains of body #15 at 1500 hrs. The remains were under and to the north of body #14. These remains were also covered from the waist upward with an opaque plastic bag. With the removal of body #14, body #15 was examined. The remains were also found face up and resting in the same direction as body #14. The remains were clothed in blue jeans, which were unzipped, purple colored socks and high top athelic shoes. Closer examination of the reminants of the shoes revealed they were Converse brand, size eight.

Dr. Stein pronounced the remains of body #15 at 1520 hrs. and issued Morgue #1330 Dec 78. The skull was located approximately 4' 6" south of the north wall, with the feet 19" south of the north wall. The skull was further positioned 16' 1" west of the east wall. Again, the plastic bag was left in place. The depth of the remains was approximately 4' 6" to the top of the floor joist and 11" to the top of the soil.

All recovered remains were removed to the Forensic Institute and the scene was secured by uniformed police officers of the Cook County Police Department, at 1650 hrs.

Page Nine
Cr #803610
Job #12555

At approximately 2200 hrs., date, Evidence Technicians NAGORSKI #430 and ROMITO #475 photographed miscellaneous items of jewelry at the Cook County Sheriff's Police facility in Niles, at the request of Investigator SMITH #205. The items of jewelry were removed by investigators from the Gacy residence, at 8213 W. Summerdale, Norwood Park Twsp., Illinois, previously. The photographs were requested in an attempt to identify any of the items as belonging to victims.

28 Dec 78

0900 hrs., Evidence Technicians on the scene were Kulovitz, Genty, Humbert, Jones, Pearson, Zekas and Lt. Taylor.

The remains of Body #16 was unearthed at approximately 1030 hrs. Dr. Stein pronounced the remains dead at 1255 hrs., at his arrival. Morgue #1377 Dec 78 was issued to the remains. The body was found with the head to the east, legs and feet to the west. The remains were face up, resting adjacent to and parallel to the unused concrete footing to the north of the body. Examination of the remains revealed cloth material in the mouth. The body was resting on the left side. The remains were positioned approximately 3' north of the south wall and 11' 5" east of the west wall. The depth of the body was noted as approximately 10" below the top of the soil and 4' 4" to the top of the floor joist.

Body #17 was discovered at 1105 hrs., approximately 9' east of the west wall and 9' south of the north wall. The remains were face down with the head to the south. The legs were extended to the north, with a slight easterly angle. The buttox of the remains were slightly elevated. Dark cloth pants and socks were in place.

The remains were resting on the east side of slab of concrete, which measured approximately 3' 3" wide by an undetermined depth. The slab was extending on an angle into the crawl space earth, with the west end jutting out of the soil, obliquely. A depth into the soil could not be made as the remains of body #17 were resting just above it. The body was approximately 4' 5" below the top of the floor joist and 8" below the top of the soil. Dr. Stein pronounced the remains dead at 1300 hrs. and issued Morgue #1378 Dec 78.

The remains of body #18 were discovered at approximately 1220 hrs., and located approximately 18" east of the west wall and 8' 5" north of the south wall. The remains were positioned with the head toward the east, legs and feet to the west. The body was face down and the skull was turned to the right. It was also observed that the skull was contained in a opaque plastic bag, was secured at the neck by a ligature. Evidence Technicians placed the remains in a plastic bag, over the head to the waist, to facilitate examination at the Forensic Institute. The depth of body #18 was recorded as approximately 8" below the top soil and 5' 8" to the top of the floor joist. Dr. Stein pronounced the remains dead at 1315 hrs. and issued Morgue #1379 Dec 78.

Page Ten
Cr #803640
Job #12555

Body #19 was unearthed at 1230 hrs., was located approximately 2' 2" east of the west wall and 5' 10" south of the north wall. The remains were face down with the head to the north, legs and feet extended to the south. A cloth material was found in the mouth. The depth of the body was approximately 10" to the top soil and 4' 3" to the top of the floor joist. The remains were pronounced dead by Dr. Stein at 1350 hrs., date, and issued Morgue #1380 Dec 78.

Discovery of the remains of body #20 was made at 1235 hrs. The remains were positioned approximately 16' east of the west wall and 2' south of the north wall, face up with the head toward the west. Several inches of rope-like cord was around the neck. Both arms were under the body. Clothing included dark pants with a leather belt. Dr. Stein pronounced the remains dead at 1355 hrs., issuing Morgue #1382 Dec 78. Dr. Stein upon examining the remains noted the condition of the abdomen, and observed it was distended. Dr. Stein then proceeded to puncture the abdomen to release the pressure. The depth of the body was approximately 4' to the top of the floor joist and 8" to the top of the soil.

The remains of body #21 was unearthed at 1420 hrs. in the southeast corner of the crawl space. The head was located to the east, face upward, legs and feet extended to the west. The skull measured 1' west of the east wall, and 3' north of the south wall. Depth from the top soil was 12" and 4' 2" to the top of the floor joist from the skull. Dr. Stein pronounced the remains dead at 1445 hrs., and issued Morgue #1385 Dec 78.

All remains were removed to the Forensic Institute and the scene was secured by uniformed police officers at 1545 hrs.

29 Dec 78

Excavation began at 0945 hrs., by Evidence Technicians Bumbert, Kulovitz, Jones, Pearson, Conty, Zekas and Lt. Taylor.

At the commencement of the days activities, a section of concrete, approximately 7½' x 4', located at the southwest edge of the sump hole was explored with hammer and chisel.

At 1120 hrs., the remains of body #22 was discovered under the remains of #21. The body was positioned face down with the skull toward the west, legs and feet were extended to the east. The position of the remains was approximately 2' 8" north of the south wall and 6' 2" west of the east wall.

Examination of the remains yielded two light blue socks from the pelvic area. A material similar to cloth underwear was found in the mouth. A black rubber shower clog was found under the rib cage area. Dr. Stein pronounced the remains dead at 1235 hrs., after his arrival and issued Morgue #1439 Dec 78. The depth of the victim was noted as approximately

(continued)

Page Eleven
Cr #803640
Job #12555

2' to the top soil and 5' 7" to the top of the floor joist.

The remains of #23 were discovered at 1400 hrs., and pronounced dead by Dr. Stein at 1405 hrs., who issued Morgue #1452. The remains were located adjacent to and just west of bodies #21 and #22. The head was to the west, legs and feet extended to the east. The body was positioned face down with the head turned to the south. A pair of cloth under shorts were found in place. The skull measured 3' 2" north of the south wall and 13' 6" west of the east wall. The depth of the skull to the top soil was approximately 1' 3" and to the top of the floor joist was 4' 3".

Body #24 was discovered at 1435 hrs., under body #23 and adjacent to the west of #21 and #22. The head was to the west with the legs and feet to the east. The body was positioned with the face down and turned slightly to the south. The position was located as approximately 2' 11" north of the south wall and 14' 3" west of the east wall.

Cloth type material was found in the mouth and two white metal jewelry type chains were found in the neck area. Both were link type chains, measuring approximately 2' in length. One chain was a large link and the second of smaller link. A cloth type shirt was also found in the area of the body. The remains were approximately 1' 9" to the top soil and 4' 9" to the top of the floor joists. Dr. Stein pronounced the remains dead at 1435 hrs., and issued Morgue #1453 Dec 78.

The remains of body #25 were discovered under the section of concrete that had been explored earlier. Remains were located at approximately 1115 hrs., however, were not unearthed until approximately 1435 hrs. The remains were buried under concrete which varied from 2-8" in thickness. The body was positioned with the head to the south, face down, turned to the west. The position was approximately 6' north of the south wall and 13' 3" east of the west wall. The covering slab of concrete extended over the feet to the upper torso. The legs extended deeper into the ground than the remainder of the body. A cloth sock was found in the mouth. The sock appeared to be a knee length, athletic type, with three red stripes at the top. The remains were pronounced dead by Dr. Stein at 1435 hrs., and issued Morgue #1454 Dec 78. The depth of the skull was recorded as approximately 1' to the top of the soil and 4' to the top of the floor joist.

Body #26 was discovered at 1545 hrs., under bodies #23 and #24, to the west of bodies #21 and #22. The remains were positioned with the head to the west, legs and feet extended to the east, face down. The skull was positioned approximately 11' 5" west of the east wall and 3' 1" north of the south wall. A depth of 2' 7" was recorded to the top soil and 5' 10" to the top of the floor joist. Closer examination of the remains revealed a cloth material in the mouth. Dr. Stein pronounced the remains dead at 1545 hrs., and issued Morgue #1455 Dec 78

Page Twelve
Cr 1803640
Job 12555

Body #27 was discovered at approximately 1415 hrs., and pronounced dead at approximately the same time, by Dr. Stein, who also issued Morgue #1456 Dec 78 to the remains. The body was positioned face up, with the head to the east, legs and feet extended to the west. The head was turned slightly to the south. The body was located approximately 3' 4" north of the south wall and adjacent to the unused concrete footing. Cloth material was found around the lower portion of the skull. Dark pants with a leather belt and metal buckle were on the remains. Two dark socks were also found in place. The victim was approximately 10" below the surface of the top soil and 4' 3" below the top of the floor joist.

All recovered remains were transported to the Forensic Institute and the scene was secured by members of the Cook County Police Department at 1700 hrs.

30 Dec 78

Evidence Technicians on the scene at 0915 hrs., were Zekas, Pearson, Genty, Kulovitz, Jones, Hale, Humbert, and Lt. Taylor.

Excavation began in the area of the back yard bar-b-que pit, where a metal tool box was found contained in the fire pit. Further examination was delayed until equipment could be obtained to break the concrete at the bottom of the fire pit.

Members of the North Investigative Unit then proceeded to examine the attic area of the residence. Access to the attic was attained through a pull down ladder in the hallway, at the bathroom. The wooden attic floor was removed and various items of physical evidence were removed, including four books, smoking materials, pipes, bongs, a bag of badges and police type stars. Also recovered was a shoe from the hallway closet, a brown bottle from the attic, a length of rope from the dining room hutch and an envelope containing unknown strips of material. Two samples of the chalky white substance were collected from the south east and northwest corners of the crawl space.

Excavation of the crawl space continued, searching for physical evidence and remains. The days activities were met with negative results.

The scene was secured at approximately 1600 hrs., by uniform members of the Cook County Police Department.

Per the directive of Chief of Police Dobbs, all work at the scene was suspended until after the New Years holiday.

2 Jan 79

Evidence Technicians on the scene at approximately 0830 hrs., were Zekas, Genty, Kulovitz and Sgt. Des Re' Maux.

Page Thirteen
Cx #803640
Job #12555

Excavation of the crawl space continued, searching for physical evidence and remains. The days activities were met with negative results.

3 Jan 79

Evidence Technicians Zekas, Jones, Sgt. Des Re' Maux, and Lt. Taylor were on the scene at approximately 0830 hrs.

The crawl space was photographed, illistrating the grave markers in place, throughout. Excavation of the crawl space continued, searching for physical evidence and remains. The days activities were met with negative results.

The scene was secured at approximately 1800 hrs., by members of the Cook County Police Department.

Evidence Technician ROSSI #344 processed a roll of Plus-X photographic film at the request of North Investigations, Sgt. ANDERSON #57. Rossi further made three sets of photographic prints, which, along with the negatives were forwarded to Anderson at North Investigations.

4 Jan 79

Evidence Technicians Jones, Zekas, Sgt. Des Re' Maux and Lt. Taylor were at the scene at approximately 1000 hrs.

Lt. BRAUN of the North Investigations Unit received information that a section of floor in the residence, specifically the utility room, may contain physical evidence. Two boxes of food stuffs were removed from the south wall floor area. A hole in the floor was observed, which measured approximately 2" X 8½", and was further located as approximately 52" east of the west wall and just east of a metal floor cabinet. The opening entered a space between the floor joists.

Closer examination in the area revealed a blue cloth material placed between the floor joists. The material was the photographed and removed, revealing that it was a nylon parka type jacket, down filled. The brand name was identified as Pacific Trail. Officer TOVAR #222 of the Des Plaines Police Department collected the coat as physical evidence.

In addition to the jacket, a plastic tooth brush and a cellophane cigar wrapper was found in the crevas. Photographs were taken of all items.

Members of the Cook County Highway Department were placed into service, digging in the crawl space. Heavy machinery was brought to the scene to facilitate the deep excavation of the crawl space. Sgt. MARINELLI #88 of the Investigative Unit recorded the names of the workers involved in the excavation.

Page Fourteen
CF JE03640
Job #12555

Excavation of the crawl space continued, searching for physical evidence and remains. The days activities were met with negative results.

5 Jan 79

Evidence Technicians at the scene were Jones, Sgt. Des Re' Maux and Lt. Taylor at approximately 0900 hrs.

Search of the crawl space yielded a work type glove from the northeast corner of the soil. Evidence Technician Jones collected same as physical evidence.

Further examination of the crawl space was met with negative results.

The scene was secured at approximately 1700 hrs., by personnel of the Cook County Police Department.

6 Jan 79

Evidence Technicians present at the scene included Jones, Sgt. Des Re' Maux, and Lt. Taylor.

Excavation of the crawl space continued, searching for physical evidence and remains. The days activities were met with negative results.

The scene was secured at approximately 1700 hrs., by personnel of the Cook County Police Department.

All activities at the scene subsequent to 6 Jan 79 will be recorded on a daily basis, by the officer handling the assignment.

Job #12555D CR 003640 Homicide CCSPD 09 Jan 79 Fisher 226

The second body to be examined was number 1323 Dec 78; CCSPD number 12. The body was determined to be that of a male, white, aged twenty-three to twenty-five, with light to medium brown hair and a medium to heavy build. Items number three through five were removed from the body and collected by R/ST.

Body number 1278 Dec 78, CCSPD number eight, was the third body to be examined. The physical characteristics of the body were determined to be that of a male, white, aged seventeen to nineteen, with black hair and a slim to medium build. Items number six and seven were removed from the body and were collected by R/ST.

Body number 1329 Dec 78, CCSPD number 14, was the last body to be examined. The body was that of a male, white, aged fifteen to seventeen, with dark brown hair, and a medium build. Items number eight, nine, and ten were removed from the body and collected by R/ST.

The recovered items will be evaluated for submission to the Illinois State Crime Lab.

No further action by R/ST.

Job #12555 (1) CR#003640 Homicide CC-PD Inv. Jettiker, Fisher 22

as numbers one through three were recovered from the body.

Body number 1454 Dec 78 was that of a male, white, with black hair and of average build. The age was estimated to be between nineteen and a half and twenty-one and a half. Items number four and five were removed from the body.

Body number 1377 Dec 78 was that of a male, white, subject with a build described by Prof. Warren as robust. The age was estimated as being between twenty-two and twenty-four. Prof. Warren noted a possible injury to the right clavical.

Body number 1330 was that of a male, white, with light brown hair. The build was described as being average, and the age was estimated to be between sixteen to eighteen years.

The examination was concluded at approximately 1930 hrs date.

NO FURTHER ACTION BY RPT.

EVIDENCE TECHNICIAN'S REPORT

Job Number	Case Report Number	Date Received
12535	803640	21 Dec 78

Assignment: Homicide Investigation (Multiple)
Time Assigned: 1840   Time Arrive: 1955

Location: 8213 W. Summerdale, Norwood Park Twsp., Illinois
Agency: C.C.S.P.D

Victim: PIEST, Robert J., et al
Sex: M   Race: W   Age: 15   D.O.B.: Unknown

Victim's Address: [redacted]

Photographs or Evidence Description and Location

#	Description	P	L	E	Inventory
1	A section of green carpet and pad			X	2418-7
2	A piece of paper found in the area of body #5			X	2446-7
3	One folding knife			X	2447-7
4	One piece of rope			X	2447-7
5	One right shoe			X	2447-7
6	One book			X	0004-7
7	One book			X	0004-7
8	One book			X	0004-7
9	One book			X	0004-7
10	One brown bottle			X	0004-7
11	One length of rope			X	0004-7
12	Twenty five badges and stars			X	0004-7
13	One envelope containing smoking materials, pipes and bongs			X	0004-7
14	One paper bag with a chalky white substance			X	0018-7
15	One paper bag with a chalky white substance			X	0018-7

Photographs B&W[ ] C[ ] S[ ] Print Cards[ ] Palm[ ] Blood[ ] Hair[ ] Nails[ ] Swabs[ ] Bile[ ]
Urine[ ] Clothing[ ] Ammo[ ] Glass[ ] Soil[ ] Paint[ ] Safe Material[ ] Scene Plat[ ]
Latents[ ] Firearms[ ] Serology[ ] Chemistry[ ] Trace[ ] Arson[ ] ToolMarks[ ] Spectro[ ]
Gunshot Residue[ ] Handwriting-Typo Analysis[ ] Other

Make-Yr-Mileage   Model   Color   Vin   Lic-Yr-St

The following is a compilation of the daily activity conducted at 8213 W. Summerdale, Norwood Park, Twsp., Illinois, by the Evidence Technician Unit. Initial contact commenced on 21 Dec 78. It should be noted that before, during and after the excavation of the residence Reporting Evidence Technicians recorded the scene with photography and video tape. The photography included color print film and color slide film. After the exhumation of each body a wooden stake with the corresponding body number was placed in the location of the skull. Body numbers were issued upon discovery of the remains and Morgue numbers issued by the Medical Examiners personnel at the scene. Measurements were taken to locate each skull as found, both as to position and depth in the crawl space soil. The interior demensions of the crawl space were approximately 28' x 38'.

...imately 1840 hrs., 21 Dec 78, Reporting Evidence Technicians were [redacted] #228 and the members of the Evidence Technician Unit.

Investigator-Agency: Cook County Sheriff's Police, North Investigations Unit

EVIDENCE REPORT Item Sheet	COOK COUNTY SHERIFF'S POLICE DEPARTMENT Criminalistics Section	Lab No. 12555	Case Report No. 803640	Date 21 Dec 7_

Item	Description and Location	P	L	E	Invent. No
6	One work type glove			X	0044-79
	** The following listings represent a roll by roll accounting of				
	the color and black & white print photography taken at the scene **				
1	Over all views of interior residence prior to excavation	B			
	Over all views crawl space area of body #1 and Dr. Stein at #2	B			
	Over all views of bodies #1 and 2	C			
	Over all views of exterior residence and areas of bodies #1&2	C			
	Close up views skull of #3 and block like stain floor of SW bedroom	C			
	Over all views of bodies #1 thru 5	C			
	Over all views of bodies #6 and 7, including recovery	C			
8	Over all and close up views of body #7	C			
9	Over all views and recoveries of bodies #8, 11, and 13	C			
10	Over all views of bodies #8, 11 and 12	C			
11	Over all views of bodies #14 and 15	C			
12	Over all views crawl space NE portion. Over all views of bodie #16	C			
13	Over all and close up views of bodies #16 thru 20	C			
14	Over all and close up views of bodies #23, 24 and 27, and close up				
	views with scale of recovered jewelry chains	C			
15	Over all and close up views of bodies #22, 23 and 25	C			
16	Over all and close up views of body #26	C			
17	Over all views of bar-b-que pit at rear of residence and close up				
	views of recovered badges	C			
18	Over all views of jewelry at Area One Investigations	C			
19	Over all views of jewelry at Area One Investigations	C			
20	Over all views of jewelry at Area One Investigations	C			
	Supplemental Photographs; Close up view of necklace, close up view of belt buckle,				
	close up view of scrap of paper and close up views of photographs found at the residen_				

Des Plaines Police Department
WITNESS STATEMENT

Date: Dec 22/78 Time: 1400 Place: DESPLAINES Police STATION R.D. # 78-35203

I, RONALD E. ROHDE, am 45 years of age and my address is ▓▓▓▓▓▓▓▓▓▓▓▓▓▓▓▓▓▓▓▓▓▓▓▓

Until this incident arose about Rohde about John Gacy I have had business dealings with him, and to my knowledge he has been normal & honest in all our dealings.

I have had him to my home and played cards with him and Rohde my wife & I went to Las Vegas with him in 1977 & 1978. I've been to parties he has thrown in his home. That is the extent of my knowledge of his personal life.

On Thursday Dec 21, he told me he killed thirty people. I called my uncle DONALD E. MAAS a Deputy Sheriff at 6:30 AM Dec 22 and he recommended I call Chief QUAGLIANO of the sheriffs dept and repeat what he had told me. I made the call at 8:30 AM Dec 22, 1978.

I have read the 1 pages of this statement and the facts contained therein are true and correct.

Page 1 of 1 pages.

Missing Person

Piest, Robert J.

22 Dec 78 0900 Hours

The following report reflects my activities in a follow up investigation of a missing person's report filed on 11 December 79 by Mrs. Elizabeth Piest.

On 21 December 1978 at approximately 2100 hours I had an occasion to be in the home of John Wayne Gacy, 8213 West Summerdale Avenue in Norwood Park Township in the process of serving a search warrant on the premises. In the process of serving the warrant, Detectives Kautz, Adams and Tovar, after having done some previous investigation regarding a black and white Motorola television set and a Sears clock radio, were able to locate the two items in the master bedroom, which would be in the northwest corner of the house of the residence of John Wayne Gacy. Recovered was (1) 12 inch Black & White Motorola Television, portable type, with a beige color and dark tan. The Serial Number on it is T31679894 and the Model Number is BP3050KH. Also recovered was (1) Sears AM/FM Digital Clock Radio with a simulated walnut wood color and a black plastic front with the Serial Number A42E21. These two items would correspond with the items previously known to us as having belonged to John A. Szyc, of 2247 Westview, Des Plaines, Illinois. The two items were inventoried and put into evidence by Detectives Tovar and Adams.

R.D. # 78-35203

22 Dec 78

Det. R. Tovar 222

22 Dec 78 1128 Hours

On the above time and date Detectives Adams and Sommerschield arrived at the Crime Lab and spoke with Chemist George Dabdoub in reference to evidence which had been submitted to the Crime Lab on 21 December 1978. The evidence submitted to the Crime Lab was retrieved by Detectives Adams and Sommerschield in addition to a letter which is directed to the Des Plaines Police Department, Lt. J. Kozenczak, Agency Case #78-35203, Laboratory Case #78-6123 which lists the findings of the Crime Lab. The above mentioned items were returned to this department and placed into evidence.

22 Dec 78

EVIDENCE REPORT

OFFENSE: MISSING - HOMICIDE
DATE-TIME THIS REPORT: 22 DEC 78 1745
DEATH REPORT: ☒ NO

LOCATION: SEE NARRATIVE

PHO	CAST	REC	LOCATION FOUND — DESCRIBE
		X	1 GOLD "CANNON" TOWEL
		X	1 MULTI-COLORED SHIRT

RB No.: 78-35203

Officer: WHETSTONE **Star No.:** 744

R/O WENT TO STATE POLICE H.Q'TS DIST #5 JOLIET AND RECOVERED ONE ITEM RECOVERED BY TROOPER LAMB #1719 ALONG I55 NEAR MILE POST MARKER 268.7 IN WILL COUNTY. THIS AREA IS APPROXIMATELY 20 MILES NORTH OF THE DES PLAINES RIVER BRIDGE. UPON R/O'S ARRIVAL BACK IN THE D.P. STATION, THE ITEM, ALONG WITH A MULTI-COLORED SHIRT FOUND ON A FRONTAGE RD OFF I55 (N/B FRONTAGE ROAD) 200' FT. SOUTH OF NORMANTOWN RD. WERE PLACED IN THE PHOTO LAB TO DRY. THESE ITEMS SHOULD BE RE-PACKAGED AFTER DRYING.

LISTED BELOW ARE PHOTO'S TAKEN OF WHERE THE TOWEL WAS F...D (PHOTO'S 1 THRU 7) AND ALSO THE AREA WHERE THE VICTIM'S BODY WAS ALLEDGEDLY DROPPED.

#1. NORTH BOUND I55 — SHUTTER SPEED 125 — MILE MARKER 268.7
#2. " " " " " " " "
#3. SOUTH BOUND I55 — SHUTTER SPEED 500 " " "
#4. " " " " " " 1000 " " "
#5. MEDIAN DITCH FACING NORTH SHUTTER SPEED 250 " " "
#6. " " " " " " 125 " " "
#7. ...... RESTURANT (S.S. 125) " " "
#8. S/B I55 DES PLAINES RIVER BRIDGE (S.S. 125)
#9. N/B I55 DES PLAINES RIVER BRIDGE (S.S. 125)
#10. N/B I55 DES PLAINES RIVER BRIDGE FROM ARSENAL RD OVERPASS (S.S. 125)
#11. " " " " " " " " " (S.S. 125)
#12. N/B I55 TOWARDS DES PLAINES RIVER BRIDGE (S.S. 125)
#13. " " " " " " (S.S. 125)
#14. N/B I55 ON BRIDGE
#15. N/B I55 ON BRIDGE
#16. N/B I55 ON BRIDGE
#17. ... BELOW BRIDGE ... SIDE BRIDGE LINE W/ AT BRIDGE

ILLINOIS STATE POLICE FIELD REPORT

Case #: OS-78-3027

Brief Description: Rec. cv of Evidence Found in Homie I-55 N3 @ MP 218

Investigating Officer: LIMB, THOMAS W. ID No. 1714 Dist. No. 05

County: WILL-DUPAGE

Date: 12-22-78

I was advised by Lt Smith to search an area along I-55 NB 4 miles Either side of Ill 53 for an orange blanket which was used in a Homicide in Cook County. While searching this designated area at 10:55 AM I found an orange beach towel in the center median closest to the south bound lanes. This location was North bound on I-55 @ MP 268.7. At this time I secured the possible evidence and transported it to Aur 1.

The towel was found on the grass with no snow on top of it. The towel was rolled up and was frozen. When I picked the towel up, I was careful to pick up near the corner, so that it would not be contaminated further.

DEPARTMENT OF LAW ENFORCEMENT EVIDENCE INVENTORY AND RECEIPT

1. Date: 12-22-78
2. Time: 2:46 P.M.
3. Case/File No.: 05-78-3027
4. District No.: 05

5. Name or Place of Business: Ill. State Police Dist. 5
6. Address and City:

ITEMIZED LIST OF EVIDENCE	LOCATION EVIDENCE FOUND
1 Plastic Bag Containing 1 Large Orange Bath Towel	I-55 N/B M.P. 268.7 Near I-55 and Joliet Rd (Found by Tpr. Lamb)
1 Paper Bag Containing 1 Small Size Shirt	Found 12:41 PM 12-22-78 I-55 N/B Frontage Rd 3/10 mi South of Nicomtown Rd

FIELD SUPPLEMENTARY REPORT / DES PLAINES POLICE

Offense: Possession of Marijuana
Offense Changed to: Possession of Controlled Substance

On arrest the defendant John W. Gacy, 8213 Summerdale, Norridge Ill, 457-1614, DOB 17 Mar 42, was arrested for possession of marijuana. In a search incident to the arrest, forty pills marked Lowe Valina were recovered from the defendant. The pills were in a bottle bearing no label or prescription.

A.S.A. Cockell O.K.'d a felony complaint for possession of controlled substance. Court date 26 Jan 79 1330 Des Plaines. The evidence to be taken to the lab to determine its exact make up.

DES PLAINES POLICE   12-22-78 1630

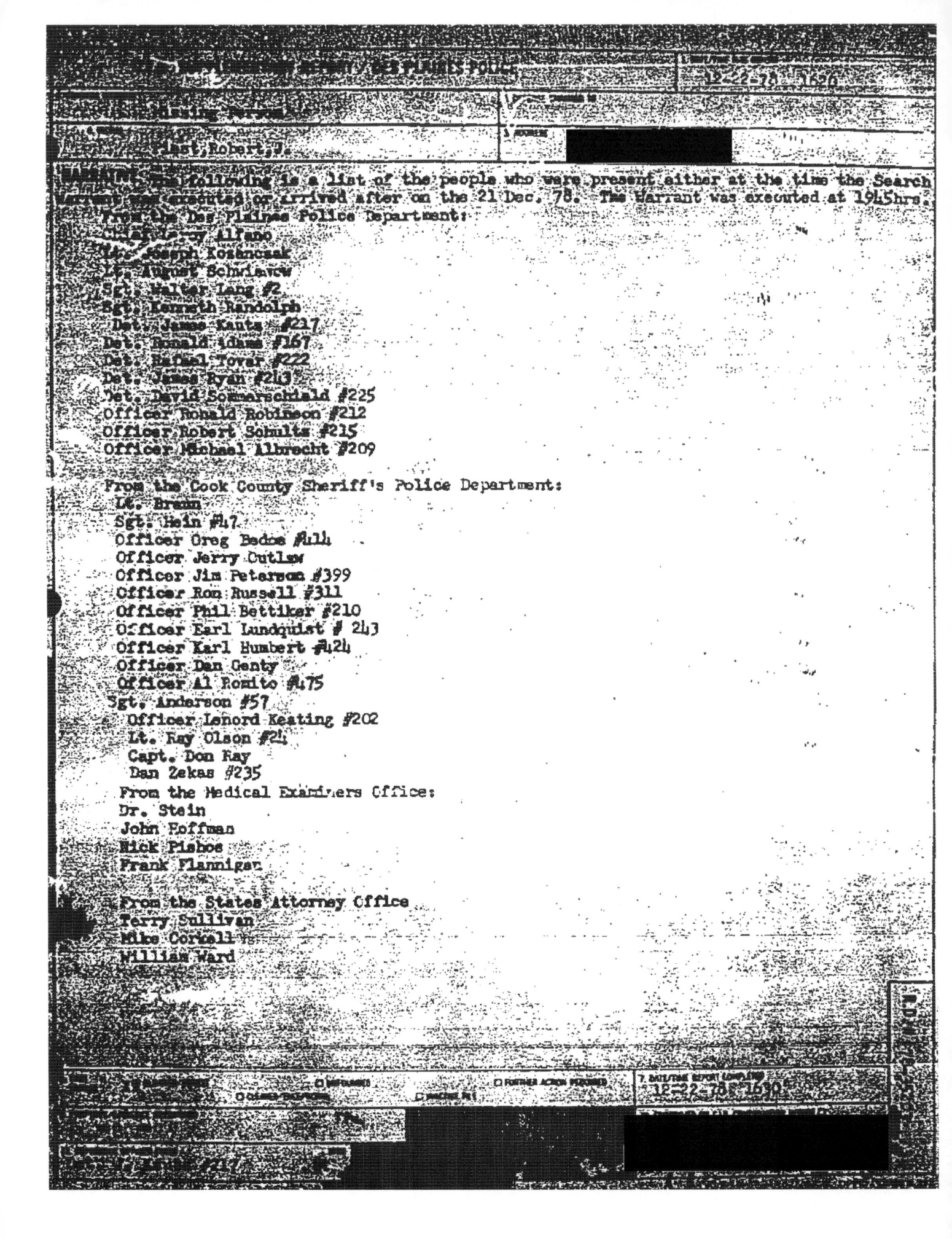

Last, Robert J.

NARRATIVE: The following is a list of the people who were present either at the time the Search Warrant was executed or arrived after on the 21 Dec. 78. The Warrant was executed at 1945hrs.
From the Des Plaines Police Department:
Chief J. Alfano
Lt. Joseph Kozenczak
Lt. August Schnieder
Sgt. Walter Lang #2
Sgt. Kenneth Randolph
Det. James Kautz #217
Det. Ronald Adams #167
Det. Rafael Tovar #222
Det. James Ryan #243
Det. David Sommerschield #225
Officer Ronald Robinson #212
Officer Robert Schultz #215
Officer Michael Albrecht #209

From the Cook County Sheriff's Police Department:
Lt. Braun
Sgt. Hein #47
Officer Greg Bedoe #414
Officer Jerry Outlaw
Officer Jim Peterson #399
Officer Ron Russell #311
Officer Phil Bettiker #210
Officer Earl Lundquist #243
Officer Karl Humbert #424
Officer Dan Genty
Officer Al Romito #475
Sgt. Anderson #57
Officer Lenord Keating #202
Lt. Ray Olson #24
Capt. Don Ray
Dan Zekas #235

From the Medical Examiners Office:
Dr. Stein
John Hoffman
Nick Pishos
Frank Flanniger

From the States Attorney Office
Terry Sullivan
Mike Corkell
William Ward

Arrest Card — Des Plaines P.D.

Name: Gacy Jr., John Wayne
Address: 8213 Summerdale, Norridge, IL 60634
Date of Arrest: 12 21 78
Date Printed: 12 21 78

Count	Chapter Article Section Subsection	Description of Offense	Class
1	56½;1402 b	Poss. Cont. Substance	3 F
2	56½;704 b	Poss. Cannabis	B M

Number of Defendants: 1
Number of Charges: 2

Judge: Judge Martay
Bond Amount: $1000.00
Initial Court Date: 22 DEC 1978 — 1330
Initial Court Location: DES PLAINES

Agency Information: ...T CERMACK HOSPITAL

COPY 1 ARRESTING AGENCY

MISCELLANEOUS INCIDENT / DES PLAINES POLICE — INFORMATION REPORT

Location: 1320 Miner Street
Offense Code: 6 Mio
Date/Time of Incident: 22 Dec 78, 2100
Beat Assigned: Desk
Time Dispatched: 0224
Day of Occurrence: Friday

Complainant: Rochford, James — M W

NARRATIVE

Complainant, a cab driver for Flash Cab Co. in Chicago, contacted R/O via telephone to relate the following information. On 22 Dec 78 at about 9 PM he picked up a very attractive looking white female with short black hair, 5'0" - 5'2", slender build, in her early 20's, in front of a clothing store on the south side of Irving Park Road at about 4819, just west of Cicero Ave. The female was carrying 9 or 10 yellow plastic shopping bags possibly from the clothing store. Complainant feels the female worked at the clothing store. The female was taken to 3300 Belle Plaine Chicago, where she apparently lives. During the ride the female had the following conversation with the cab driver. She related her and her boy friend were real good friends with John Gacy, and that Gacy had given him, the boy friend, used clothing, that they knew could never had fit Gacy. She also related that Gacy asked her boy friend if he wanted some watches, she didn't say he had accepted the watches, but he apparently took the clothing. Gacy also asked both her and her boy friend if they wanted to go to Wisconsin, which they refused because he was acting very suspicious. The female mentioned the fact that she was from France (no accent).

FWD at Division.

DO NOT PUBLISH

RD# 78-0255

		HOMICIDE		22 DEC 78	1440
				□ FOUND □ RECOVERED ☒ EVIDENCE	

UNKNOWN

QTY	DESCRIPTION	VALUE	RELEASED TO (SIGNATURE)
1	GOLD CANNON TOWEL	?	
1	MULTI COLORED STRIPED SHIRT	?	

J WHETSTONE #19F

PRESS RELEASE

FOR IMMEDIATE RELEASE

8:15 P.M. December 22, 1978

At 11:30 P.M. December 11, 1978, Elizabeth Piest called this Department to report her son, Robert Piest, male white, age 15, 2722 Craig Dr, Des Plaines missing under unusual circumstances. She related that she went to Nisson's Pharmacy, 1920 Touhy Ave Des Plaines, Ill. at about 9:00 P.M., December 11, to pick up her son who was employed at this drug store. He requested that she wait a few minutes while he spoke to an individual about a job for summer employment. Robert Piest went outside the store and disappeared.

After 20 minutes Mrs. Piest became alarmed and contacted friends of Robert Piest to no avail. She was able to learn from her son's employer that Robert Piest may have gone outside the building to speak to a Mr. Gacy of P.D.M. Construction Chicago about a summer job. A Missing Person's Police Report was completed at 11:50 P.M., December 11, 1978. The appropriate information was entered into the State and National Computer at 1:54 A.M., December 12th.

The next morning, December 12th, at about 9:00 A.M. Mrs. Piest came to the Des Plaines Police Station with members of her family. Her son had still not returned home and none of his friends had heard from him. The Criminal Investigations Division of the Department initiated an investigation into the matter.

Page 2, Cont.

Early in the investigation, speculation was that Mr. Gacy may have had contact with the Piest boy outside the Nisson Pharmacy on the night of December 11th. Our investigation revealed that Mr. Gacy had a criminal history with a conviction for a sex crime in Iowa in 1968.

Lt. Kozenczak, Commander of the Criminal Investigation Division then intensified the investigation of the missing Piest boy. Many people were contacted and interviewed. Mr. Gacy was placed under a continuous, round the clock surveillance during much of this period of time.

Page 3, Cont.

From information and physical evidence gathered by investigators, Mr. Gacy was arrested by members of this Department at 12:15 P.M. December 21, 1978 and brought before Judge Marvin Peters of the Circuit Court of Cook County., Des Plaines Court branch on Dec. 22, 1978 for the charge of murdering Robert Piest. Judge Peters refused the defendant bail and continued his case to December 29, 1978 in the Des Plaines Court. Mr. Gacy will be transferred to the Cook County Jail, Chicago sometime during the day of December 23rd.

During the progress of the investigation, leads were developed by this Department that bodies of other victims may be buried in the home of Mr. Gacy at 8213 Summerdale, unincorporated Norridge, Ill. Since this is the Police jurisdiction of the Cook County Sheriff, they were requested to assist this Department in the searching of Mr. Gacy's home pursuant to a search warrant. At this time, they are conducting this search, and it is expected to continue for sometime.

As of this date and time, the body of Robert Piest has not been recovered. This Department is continuing it's investigation.

Chief Alfano and Lt. Kozenczak wish to acknowledge the exceptionally fine cooperation of the State's Attorneys investigators staff and the Cook County Sheriff's Police Department in this matter.

Page 3, Cont.

Arrested was John Wayne Gacy, Jr., male, white, age 36, divorced, residing at 8213 Summerdale Ave., Norridge, Ill.

Lieutenant Michael Clark
Des Plaines Police Dept.

FELONY MINUTE SHEET
Form 101

BINDERS MARGIN (DO NOT WRITE ABOVE THIS LINE)

ASSISTANT STATE'S ATTORNEY: (For State's Attorney Use Only)
Enter each continuance here. In cases of multiple defendants indicate which defendants, if any, did not join in the continuance. Also indicate dates of all demands for trial, and by whom demands were made.

COURT: _____

I.R. NUMBER	DEFENDANTS	AGE	DATE OF ARREST	CHARGE
	GACY, JOHN	36	21 DEC 78	POSSESSION OF CONTROLLED SUBSTANCE

Date of Offense: 21 DEC 78 Time: 12:15 Place: MILWAUKEE & OAKTON NILES Illinois

The facts briefly stated are as follows: DEFENDANT WAS ARRESTED FOR DELIVERY OF MARIJUANA. IN SEARCH INCIDENT TO THE ARREST 40 ROCHE VALIUM 10 MILIGRAMS WERE RECOVERED FROM A BOTTLE CARRYING NO PRESCRIPTION OR LABEL.

WITNESSES: SPELL OUT FIRST AND LAST NAME; FIRST NAME FIRST
ALSO FURNISH ADDRESS AND PHONE NUMBER OF EACH WITNESS

PROSECUTING WITNESS: OFF. DAVID HACHMEISTER, OFF. ROBERT SCHULTZ, OFF. RONALD ROBINSON, SGT. WALTER LANG ALL OF THE DES PLAINES POLICE DEPARTMENT 1420 MINER ST. DES PLAINES.

BOND, $ _____ ASST. STATE'S ATTY. _____ DATE _____

(Do Not Write in this Space — For State's Atty. Use Only)

FELONY MEMORANDUM

DEFENDANT (S) Gacy John Wayne Jr.

CHARGE (S) Possession Controlled Substance

POLICE DEPT. Des Plaines P.D.

DATE OF OFFENSE 21 Dec 78

DATE OF ARREST 21 Dec 78

IN CUSTODY OR OUT ON BOND _____

COURT DATE Jan 26, 979 1:30 PM

DATE 21 Dec 78   OFFICER Hachin Ster. 231

PLEASE MAIL TO
OUR OFFICE ON
DATE OF ARREST.

3rd District Circuit Court
Criminal Branch
7166 N. Milwaukee Avenue
Niles, Illinois 60648
647-7324

Piest, Robert J.

NARRATIVE:

The following report reflects my activities in a follow up investigation of a missing person's report which was originally filed by Mrs. Elizabeth Piest on December 10, 1978.

On today's date, December 22, 1978, Detectives Ryan, Youth Officer Detective Adams and myself were assigned to transport John Wayne Gacy Jr to the Cook County Jail Compound at 26th and California, where he was to be turned over to Jail personnel pending his next court appearance. While en route to the location of the Cook County Jail, John Gacy was quite talkative with the Officers who were transporting him to the location, making numerous remarks about the tenacity of the news media who were around when we placed him in the vehicle to transport him to the Cook County Jail. Gacy started talking about various things revolving around the case and it was at this time that I stopped him and advised him that he should remember that anything he said to us would be putting in our report and it could be used against him in court. I indicated to him that he did have his rights still to remain silent and he indicated that he knew his rights and would continue speaking with the Officers. In the conversation Gacy was asked by myself whether it was a fact that the last five people he had told the other officers he killed were dumped into the Des Plaines River, and he stated that as far as he could remember the last five were the ones he had thrown off the bridge into the Des Plaines River. He further indicated that this was those that he had killed since July of 1978 to the present date. I further asked him if Rob Piest was the last subject he had thrown off the bridge. He indicated that he was. I asked him who was the one just prior to him, trying to work backwards as to the identities of the various individuals, and he indicated that it was a guy from Elmwood Park he knew only as something Joe. I questioned as to what he meant by something Joe and he indicated that it was part of the name that he could not remember. I asked him if it was something like Little Joe or Big Joe, and he indicated that no it was all together but couldn't remember the exact name. I asked him if it was part of the name, and he said no that as far as he knew it was only a nickname, as I should realize that most of these that were into this type of sex were known only by nicknames. I asked him if he knew anything further on the name and he said no, but that he was sure that that Joe part was not his real name. He further told me that as far as he knew the subject was from Elmwood Park and that he was sure of, but that at the time the guy was living somewhere in the area of Clark and Sheridan in the Chicago area. I asked him if he could remember how long prior to Piest he had been thrown into the river, and he could not remember. I asked him if he could tell me anything else about the subject, and he said that this guy Joe was a small guy and that he was into masochism, and that he had taken care of him. I asked him what he meant by taking care of him and he said he had tended to his particular sex inclination. He further elaborated that the board he had previously told us about, making reference to a three foot long two-by-four with four holes in it which he used to tie people up with chains, was one that he had used on this subject Joe. He told us that Joe liked pain inflicted upon him and he had really done a number on him using the board. I asked how he got the idea of the board and he said he had gotten the idea from Elmer Wayne Henley from Texas who was convicted of mass murder in 1973. In the conversations with Gacy about the subject known as something Joe, he also mentioned that Joe was a real short individual, not very big at all. In other conversation with Gacy, he wanted to know whether Mike Royko or Walter Jacobsen, of the Sun-Times and

NBC-Television respectfully, had telephoned for him. He said that they were his friends and that he knew them quite well and figured they would be calling for him. We advised that they had not called as of yet and that we would relay any message to him if they did, in fact, call. Detective Adams, of the Youth Bureau, also asked him whether he knew if Rob Piest had suffered any pain after he had strangled him, and he stated that he did not remember at this time. He said that he had had a phone call and was not sure if he had at all. However, then he changed his mind and said he didn't think Piest had suffered any. Other conversation was general in nature and not anything of evidentiary value, therefore, that is all the information for this report. Further action to follow.

CONFIDENTIAL

Piest, Robert J. — Murder

This is a continuing report in regards to the investigation of the disappearance of Robert J. Piest, a M/W, age 15, DOB: 16 March 1963, 5'8", brown hair with a slim build. During the course of my investigation evidence was gathered through a search warrant indicating that the missing boy, Piest, was in the residence belonging to John W. Gacy located at 8213 West Summerdale, Norridge, Illinois, within 48 hours after he was reported missing from Nisson Drugs at 1920 Touhy Avenue, Des Plaines. The search warrant referred to above was a search warrant executed on 13 December 1978 at 8213 West Summerdale Avenue, Norridge, Illinois, signed by Judge Marvin J. Peters. Recovered during that search was a customer receipt #36119 from a film developing envelope with the name and address of Nisson Pharmacy stamped on it in ink. Further investigation revealed that this receipt had last been in the possession of Robert Piest immediately prior to the time he had disappeared.

On December 21, 1978 I had occasion to speak to Officer Robert Schultz/Star #215, of the Des Plaines Police Department. Officer Schultz has been a Des Plaines Police Officer for the past 8½ years. He told me that on Tuesday, December 19, 1978, at 7:30 p.m. he was at the John Gacy residence at 8213 West Summerdale, Norridge, Illinois, on surveillance assignment. At that time John Gacy approached Officer Schultz's police vehicle and asked him if he would like to enter his residence. Officer Schultz responded in the affirmative and entered the Gacy residence, via the kitchen entrance with Mr. Gacy. Once inside, Officer Schultz immediately detected an odor similar to that of a putrefied human body. Officer Schultz further indicated that during his tenure as a Des Plaines Police Officer, he has smelled the odor of at least forty putrefied human bodies and that the odor he detected in the Gacy residence smelled similar to the odor of putrefied bodies he has smelled in the past.

Based on all of the information given and with the approval of the Cook County State's Attorney's Office, Assistant State's Attorney Larry Finder, this Reporting Officer prepared a complaint for search warrant and a search warrant and said documents were taken in front of Judge Marvin Peters on this date and, upon review of the complaint for search warrant, Judge Marvin Peters approved said warrants and the Reporting Officer, along with other officers from the Des Plaines Police Department and Cook County Sheriff's Police Department, went to the residence of John Wayne Gacy located at 8213 West Summerdale, Norridge, Illinois, and entered the residence per the authority of the warrant issued earlier this evening. The warrant in question was issued for the search for the body of Robert Piest and/or remains thereof. Warrant dated December 21, 1978.

After entering the house in question a search of the crawl space area was started by investigators, and after a brief time period a bone was unearthed which appeared to be that of a human arm. At this time digging was stopped, pending the arrival of the Cook County Medical Examiner.

CONFIDENTIAL

On Saturday, December 23, 1978, John W. Gacy Jr. was transported to the Cook County Jail by Detectives Adams, Tovar and Ryan. We arrived at the jail at approximately 1128 hours, at which time we met with the Director of Security, Mr. Patrick, and were advised that it would be necessary to escort Mr. Gacy to the Cermak Memorial Hospital. Mr. Gacy was **** Doctor Cone at 1156 hours, at which time the above mentioned Officers left the hospital.

FIELD SUPPLEMENTARY REPORT - DES PLAINES POLICE

MISSING PERSON / HOMICIDE
PIEST, ROBERT

NARRATIVE:

On 22 Dec 78 R/O and Officer Robinson transported offender (Gacy, John Wayne) and his attorney (Sullivan, Leroy) from station in squad #76 to a bridge on Rowell Rd. just south of I-80 where offender agreed to point out the exact location that he threw the missing Piest boys body into the Des Plaines River. R/O's and offender walked along the inside portion of the northbound bridge and using the upright structural beams as markers, walked until we reached the fifth one. From this point, looking across at the southbound bridge R/O's located a second marker which was a dingy white beach towel hanging from the metal structure below the roadbed area. Offender then described the method of discarding the bodies which was merely throwing them over the two foot high rail between N/B and S/B sides of the bridges.

Offender had originally informed R/O that the bridge was 63 miles from station, however an accurate clock pointed out the distance was 53 miles. From the bridge R/O's drove to 8213 Summerdale in Norwood Park, and once there offender outlined another victims body with spray paint indicating the exact position the body would be buried under the concrete floor.

SCHULTZ / 915

to the ??? ??? the tool room which was an addition to the garage. Offender was then brought back into the station

Piest, Robert J.

NARRATIVE:
The following is a list of people pertaining to the investigation along with information on them:

CONFIDENTIAL

John Wayne Gacy Jr.
M/W, D.O.B. 03-17-42
5'09", 200, Hair Brown, Eyes Blue
DL# G200-4794-2079
SS# 344-34-3840
F.B.I.# 5851810
I.S.B.# 1377836
I.R.# 273632
Alias Colonel
8213 West Summerdale, Norwood Park Township, Illinois
TL 457-1614

Vehicles 1) 1979 Oldsmobile 4dr. sedan black
Vin# 3N69R9Y105706
Illinois 1978
PDM Contractors-firm owned-8213 W. Summerdale Norwood Park

2) 1978 Chevrolet Van black
Vin# CGL258L118817
Illinois 1979
PDM Contractors-firm owned-8213 W. Summerdale Norwood Park

3) 1978 Chevrolet Pickup black
Vin# CKL248J192155
Illinois 1979
PDM Contractors 8213 W. Summerdale Norwood Park

4) 1977 Plymouth 4dr. sedan silver
Illinois 1978
Drive Okar Corporation-firm owned-5440 N. River Rd. Rosemont, Ill. leased

John Gacy is the owner of PDM Contractors, 8213 W. Summerdale Norwood Park Township, Illinois, and is also the apparent Vice-President of, Charo Raphael, President, Raphco Inc. 831 East Lake Ave. Glenview, Illinois 60025. Incharge of operations. Raphco Inc. are Contractors/Developers.

Arrested Waterloo Iowa, 05-20-68, Sodomy, sentenced 10yrs., paroled 06-18-70 to Chicago. He was also arrested in Northbrook, Illinois, for Aggravated Battery, 06-22-72, and also Reckless Conduct, discharged the Agg. Battery and S.O.L. motion to reinstate Reckless Conduct. He was further arrested in Chicago, 07-15-78, for Battery and the case is still pending.

27 Dec. 78 - 1200

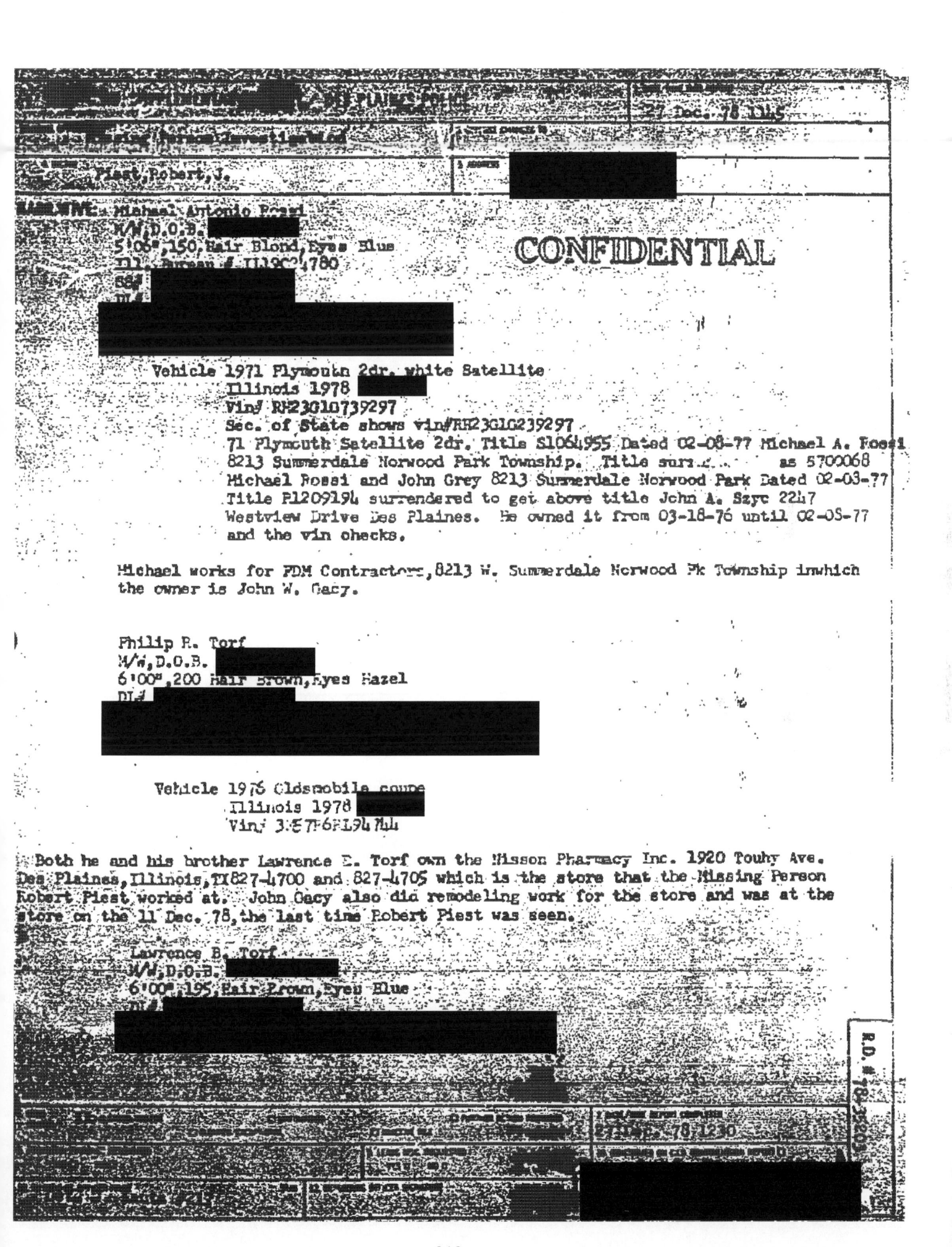

27 Dec. 78

Piest, Robert, J.

Michael Antonio Rossi
M/W, D.O.B.
5'06", 150, Hair Blond, Eyes Blue
DL Bureau # I119024780

CONFIDENTIAL

Vehicle 1971 Plymouth 2dr. white Satellite
Illinois 1978
Vin# RH23G10739297
Sec. of State shows vin#RH23G1G239297
71 Plymouth Satellite 2dr. Title S1064955 Dated 02-08-77 Michael A. Rossi
8213 Summerdale Norwood Park Township. Title surr... as 5700068
Michael Rossi and John Grey 8213 Summerdale Norwood Park Dated 02-08-77
Title P1209194 surrendered to get above title John A. Szyc 2247
Westview Drive Des Plaines. He owned it from 03-18-76 until 02-08-77
and the vin checks.

Michael works for PDM Contractors, 8213 W. Summerdale Norwood Pk Township inwhich the owner is John W. Gacy.

Philip R. Torf
M/W, D.O.B.
6'00", 200 Hair Brown, Eyes Hazel
DL#

Vehicle 1976 Oldsmobile coupe
Illinois 1978
Vin# 3J57R6R194744

Both he and his brother Lawrence E. Torf own the Nisson Pharmacy Inc. 1920 Touhy Ave. Des Plaines, Illinois, PX827-4700 and 827-4705 which is the store that the Missing Person Robert Piest worked at. John Gacy also did remodeling work for the store and was at the store on the 11 Dec. 78, the last time Robert Piest was seen.

Lawrence B. Torf
M/W, D.O.B.
6'00", 195, Hair Brown, Eyes Blue

Missing Person Investigation

Piest, Robert J.

NARRATIVE:
Vehicle 1977 Oldsmobile station wagon
Illinois 1978
Vin# 3J45KM203098

1977 Chevrolet Coupe
Illinois 1978
Vin# 1Z37L7S445615

Both he and his brother Philip R. Torf own the Nisson Pharmacy Inc. 1920 Touhy Ave. Des Plaines, Illinois, T.827-4700 and 827-4705 which is the store that the Missing Person Robert Piest worked at. John Gacy also did remodeling work for the store and was at the store on the 11 Dec. 78, the last time Robert Piest was seen.

Gordon E. Nebel
M/W, D.O.B.
6'01", 190, Hair Brown, Eyes Blue
TL#

Unable to locate and TX

Vehicle 1968 Oldsmobile coupe yellow
Illinois 1979
Vin# 332778M4612?

Gordon is apparently the book keeper for John Gacy and is also a very close friend of his.

Richard A. Raphael
M/W, D.O.B.
5'11", Hair Brown, Eyes Brown
DL#

Vehicles 1) 1977 Dodge Station Wagon
Illinois 1978
Vin# NL4507B463444
Raphael Henber Const. Co.-firm owned
281 Waukegan Road, Northfield

2) 1966 Pontiac 2dr.
Illinois 1978
Vin# 266576E118359
Raphael Henber Const. Co.-firm owned
281 Waukegan Rd., Northfield

3) 1976 Chevrolet Coupe
Illinois 1978

27 Dec. 78 1300

SUPPLEMENTARY REPORT / DES PLAINES POLICE   27 Dec. 78 1300

Missing Person Investigation

Piest, Robert J.

NARRATIVE:
Vin#12371692421693
Raphael Henber Const. Co.-firm owned
281 Waukegan Rd. Northfield

He owns Charo Raphael, President
Raphco Inc.
831 E. Lake Ave.
Glenview, Illinois 60025
Contractors/Developers

CONFIDENTIAL

He is also apparently involved in Raphael Henber Construction Corp. 281 Waukegan Road Northfield, Illinois, TX446-5295. John Gacy apparently was the Vice-President of Operations for the Raphco Inc..

David F. Cram Jr.
AKA David Frederick Cram
M/W, D.O.B.
5'09", 140, Hair Brown, Eyes Brown, Skin Medium

FBC/124A081212107TTTC913

The IX checks to Donald E. Weber, 3300 W. Belleplaine, Chicago, M/W, D.O.B. 05-08-35, 6'00", 220, Hair Black, Eyes Blue, DL#W160-1853-5132. Weber is the Stepfather to David. David was employed by John Gacy PDM Contractors.

James G. O'Toole
M/W, D.O.B.
5'07", 160, Hair Brown, Eyes Brown

His DL was found in Gacy's residence in a jewelery box ontop of a dresser in Gacy's bedroom.

Michael B. Baker
M/W, D.O.B.
5'10", 160, Hair Brown, Eyes Blue

27 Dec. 78 1315

SUPPLEMENTARY REPORT / DES PLAINES POLICE

Date/Time: 27 Dec. 78 1315

Missing Person Investigation

Piest, Robert J.

NARRATIVE: Baker's Temporary DL#0784008 was issued 5 Nov. 75 and was good to 5 Feb. 76. This was found in Gacy's residence in a coffee can that was in Gacy's bedroom in a dresser.

    Charles Antonio Hattula
    M/W, D.O.B.
    6'00", 175, Hair Blond, Eyes Blue

CONFIDENTIAL

    Texas License Operator

Charles worked for P.D.M. Contractors and was found dead in the Pecatonica River off of Winneshiek Bridge in Harlem Township, Stephenson County, Illinois. He was found on the 23 May 78 and the incident apparently happened 13 May 78. Apparently he fell off of the bridge after attempting to help get a vehicle loose that became stuck on the bridge that was under repair in which he was riding in. The cause of death was Asphyxia-Due To Drowning. Jury found the death accidental. Inquest held 31 May 78, Schwarz Funeral Home, 316 S. Galena Ave., City of Freeport, County of Stephenson. The Sheriff's Department handled it TX 815-232-2108, Freeport, Illinois, case#780559, Capt. Currier and Inv. Volkert.
    His mother is Margaret Hancock (maiden name Margaret Kramer) 332 Lorraine Drive, Freeport, Illinois, TX 815-235-3318, father Carl Hattula and his aunt is Alice Hattula, 5067 Valverde, Texas, TX 713-960-1485. Subjects in the vehicle at the time of the accident are Charles Hattula, Bobby Hattula, brother, Norman Smeathers, driver, Karen Johnson, Glenn Miller, Sue Schmoll and Randy Saxby. From all the facts there didnot seem to be any foul play involved.

    Ronald E. Rohde
    M/W, D.O.B.
    5'06", 200, Hair Brown, Eyes Green

    Vehicle 1) 1978 Ford Pickup
        Illinois 1979
        Vin#F14HL8R5574

    2) 1976 Buick Coupe
        Illinois 1978
        Vin#4J57J6H189309

Ronald is a good friend of Gacy's and ran a Christmas Tree Lot on Cumberland Ave., just North of St. Joseph Ukrainian Catholic Church, 5000 N. Cumberland, Chicago, Ill..

Date/Time Report Completed: 27 Dec. 78 1330

Missing Person Investigation

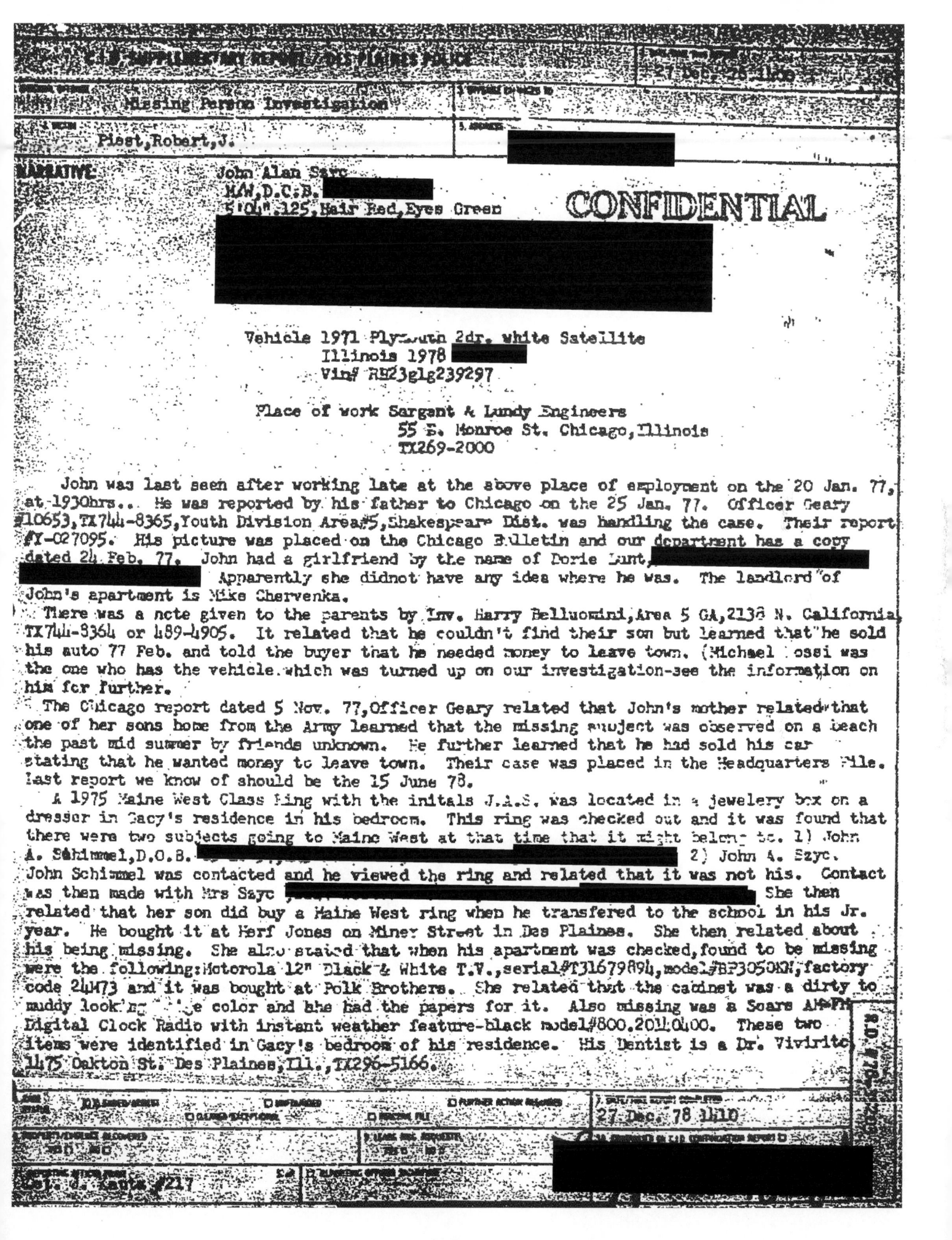

Piest, Robert J.

John Alan Szyc
M/W, D.O.B. [REDACTED]
5'04", 125, Hair Red, Eyes Green

CONFIDENTIAL

Vehicle 1971 Plymouth 2dr. white Satellite
Illinois 1978 [REDACTED]
Vin# RH23g1g239297

Place of work Sargent & Lundy Engineers
55 E. Monroe St. Chicago, Illinois
TX269-2000

John was last seen after working late at the above place of employment on the 20 Jan. 77, at 1930hrs.. He was reported by his father to Chicago on the 25 Jan. 77. Officer Geary #10653,TX744-8365,Youth Division Area#5,Shakespeare Dist. was handling the case. Their report #Y-027095. His picture was placed on the Chicago Bulletin and our department has a copy dated 24 Feb. 77. John had a girlfriend by the name of Dorie Lunt, [REDACTED] Apparently she didnot have any idea where he was. The landlord of John's apartment is Mike Chervenka.

There was a note given to the parents by Inv. Harry Belluomini, Area 5 GA, 2138 N. California, TX744-8364 or 489-4905. It related that he couldn't find their son but learned that he sold his auto 77 Feb. and told the buyer that he needed money to leave town. (Michael Rossi was the one who has the vehicle which was turned up on our investigation-see the information on him for further.

The Chicago report dated 5 Nov. 77, Officer Geary related that John's mother related that one of her sons home from the Army learned that the missing subject was observed on a beach the past mid summer by friends unknown. He further learned that he had sold his car stating that he wanted money to leave town. Their case was placed in the Headquarters file. Last report we know of should be the 15 June 78.

A 1975 Maine West Class Ring with the initals J.A.S. was located in a jewelery box on a dresser in Gacy's residence in his bedroom. This ring was checked out and it was found that there were two subjects going to Maine West at that time that it might belong to. 1) John A. Schimmel,D.O.B. [REDACTED] 2) John A. Szyc. John Schimmel was contacted and he viewed the ring and related that it was not his. Contact was then made with Mrs Szyc [REDACTED] She then related that her son did buy a Maine West ring when he transfered to the school in his Jr. year. He bought it at Herf Jones on Miner Street in Des Plaines. She then related about his being missing. She also stated that when his apartment was checked, found to be missing were the following: Motorola 12" Black & White T.V., serial#T31679894, model#BP3050KH, factory code 24473 and it was bought at Polk Brothers. She related that the cabinet was a dirty to muddy looking olive color and she had the papers for it. Also missing was a Sears AM-FM Digital Clock Radio with instant weather feature-black model#800.2014.0400. These two items were identified in Gacy's bedroom of his residence. His Dentist is a Dr. Vivirito 1475 Oakton St. Des Plaines, Ill., TX296-5166.

27 Dec. 78 1410

SUPPLEMENTARY REPORT / DES PLAINES POLICE

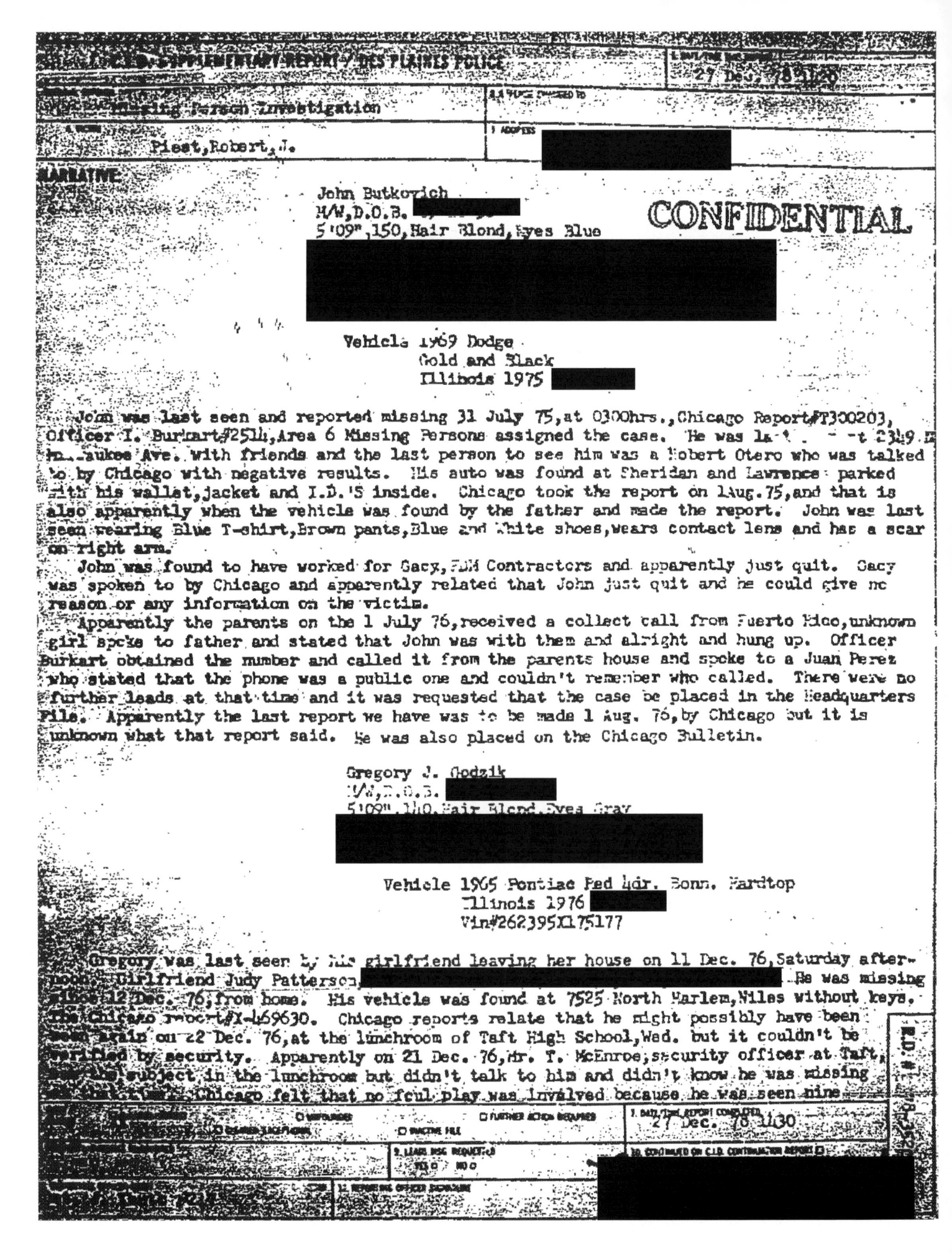

Missing Person Investigation

Piest, Robert J.

NARRATIVE

John Butkovich
M/W, D.O.B. [redacted]
5'09", 150, Hair Blond, Eyes Blue

CONFIDENTIAL

Vehicle 1969 Dodge
Gold and Black
Illinois 1975

John was last seen and reported missing 31 July 75, at 0300hrs., Chicago Report #T300203, Officer I. Burkart #2514, Area 6 Missing Persons assigned the case. He was last seen at 2349 N. Milwaukee Ave. with friends and the last person to see him was a Robert Otero who was talked to by Chicago with negative results. His auto was found at Sheridan and Lawrence parked with his wallet, jacket and I.D.'S inside. Chicago took the report on 1 Aug. 75, and that is also apparently when the vehicle was found by the father and made the report. John was last seen wearing Blue T-shirt, Brown pants, Blue and White shoes, wears contact lens and has a scar on right arm.

John was found to have worked for Gacy, PDM Contractors and apparently just quit. Gacy was spoken to by Chicago and apparently related that John just quit and he could give no reason or any information on the victim.

Apparently the parents on the 1 July 76, received a collect call from Puerto Rico, unknown girl spoke to father and stated that John was with them and alright and hung up. Officer Burkart obtained the number and called it from the parents house and spoke to a Juan Perez who stated that the phone was a public one and couldn't remember who called. There were no further leads at that time and it was requested that the case be placed in the Headquarters File. Apparently the last report we have was to be made 1 Aug. 76, by Chicago but it is unknown what that report said. He was also placed on the Chicago Bulletin.

Gregory J. Godzik
W/M, D.O.B. [redacted]
5'09", 140, Hair Blond, Eyes Gray

Vehicle 1965 Pontiac Red 4dr. Bonn. Hardtop
Illinois 1976
Vin#262395X175177

Gregory was last seen by his girlfriend leaving her house on 11 Dec. 76, Saturday afternoon. Girlfriend Judy Patterson, [redacted]. He was missing since 12 Dec. 76, from home. His vehicle was found at 7525 North Harlem, Niles without keys. The Chicago report #X-469630. Chicago reports relate that he might possibly have been seen again on 22 Dec. 76, at the lunchroom of Taft High School, Wed. but it couldn't be verified by security. Apparently on 21 Dec. 76, Mr. T. McEnroe, security officer at Taft, saw subject in the lunchroom but didn't talk to him and didn't know he was missing at that time. Chicago felt that no foul play was involved because he was seen nine

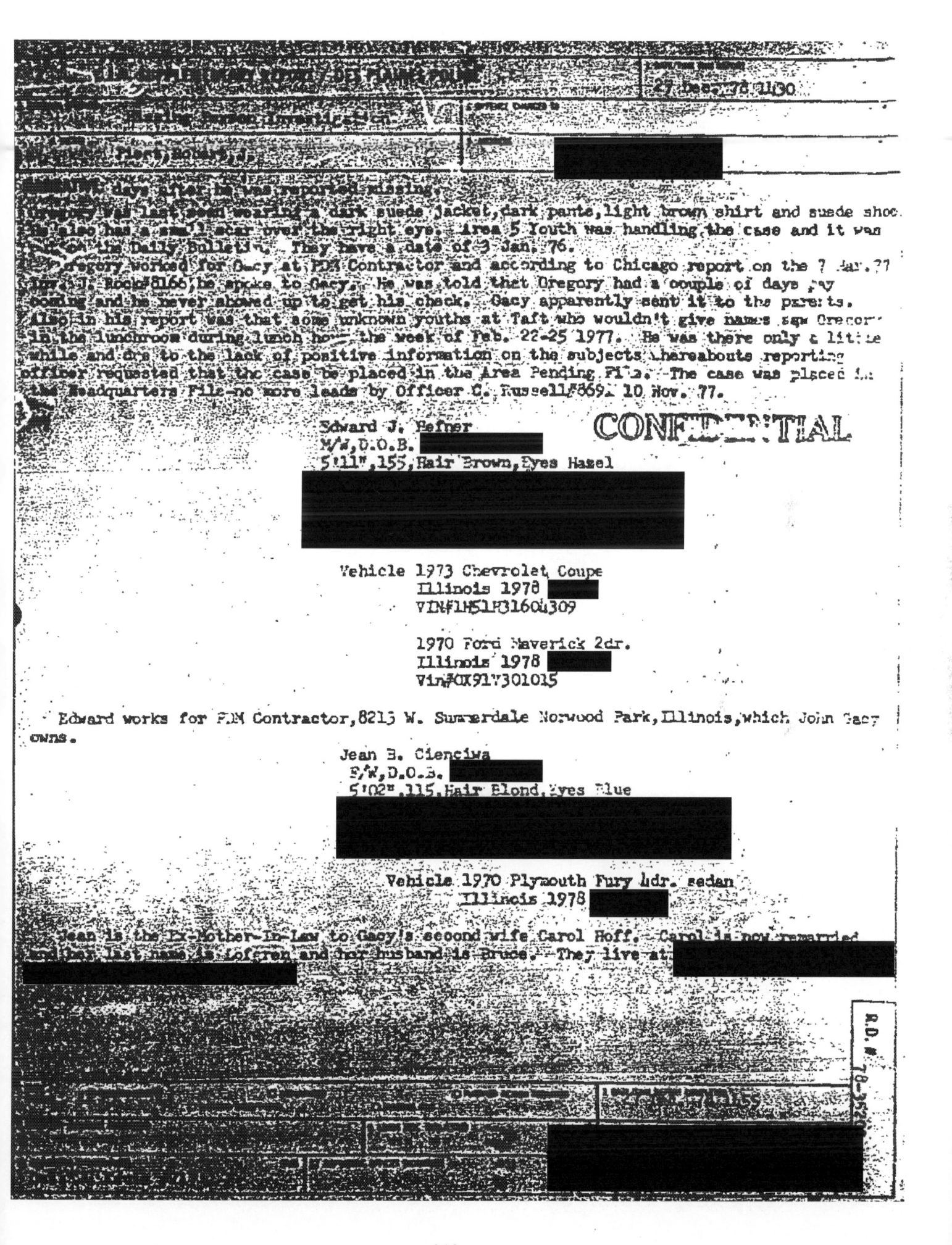

days after he was reported missing.
Gregory was last seen wearing a dark suede jacket, dark pants, light brown shirt and suede shoes. He also had a small scar over the right eye. Area 5 Youth was handling the case and it was on the Daily Bulletin. They have a date of 9 Jan. 76.
Gregory worked for Gacy at PDM Contractor and according to Chicago report on the 7 Jan. 77 by J. Bock #8166, he spoke to Gacy. He was told that Gregory had a couple of days pay coming and he never showed up to get his check. Gacy apparently sent it to the parents. Also in his report was that some unknown youths at Taft who wouldn't give names saw Gregory in the lunchroom during lunch hour the week of Feb. 22-25 1977. He was there only a little while and due to the lack of positive information on the subjects whereabouts reporting officer requested that the case be placed in the Area Pending File. The case was placed in the Headquarters File-no more leads by Officer C. Russell/8669. 10 Nov. 77.

        Edward J. Hefner
        M/W, D.O.B.
        5'11", 155, Hair Brown, Eyes Hazel

CONFIDENTIAL

        Vehicle 1973 Chevrolet Coupe
        Illinois 1978
        VIN#1H51H316011309

        1970 Ford Maverick 2dr.
        Illinois 1978
        Vin#0X91Y301015

Edward works for PDM Contractor, 8213 W. Summerdale Norwood Park, Illinois, which John Gacy owns.

        Jean B. Cienciwa
        F/W, D.O.B.
        5'02", 115, Hair Blond, Eyes Blue

        Vehicle 1970 Plymouth Fury 4dr. sedan
        Illinois 1978

Jean is the Ex-Mother-In-Law to Gacy's second wife Carol Hoff. Carol is now remarried and her last name is Lofgren and her husband is Bruce. They live at

SUPPLEMENTARY REPORT / DES PLAINES POLICE
27 Dec. 78 0945

Missing Person Investigation

Piest, Robert J.

NARRATIVE: On 26 Dec. 78, reporting officers went to the Goodwill Rehabilitation Center, 120 S. Ashland Blvd., Chicago, Illinois, TX 738-3860. This was after Det. Adams had found out from John Gacy that he had apparently thrown Robert Piest's clothes into a goodwill box either at Cumberland and Lawrence or at Harlem and Irving. Det. Adams had first called the Goodwill and spoke to a female subject by the name of Bernice, TX 738-3860 Ext. 259 and also the Transportation Manager Manuel DeGuzman Ext. 326 4331. He was informed that they have eight stores to which they send out items to sell and that their trucks are out every day but do not always pick up from their different pickup locations due to the fact that there may not be enough clothes to pick up. There are about 20-40 people on the production end of the company. Apparently, the clothes are sent on a conveyer to the fifth floor where they are priced and gotten ready for shipment. The shoes also go to the fifth floor and are boxed. The pants are put into boxes of fifty.

Reporting officers upon arrival were taken to the fifth floor and allowed to look through the jackets and coats that were hanging and already being gotten ready to ship out with negative results.

Reporting officers then spoke to Mr. DeGuzman who related that they do not have a box at Harlem and Irving but that there is a box located at 4900 N. Cumberland next to a Kinney Shoe Store in Norridge. He checked his records and found that the driver for that route #5 is a Derrick Washington, truck #11. Pickups were made at that location supposedly on the 18th Dec., Monday and on the 21 Dec., Thursday. He further related that once items come into the center, it takes about four to five days not counting Sunday, which no one works, for the items to be sent out to the various stores. There is no set pattern in which the items are sent out to the stores and it would be impossible to trace any item down.

Reporting officers next checked the store they have in the building and could come up with only a pair of pants which looked something like the ones Robert Piest was wearing. These were recovered and an attempt will be made to see if they can be identified. No other items could be located and reporting officers showed the sales clerks the picture of Piest with the clothes he was wearing when he was reported missing and they related that they could not remember seeing any of the items.

The following is a list of the stores that Goodwill has:

Milwaukee
1474 N. Milwaukee Ave. TX486-9035

Ashland
4834 S. Ashland TX847-9211

Commerical
8936 S. Commerical Ave. TX933-9793

Stony Island
6840 S. Stony Island TX667-9467

Belmont
3315 N. Marshfield TX525-9591

Albany Park
3224 W. Lawrence TX588-9347

Broadway
N. Broadway TX334-9410

27 Dec. 78 0930

DES PLAINES POLICE
27 Dec 78

Missing Person Investigation
Piest, Robert J.

NARRATIVE: Reporting officers went out to the Goodwill store at 4834 S. Ashland and looked through the clothes with negative results. Again the clerk was shown the picture of Piest with the clothes he was wearing and again reporting officers were informed that the clothes had not been seen.

Reporting officers next went to the Goodwill box at 4900 N. Cumberland, Norridge, and found that there were two boxes and that they were both full and did not appear as if they had been picked up for sometime. Lt. Kozenczak was informed of this and he requested that a City truck be sent out and the items brought into the station and checked to see if any of the missing clothes were among the items. The items were brought into the station and checked with negative results.

Det. Adams talked to the driver of the route later on when he had returned from his route and he could give no information on the missing clothes having possibly seen them during his pickups.

It should be noted that if the jacket did go through the Goodwill and to one of their stores, since this was a very good jacket and since this is the Christmas holiday and since the stores sell their items at very low prices, the jacket would have probably been sold almost immediately and further checking of their stores would be useless.

C.P.D. SUPPLEMENTARY REPORT CHICAGO POLICE   28 Dec 78   1215 Hours

Missing Youth

Piest, Robert

NARRATIVE

On the above time and date Mr. Boso was contacted at the Salvation Army Warehouse, 2258 North Kilbourn, Chicago, tx 477-1300, in reference to pick up boxes which might be owned by their organization. We specifically requested information regarding the pick up boxes at the following locations, Harlem and Irving, Harlem and Golf, Belle Plaine Avenue, and 4880 North Milwaukee Avenue. Mr. Boso stated that the boxes at those locations are emptied every evening, in which case the items collected at those locations are moved to their warehouse and are shipped from the warehouse on the following morning. The items that are of some value are shipped to the Salvation Army Outlet Stores and the articles of clothing which are of no value are packaged in large bundles and are used as rags. Mr. Boso stated that he would direct a memo to their various stores in an attempt to locate the items which had been worn by the missing youth and were allegedly discarded by Mr. Gacy in a collection box at either Harlem and Irving or Lawrence and Cumberland.

Des Plaines Police Department
WITNESS STATEMENT

Date 12/08/7_ Time 12:33 Place Desplaines PD R.D. #_____

I, RJ Miller, am 13 years of age and my address [REDACTED] left my house about 6:35 p.m. to go to pick up some friends at Mike Carongo's house when I got there they had already left for the christmas concert at Iroquois Jr. High school. I started walking and met up with Mike Carongo, John Budil, Ken Theeser, Mark Braswood at the corner of Maple & Howard, we resumed walking. We went strait to the christmas concert. We walked around the school for about twenty minuts. Mr. Gunn the principal told us to leave. We left the school about 7:00 pm. we headed for 7 eleven before two new kids entered our group there names were Dan Blanco, Mike Harding. we went to 7 eleven for about 20.00 minnut left and went to John Badil house, it took us about 20 to 30 minutes to walk there he lives on pimits a. We stayed there for a while and had something to eat. We left his house headed back tward school went prist Mission pharmacy saw Robert

I have read the __2__ pages of this statement and the facts contained therein are true and correct

Witness [REDACTED]   [Signature by witness]

Des Plaines Police Department
WITNESS STATEMENT

Date 12/28/78 Time 1:00 Place DPPD

I, R.T. Miller, am 13 years of age and my address is ▮▮▮▮▮▮▮▮▮▮. I went with two or three other kids about same age all males, and white from there proceeded to Iroquois Jr High when we got there the concerts just ended a little bit before we got there. When I looked at the clocke it said 9:00 we & called Ken throdes's (said) mom for a ride

I have read the 2 pages of this statement and the facts contained therein are true and correct.

SUPPLEMENTARY REPORT — DES PLAINES POLICE

28 Dec 78   1515 Hours

Missing Youth

Piest,

NARRATIVE:

On the above time and date Robert L. Steinberg, of ███████████████████████ was interviewed in reference to the above captioned incident. Mr. Steinberg indicated that he may have information pertinent to the investigation regarding John Gacy and that although he was not a victim in this particular incident, his friend or associate Loren Itkin, of ███████████████████████ ██████████ had been chased by John Gacy and, although he was uncertain of the exact date the incident occurred, he does recall that approximately three days after that particular incident his friend, Loren Itkin, had been involved in a traffic accident and Mr. Itkin was going to request that the Cook County Sheriff's Police check the registration on the vehicle which had been driven by Mr. Gacy and as best Robert can recall the plate was ██████ Illinois '77 registration. Upon further speaking with Mr. Steinberg, Mr. Steinberg described the vehicle driven by Mr. Gacy as perhaps a '73 or '74 dark colored Oldsmobile and although the vehicle did not have any spotlights, it did have a red light behind the grill on the right hand side of the grill work. Mr. Steinberg informed this Officer the incident began in a gas station located at 2351 West Howard in Chicago, which is the corner of Howard and Western, when Itkin was to go to ███████████ to pick up an item for Robert Steinberg. After leaving the Mobil Station, Itkin proceeded and was followed to the Steinberg residence by the vehicle, which was later identified as having been driven by John Gacy. According to Mr. Steinberg, Itkin made several maneuvers in an attempt to elude Gacy's vehicle and subsequently returned to the Mobil Station, at which time Gacy pulled his automobile in close proximity to the vehicle being driven by Loren Itkin. Itkin then exited his vehicle at approximately the same time Gacy exited his vehicle and at that point Gacy removed what is described as a revolver from his belt or waistband and pointed the weapon in the direction of Loren Itkin. Gacy then asked Itkin why he came to that gas station and if, in fact, if he had robbed the gas station. Itkin then made some type of reply to Mr. Gacy, at which time Gacy mumbled something and then left the area of Howard and Western. Robert Steinberg stated that was the first and the last time that he had ever seen John Gacy, and to the best of his knowledge Loren Itkin had never seen Gacy before nor has he seen him since.

28 Dec 78

Missing Youth

Piest, Robert

R/O received information that the body of Robert Piest might be buried in a dirt mound located at the Maryhill Cemetary located at Dempster & Cumberland in Niles, IL. Upon receiving this information r/O went to the Maryhill Cemetary and spoke with the Sexton who advised R/O that one of Gacys first victims was buried in a paupers grave along the North boundry of the cemetary. R/O was directed to this area and observed the grave marker of a subject named LONIGAN who was in fact identified as one of Gacys victims that was recovered from the river in Grundy County.

R/O noted that about 200 yards south of the grave site was a large dirt mound that was used by the cemetary to store extra dirt. The mound in question was about 50' wide 30' across and about 30' high. According to R/Os information this was the area that could be the burial site. At this time R/O contacted Capt. Edward Dennis of the Niles P.D. and requested his assistance in this matter.

Capt. Dennis received approval from the Archdiocese of Chicago for us to search the dirt mound.

With the help of the staff at Maryhill Cemetary and in the presence of R/O and Capt. Dennis the dirt mound was excavated with a bull dozer at about one foot levels. The entire mound was taken down to grade level, with no evidence of any body present.

THE PEOPLE OF THE STATE OF ILLINOIS
vs.

JOHN W. GACY JR.

Violation: 38-19 a-1

NO. 78-3-008080-01

Complaint Filed: [illegible]

DATE	JUDGE	ORDERS ENTERED	DATE
		Leave to ___ to file ___	
		Complaint for preliminary examination. Bail: $	
		Court takes jurisdiction of defendant in court on complaint. Red.	
12-29-78	[illegible]	BQ 1-10-79 Transfer to Presiding Judge Circuit for further reassignment to Chief Judge Richard Fitzgerald.	
		(1) Motion for Protective Order — entered [illegible]	
		(2) Motion for Psychiatrist exam — entered & continued	
		(3) PC Dr. K exam	
		(4) Motion to set Bail — entered & continued	
		(5) Motion to dismiss Complaint — entered & continued	
		(6) Motion to Permit Defense Counsel to be present at psychiatric exam of defendant [illegible]	

Missing Person

Piest, Robert J.

CONFIDENTIAL

The following report reflects my activities in a continuing investigation of a missing person (murder) of Robert Piest, which was originally filed by his mother on December 11, 1978.

On today's date at approximately 0945 hours I was advised by Lt. Frank Braun, of the Cook County Sheriff's Police, that after having interviewed John Wayne Gacy at the Cook County Jail Complex, Cermak Hospital, in the presence of his attorney, he had advised them where the jacket of Robert Piest could be located within the house. Lt. Braun pointed out the location to me, which is in the area which was commonly known as the pantry area, and after having removed two boxes of food stuffs; one of Pine-Sol Cleaner and one of Stewed Tomatoes, a small hole at the base of the south wall was observed. This hole is approximately 12 inches west of the joist directly underneath the west side of the door jamb that leads to the dining area. The hole is 2"x2" and from there once a light was shone into the area, you could observe the blue material of the jacket within. At this time I went into the area below the level of the crawl space of the addition and from the crawl space under the pantry I could observe a paper bag covering same. This paper bag turned out to be a large grocery type bag from Dominicks Finer Foods and, once it was moved over to the side, the blue ski jacket could be observed more clearly. Photographs were then taken by Lt. Al Taylor, of the Cook County Sheriff's Police, Evidence Technician Department, and at this time I went upstairs again to remove said item. The item is a light blue ski jacket with a hood of the brand name of Pacific Trail. The jacket was removed from the hole and in the immediate locale of it was also recovered an Oral B-20 yellow toothbrush in a small piece of foil that appears to be packaging for a cigar. All items were recovered, initialed by the recovering officer, Detective Rafael Tovar/Star #222, and witnessed by Evidence Technician Tom Richard/Star #240. Items were initialed by both officers and recovered at 1000 hours on January 4, 1979. Items were further photographed by Lt. Taylor and then were transported to the Des Plaines Police Department, where they were held in evidence at this time. They were inventoried under the file number of 78-35203. The exact area where the jacket was found is between the second and third joists in quadrant 4-S of the coordinates drawn by the Cook County Sheriff's Police Evidence Technicians. This would have been directly underneath the entrance of the dining area, which is the new addition to the house. Further reports to follow.

CONFIDENTIAL

	QUANTITY		DESCRIPTION		VALUE	RELEASED TO
	One (1)		Blue Ski Jacket Prairie Trail Brand, initialed by recovering officer (JRT) and witnessed by V. Thomas Richard.		Unk	
	One (1)		yellow oval B-20 tooth brush		Unk	
	One (1)		small piece of clear cellophane		Unk	
	One (1)		large grocery type paper bag from Dominicks Finer Foods (used to cover the jacket)		unk	

REPORTING OFFICERS AND STAR NOS.
Det. J. Rafael Tovar #822

C.I.C. SUPPLEMENTARY REPORT — DES PLAINES POLICE

Date: 4 Jan, 1979 2030

Offense: Missing Person

Victim: Piest, Rob

NARRATIVE:

CONFIDENTIAL

At approximately 1915 hours, 4 Jan, 1979, Det Pickell went to the Piest home and spoke with Mr & Mrs Piest and their son, Ken, and their daughter, Kerry. In summary, R/O advised the Piest family that a jacket similar to that which Rob had been wearing on the night of his disappearance had been recovered.

Prior to showing the family the jacket, R/O asked the family where the jacket had been purchased. Mrs Piest advised that the jacket had been purchased about two years ago at Spieglers Department store in Des Plaines. The jacket was a down filled jacket, light blue in color, with an attached hood.

The family was asked if they recalled any rips or tears in the jacket and they replied negatively. They were asked if they recalled any mending or sewing that had been done on the jacket and they replied negatively. They were asked if they knew of any stains, marks, or other distinguishable marks on the jacket and they again replied negatively.

Upon viewing the jacket, Ken and Kerry Piest said that without a doubt, the jacket was their brothers. They both said that they had worn this jacket several times themselves. They also specifically remember the brand name, "Pacific Trail".

Mr & Mrs Piest examined the jacket and they said that they were positive that this jacket was their sons.

The Piest family examined three other items recovered, a yellow toothbrush, a small piece of cellophane, and a brown grocery-type bag. They said that these items were not familiar to them and they meant nothing to them.

Mr & Mrs Piest advised R/O that their son, Rob, had been wearing "Young Jockey" undershorts. The undershorts were colored, not white. They said the color was most probably blue in color, but they couldn't be 100% certain. The size was 18-20 waist.

Mr & Mrs Piest also said that their son may have been wearing white tube socks or colored terry-cloth socks, both of mid-calf length.

The Piest family was advised that they would be kept informed of the progress of our investigation.

It should be noted that yellow soiled undershorts were recovered from the Gacy residence on 12/13/78.

CONFIDENTIAL

4 Jan, 79 2055

Pickell 229

	Job Number	Case Report Number	Date Received
	12555 B	803696	8 Jan 78

Assignment	Time Assigned	Time Arrived
Homicide Investigation	1245 hrs	1245 hrs

Location	Agency	Beat
Maybrook Square Evidence Section	CCSPD – North Inv	

Victim	Sex	Race	Age	D.O.B.

Victim's Address	Telephone Number

#	Photographs or Evidence Description and Location	P	L	E	Inventory
1	envelope alleged to contain carpet fibers from living room			x	0065-79
2	envelope alleged to contain carpet fibers from kitchen			x	"
3	envelope alleged to contain carpet fibers from NE Bedroom			x	"
4	plastic bag alleged to contain axillary hair samples			x	"
5	plastic bag alleged to contain pubic hair examplers			x	"
6	plastic bag alleged to contain fibers from left cheek			x	"
7	plastic bag alleged to contain foreign matter from anus				
8	plastic bag alleged to contain perianal hair examplers			x	"
9	plastic bag alleged to contain head hair examplers			x	"
10					
11					
12					
13					
14					
15					

Photographs B&W[ ] C[ ] S[ ] Print Cards[ ] Palm[ ] Blood[ ] Hair[ ] Nails[ ] Swabs[ ] File[ ]
Urine[ ] Clothing[ ] Ammo[ ] Glass[ ] Soil[ ] Paint[ ] Safe Material[ ] Scene Plat[ ]
Latents[ ] Firearms[ ] Serology[x] Chemistry[ ] Trace[ ] Arson[ ] ToolMarks[ ] Spectro[ ]
Gunshot Residue[ ] Handwriting-Type Analysis[ ] Other

Make-Yr-Mileage   Model   Color   Vin   Lic-Yr-St

R/ET met with Investigator Kipp of the Mundelein Police Department who delivered to R/ET items one through three, and requested that these itmes be compared with items already submitted to the State Crime Lab. Investigators Powers and O'Neill of the Wauksha Wisconsin Sheriffs Office delivered to R/ET items four through nine and requested that these items be compared with samples collected in this investigation. All items were submitted to the State Crime Lab in Maybrook.

No further action was taken at this time.

ET	Investigator-Agency
Ronald Hale #264	Inv Kipp – Mundelein Police
	Invs Powers & O'Neill – Wauesha County Police

COOK COUNTY SHERIFF'S POLICE DEPARTMENT
EVIDENCE TECHNICIAN'S REPORT

Job Number	Case Report Number	Date Received
12555(C)	R03640	8 Jan. 79

Assignment: Homicide
Location: Cook County Forensic Institute
Victim: Unknown

Time Assigned	Time Arrived
1600	16:15

Agency: CCSPD/North

Photographs or Evidence Description and Location

1) Socks, chain-link bracelet and waistband from underpants, Body #7
2) Socks, 1-black 1-burgandy, from body #9
3) END

R/ET was assigned to proceed to the Forensic Institute and be present while the bones of bodies #7, 9, 13 were examined by Prof. Warren and his assistant Mr. Anapol. The examination was completed and the following information obtained:

Body #7 (Morgue #1277 Dec. 78)
Male, white, age: 15-17 years, muscularity: medium, hair: brown
Recovered two brown socks, a chain-link bracelet, and an elastic waistband from a pair of underpants.

Body #9 (Morgue #1279 Dec. 78)
Male, white, age: 17½-19½ years, muscularity: medium to robust, hair: med. brown
Recovered two socks, 1-black, 1-burgandy.

Body #13 (Morgue #1325 Dec. 78)
Male, white, age: 20-22 years, muscularity: medium, hair: long dark brown.
Note: third left rib has signs of possible old injury.

A. Kulovitz #341

Investigator-Agency
Inv. Bettiker
North Investigations

		0074-79	77
	09 Jan 79	803640/12555D Homicide CCSPD	
#	QUANTITY	DESCRIPTION OF PROPERTY	CASH
1	(1)	A sealed bag containing belt with no buckle, 1322 Dec 78.	None.
2	(1)	A sealed bag containing a garment resembling slacks and a garment resembling a shirt, 1322 Dec. 78.	None.
3	(1)	A sealed bag containing a ligature from 1323-78 Dec.	None.
4	(1)	A sealed bag containing a blk. pocket comb and case, 1323-Dec 78.	None.
5	(1)	A sealed bag containing a garment resembling slacks, 1323 Dec. 78.	None.
6	(1)	A sealed bag containing a ligature, 1278-Dec 78.	None.
7	(1)	A sealed bag containing two canvas shoes, two socks, and a pair of slacks 1278-Dec 78.	None.
8	(1)	A sealed bag containing a belt with buckle, 1329-Dec 78.	None.
9	(1)	A sealed bag containing a pad lock and chain 1329-Dec 78.	None.
10	(1)	A sealed bag containing two canvas shoes, two socks, and a pair of slacks 1329-Dec 78.	None.
11		NO FURTHER ITEMS.	None.

PRINT VERY HARD

Recovered from: Bodies 1322, 1323, 1278, 1329 Dec 78 Forensic Inst.

R/ET

Inv. Phil Bettiker #210 NOIS

David Fisher 226

CTU

None.

COPY 1 - KEEP WITH PROPERTY

	Job Number	Case Report Number	Date Received
	125550	803640	09 Jan 79

Assignment: Homicide
Time Assigned: 1600
Time Arrived: 1600

Location: Forensic Institute of Cook County
Agency: CCSPD
Beat: 99

Victim: Unknown
Sex: M **Race:** W **Age:** — **D.O.B.** —

Victim's Address: Unknown
Telephone Number: Unknown

Photographs or Evidence Description and Location

#	Description	P	L	E	Inventory
1)	A belt from 1322 Dec 78.			X	0092-79
2)	Garments resembling slacks and a shirt from 1322 Dec 78.			X	0092-79
3)	A ligature from 1323 Dec 78.			X	0092-79
4)	A black pocket comb and case from 1323 Dec 78.			X	0092-79
5)	A garment resembling slacks from 1323 Dec 78.			X	0092-79
6)	A ligature from 1278 Dec 78.			X	0092-79
7)	Two canvas shoes, two socks and a pr. of slacks, 1278 Dec 78.			X	0092-79
8)	A belt with buckle from 1329 Dec 78.			X	0092-79
9)	A pad lock and chain from 1329 Dec 78.			X	0092-79
10)	Two canvas shoes, two socks, a pr. of slacks from 1329 Dec 78.			X	0092-79
11)	NO FURTHER ITEMS.				
12)					
13)					
14)					
15)					

Photographs B&W [ ] C [ ] S [ ] Print Cards [ ] Palm [ ] Blood [ ] Hair [X] Nails [ ] Swabs [ ] Bile [ ] Urine [ ] Clothing [X] Ammo [ ] Glass [ ] Soil [ ] Paint [ ] Safe Material [ ] Scene Mat [ ] Latents [ ] Firearms [ ] Serology [X] Chemistry [ ] Trace [ ] Arson [ ] ToolMarks [ ] Spectro [ ] Gunshot Residue [ ] Handwriting-Typo Analysis [ ] Other

Make-Yr-Mileage   Model   Color   Vin   Lic-Yr-St
D - S - A.

On 09 Jan 79 at 1600 hrs., R/ET arrived at the Forensic Institute of Cook County to observe the examination of Medical Examiner's cases numbers 1322 Dec 78, 1323 Dec 78, 1278 Dec 78, and 1329 Dec 78. Professor Charles P. Warren and his assistant Mr. Fred Anapol both of the University of Illinois Circle Campus did the primary examination. Dr. Stein and Dr. Deaner of the Forensic Institute were also present and assisted in the examination.

Body number 1322 Dec 78 was the first to be examined. This body was also identified as CCSPD body number eleven. The following determinations were made concerning the physical characteristics: Male, white, sixteen to eighteen years old, dark brown hair and slight of build. Items number one and two were removed from the body and collected by R/ET for identification purposes.

Investigator-Agency: Inv. Phil Bettiker #210

SUPPLEMENTARY REPORT / DES PLAINES POLICE

Date: 9 Jan 79

Missing Person / **Murder**

Piest, Robert J.

NARRATIVE

The following report reflects my activities in a follow up investigation of a missing person (murder) case originally filed on December 10, 1978.

On Saturday, 6 January 1979, at approximately 1000 hours while working at the murder scene, 8213 West Summerdale Avenue in Norwood Park Township, Illinois, I found three pieces of paper with various notes on them behind a washing machine in the pantry area of the house. These three pieces of paper had been either pushed or hidden behind the washing machine and are attached to the property inventory sheet which is dated 01-06-79 by the undersigned Officer. The one slip shows the name of Jim and Rex at 3168 Hudson, Belmont and Hudson area. It also shows a number of drinking establishments, including Alfies, Broadway Limited, Crystal Blinkers, The Gold Coast, and Bistro. The other pieces of paper, the second one, shows the name of Luis A. Gonzalez, shows an age of 21, court date apparently of 29 April at 9:30 in the morning, assault and battery charge, attempted theft at Western and Belmont. The other one shows some directions, which appear to be to a Moose Lodge at 2500 Fullerton Avenue. These notes were recovered, as there is the possibility of a connection between the bar Blinkers and the disappearance of one of the bodies that has been identified, that one being the subject from Minnesota.

78-35203

Jim & Rex 3168 Hudson
Belemont & Hudson (North

Alfies 900 No. Rush

Broadway Limited
Clark & Briar

Crystal Blinkers
Clark & Briar

Gold Coast
Clark & Hubbard
Sundays

Bistro
Dearborne

10 Jan 79 1500 Hours

Piest, Robert

Reporting Officer was directed by Assistant State's Attorney Terry Sullivan to appear in front of Judge Fitzgerald, the Chief Judge of the Cook County Circuit Court, for the purpose of returning warrants on the John Wayne Gacy case. Also at this time a preliminary hearing was held, at which Mr. Gacy was denied bail, and there were 7 indictments for murder that were read against him; at which time he responded with a not guilty plea. The original Des Plaines Complaint for Murder against John Wayne Gacy will be superseded by a Grand Jury Indictment 79-C69. At this time numerous motions were presented by Mr. Amirante, the Attorney for John Wayne Gacy, and the motions were held in abeyance pending the assignment of an actual trial judge. At this time Judge Fitzgerald assigned Judge Garripo as the trial judge for this case and the various motions made by Mr. Amirante will be taken up by Judge Garripo. One of the primary motions that was, in fact, heard at this time was that of a psychiatric evaluation, which was requested by defense counsel for John Gacy, and the psychiatric evaluation should be returned to Judge Garripo by January 24, 1979. Present at this hearing were Mr. & Mrs. Piest and their two children, Reporting Officer and various other state's attorneys and investigators from the Cook County Sheriff's Police. A new date for the next hearing will be February 28, 1979 at 11 a.m. This was by agreement between defense counsel and the State's Attorney's Office. The hearing again will be held at 26th and California, the Criminal Courts Building.

10 Jan 79 1515 Hours

COOK COUNTY SHERIFF'S POLICE DEPARTMENT
EVIDENCE TECHNICIAN'S REPORT

Job Number	Case Report Number	Date Received
125557	803640	10 Jan 79

Assignment: Homicide Investigation (Multiple)
Time Assigned: 0800 Hrs
Time Arrived: 0800 Hrs

Location: 8213 Summerdale, Norwood Park, Ill.
Agency: CCSPD A-1

Victim: Unknown
Victim's Address: Unknown

Photographs or Evidence Description and Location

[1] Photos of SW and S areas of crawl space.
[2]
[3]
[4]
[5]
[6]
[7]
[8]
[9]
[10]
[11]
[12]
[13]
[14]
[15]

Photographs B&W[ ] C[X] S[ ] Print Cards[ ] Palm[ ] Blood[ ] Hair[ ] Nails[ ] Swabs[ ] Bile[ ] Urine[ ] Clothing[ ] Ammo[ ] Glass[ ] Soil[ ] Paint[ ] Safe Material[ ] Scene Plat[ ] Latents[ ] Firearms[ ] Serology[ ] Chemistry[ ] Trace[ ] Arson[ ] ToolMarks[ ] Spectro[ ] Gunshot Residue[ ] Handwriting-Typo Analysis[ ] Other

Make-Yr-Mileage Model   Color   Vin   Lic-Yr-St
Does Not Apply

R/ET was assigned to observe the continual excavation and collect any evidence relating to the above investigation. The area being excavated on this date was the southwest portion of the crawl space. Two bones approximately 10" in length were found in the area of grave location #16 at coordinates 7S and 5W. One bone approximately 15" in length was found in the area of grave location #13 at coordinates 8S and between 5W and 6W. These bones will be packaged and turned over to Dr. R. Stein, Medical Examiner of the Forensic Institute of Cook County for proper identification.

No further action taken..........

ET T. Nagorski #430

Investigator-Agency
Cook County Sheriff's Police Dept.
Area I Investigations

COOK COUNTY SHERIFF'S POLICE DEPARTMENT
EVIDENCE TECHNICIAN'S REPORT

Job Number	Case Report Number	Date Received
12555G	803640	10 JAN. 79

Assignment	Time Assigned	Time Arrived
Homicide	1600	1600

Location	Agency
Forensic Institute, Cook County	CCSPD

Victim	Sex	Race	Age	D.O.B.
Unknown	see nar	cav		

Victim's Address	Telephone Number
Unknown	Unknown

Photographs or Evidence Description and Location

#	Description	P	L	E	Inven
1	An envelope of unknown substance, from mouth of 1380 Dec. 78			X	0101-
2	A bag containing a ligature from 1382 DEC. 78			X	0101-
3	A bag containing a garment resembling blue jeans 1382 DEC			X	0101-
4	A bag containing unknown substance from mouth, 1382 DEC. 78			X	0101-
5	A bag containing three socks and unknown cloth, 1453 DEC 78			X	0101-
6	NO FURTHER ITEMS.				

Photographs B&W [ ] C [ ] S [ ] Print Cards [ ] Palm [ ] Blood [ ] Hair [ ] Nails [ ] Swabs [ ] Ellc
Urine [ ] Clothing [X] Ammo [ ] Glass [ ] Soil [ ] Paint [ ] Safe Material [ ] Scene Plat [ ]
Latents [ ] Firearms [ ] Serology [X] Chemistry [ ] Trace [ ] Arson [ ] ToolMarks [ ] Spectro [ ]
Gunshot Residue [ ] Handwriting-Typo Analysis [ ] Other

Make-Yr-Mileage Model D.M.A. Color Vin Lic-Yr-St

On 10 JAN. 79 1600 hrs. R/ET arrived at the Forensic Institute of Cook County to observe the examination of the Medical Examiners cases numbered 1380 DEC. 78, 1382 DEC. 78, 1385 DEC. 78, and 1453 DEC. 78.

The examination being done by Professor Charles P. Warren, of Illinois Circle Campus.

Body number 1385 DEC. 78 was the first to be examined. This body is also identified as CCSPD body number 21. The following determinations were made concerning the physical characteristics: A male Caucasoid, aprox. age, 24 to 26 years old. medium to robust muscularity, Light brown hair. No clothing or other items found.

The second body being number 1380 DEC. 78, also identified as CCSPD body number 19. This body was determined to be a male caucasoid of aprox. age 16 to 18 years old, medium muscularity, brown hair. A notation of possible old injury to the right cirvicle paoximal. Item number one was collected by R/ET

J.W. Coakley 256

Investigator-Agency
Inv. Bettiker #210

	Job Number	Case Report Number	Date Received
	12555 H	BD3860	11 Jan 79

Assignment	Time Assigned	Time Arrive
Homicide	1100 hrs	1100 hr

Location	Agency	Be
Maybrook Square Photo Lab	CSPD - North	

Victim	Sex	Race	Age	D.O.B.

Victim's Address	Telephone Number

	Photographs or Evidence Description and Location	P	L	E	Inventory
1)	photo two bones with scale	x			
2)	photo one bone with scale	x			
3)					
4)					
5)					
6)					
7)					
8)					
9)					
10)					
11)					
12)					
13)					
14)					
15)					

Photographs B&W[X] C[ ] S[ ] Print Cards[ ] Palm[ ] Blood[ ] Hair[ ] Nails[ ] Swabs[ ] Bile[ ]
Urine[ ] Clothing[ ] Ammo[ ] Glass[ ] Soil[ ] Paint[ ] Safe Material[ ] Scene Plat[ ]
Latents[ ] Firearms[ ] Serology[ ] Chemistry[ ] Trace[ ] Arson[ ] ToolMarks[ ] Spectro[ ]
Gunshot Residue[ ] Handwriting-Typo Analysis[ ] Other

Make-Yr-Mileage   Model   Color   Vin   Lic-Yr-St

R/ET was requested by Sgt. Des Re maux to photograph the bones which
ad been recovered from the crime scene and was the subject of report 12555 F
hese items were photographed in black and white with a scale.

o further action was taken at this time.

ET Ronald dale 3264

Investigator-Agency
Sgt Donald Des Re maux - ETU

COOK COUNTY SHERIFF'S POLICE DEPARTMENT
EVIDENCE TECHNICIAN'S REPORT

Job Number	Case Report Number	Date Received
12555 (1)	303640	11 Jan 79

Assignment: Homicide
Time Assigned: 1600
Time Arrived: 1600

Location: Forensic Institute of Cook County
Agency: CCSPD
Beat: 99

Victim: Unknown
Sex: / **Race:** / **Age:** Sgt Nark.
D.O.B.:

Victim's Address: Unknown
Telephone Number: Unknown

Photographs or Evidence Description and Location

#	Description	P	L	E	Inventory
1)	A ligature from 1378 Dec 78.			X	0116-79
2)	Slacks and socks from 1378 Dec 78.			X	0116-79
3)	A piece of paper from 1378 Dec 78.			X	0116-79
4)	Socks from 1454 Dec 78.			X	0116-79
5)	A cloth like garment from 1454 Dec 78.			X	0116-79
6)	NO FURTHER ITEMS.				

Photographs B&W [ ] C[ ] S[ ] Print Cards[ ] Palm[ ] Blood[ ] Hair[ ] Nails[ ] Swabs[ ] Bile[ ]
Urine[ ] Clothing[X] Ammo[ ] Glass[ ] Soil[ ] Paint[ ] Safe Material[ ] Scene Plat[ ]
Latents[ ] Firearms[ ] Serology[ ] Chemistry[ ] Trace[ ] Arson[ ] ToolMarks[ ] Spectro[ ]
Gunshot Residue[ ] Handwriting-Type Analysis[ ] Other

Make-Yr-Mileage Model Color Vin Lic-Yr-St
D-B-A.

On 11 Jan 79 at approximately 1600 hrs., R/ET arrived at the Forensic Institute of Cook County to observe the examination of the bodies which are identified as Medical Examiner's case numbers 1378 Dec 78, 1454 Dec 78, 1330 Dec 78, and 1377 Dec 78. These bodies were also assigned CCSPD numbers 17, 25, 15, and 16 respectively. The examination of the bodies was conducted under the supervision of Professor Charles P. Warren and his assistant Mr. Fred Anapol, both of the University of Illinois Circle Campus Anthropology Department. Mr. Warren was also assisted by Douglas Childress of the Forensic Institute. The following information concerning the bodies was provided by Prof. Warren.

Body 1378 Dec 78 was described as being that of a male, white, of medium build with dark brown hair. The age was believed to be between approximately nineteen and a half to twenty-one and a half. Items list

ET: David Fisher 226
Investigator-Agency: Inv. Phil Bettiker #210 NOIS

REPORT / DES PLAINES POLICE — 8 Feb 79   1045 hours

Murder

Plest, Robert J.

NARRATIVE:

The following report reflects my activities in a follow up investigation of a homicide reported on 11 December 1978.

On today's date, February 8, 1979, I had a conversation with Detective Irv Kraut and Investigator Jerry Lawrence, of the Cook County Sheriff's Police and Chicago Police Department/Homicide Divisions, and it was at this time that for the purpose of taking a handwriting comparison of a note which was recovered by this Officer on January 6, 1979 at the home of John Gacy that the note in question, which was inventoried under our P.D. Number, was signed over to Investigator Jerry Lawrence of the Chicago Police Department/ Area 6 Homicide. He signed for it on our evidence recovery sheet and it was turned over to him. An attached copy of it is attached to this report. Also the two other notes with the name of Luis A. Gonzalez and some directions were also turned over to them. The change of custody of evidence has been maintained, being turned over from one to the other and being held in property inventory. More reports to follow.

8 Feb 79

Forest Toxicology Laboratory

555 Wilson Lane
Des Plaines, Illinois 60016
(312) 635-4100

Director:
 Robert Simon, M.D.
Chief Chemist:
 Ernest Patel

Des Plaines Police Department
Des Plaines, IL.

DATE 2-13-79

CASE NUMBER 5794-78-PD

Name or Case Number: 78-36160

Time and Date Received: 12-22-78 11 AM

Received From: Des Plaines Police Department

Received By: Laboratory Staff

Type of Specimen: Pills and Vegetable Material

Test Required: Weight and Analysis

Telephone Report Given To:

DATE COMPLETED: 2-13-79

RESULTS:

Pills: Valium (Diazepam) were present.

Vegetable Material: 2.58 gms Marijuana Constituents present.

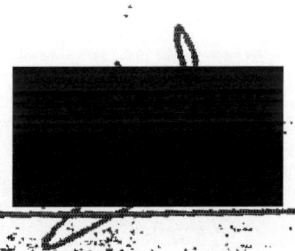

CHEMIST

SUPPLEMENTARY REPORT / DES PLAINES POLICE 5 Mar 79 2055 Hours

Missing Person / Murder

Piest, Robert J.

NARRATIVE:

The following report reflects a summary of court appearances that pertain to this case; the case of John Wayne Gacy.

December 22, 1978, Des Plaines Court, Judge Marvin J. Peters, charged with Murder, No Bond.

December 29, 1978, Des Plaines Court, Judge John L. White, John Wayne Gacy did not appear on orders of Judge Richard J. Fitzgerald, who transferred his case to his court at 26th & California for the prisoner's protection. The defense at this time asked that John Gacy be allowed to make bond and that the charges be dropped, due to the fact that the body of the victim had not yet been located. As far as the bond was concerned, Judge White tabled this motion to be decided on by the Judge who gets the case assigned.

On January 8, 1979 the Grand Jury met and a True Bill was returned on 7 counts of murder.

On January 10, 1979 John Gacy was brought to court before Judge Richard J. Fitzgerald for arraignment at 26th & California, where the defense brought up motions to quash the indictments; this was denied. They also asked that the search be stopped at the residence; this also was denied. However, the case was then assigned to Judge Louis B. Garippo, who ordered that a psychiatric work up be done, he denied bond, and when the State asked for writing exemplars, as well as blood and hair samples from John Gacy, he ordered that this was to be taken under advisement and be ruled on at a later date.

On February 16, 1979 court was held again in front of Judge Louis Garippo, 26th & California. The defense brought up motions to quash the arrest, which was denied, and also a ruling was made that John Wayne Gacy was fit to stand trial and to assist in his defense.

On February 21, 1979 Gacy was again before Judge Louis Garippo at 26th & California, where the motions were heard in the case of the search warrants. The defense asked and made motions that the search warrants Numbers 1 through 5 be quashed, which was denied by Judge Garippo, however he did not rule on the evidence that was seized. The State asked that the Judge order that the digging be continued, which was approved by the Judge, and he held over the request of the State to draw blood and hair samples.

On February 28, 1979 Judge Louis Garippo at 26th & California again held court for John Wayne Gacy, where other motions were heard. Among the motions were a request by the defense that the Grand Jury that was impaneled at the time of the indictments be brought back to check to see how much, if at all, they were tainted by the adverse publicity. The Judge ruled there was no way this could be done and thus denied the motion. Again, the defense brought up the items of news leaks and asked that the Judge also find Chief Lee Alfano in contempt for having made a statement to the secret service reference the security check on John Wayne Gacy. Also, it was asked that Doctor Stein also be included in this contempt citation for his remarks. Judge Louis Garippo at this time ruled on the State's request for handwriting exemplars and blood and hair samples, which are to be drawn and completed on March 16, 1979. The case was continued to April 25, 1979.

5 Mar 79

Det. J. Toyar 222

This, in fact, is a summary of court action and appearances by John Wayne Gacy in Case #78-3520

CID SUPPLEMENTARY REPORT / DES PLAINES POLICE	19 March 1979
Missing Youth	Murder
Piest, Robert	

NARRATIVE:

During the course of this investigation information was received from Mr. Gacy that he had disposed of Robert Piests body by throwing it over a bridge on Interstate 55 and the Des Plaines River.

At the request of the Piest family and as a followup on the investigation R/O and the father of the missing boy spent the first two week period in March of this year searching the bridge and river area of the Des Plaines River at the area were Int. 55 intersects with the river.

Numerous road and shoreline areas were searched with no success and this search process was hampered by heavy snowfall during the several weeks preceeding the start of this process.

Date/Time Report Completed: 19 March 1979 1400

Reporting Officer: J. Kozenczak Commander/CID

The following report reflects my activities in the follow-up investigation of the murder of the Robert Piest reported originally as a missing person on Dec. 11 1978 by his mother Mrs Elizabeth Piest.

On Thursday the 15th of March 1979 I recieved a telephone call from Mrs Richard Szyc of 2247 Westview in Des Plaines who is the mother of John A. Szyc another of the victims found at the residence of John Wayne Gacy Jr. The call was from an earlier request for her to call when she located the receipt for the purchase of Johns class ring. Mrs Szyc told me that she had found the receipt and the small plastic container in which the ring had been recieved. I told her that I would pick up the two items right away. I then went to her home where she turned over to me a HERFF-JONES CO. receipt number 40008ch made out to John A. Szyc at the 2247 Westview address and dated on the 26th of August 1974. The receipt was also marked paid in full on the 5th of October 1974. The second item recieved was the small plastic (zip-lock type) container that the ring had come in. It had a sticker on the bag which indicated that the class ring contained therin... size nine (9) MAINE WEST ring. The items were inventoried and turned over to property officer Leo Boyer.

Missing

Piest, Robert

NARRATIVE

On the above time and date Mrs. Marion Neseth, of ████████████████ of the Illinois Search and Rescue Unit, came to the police station and requested permission to search an area south of Axehead Lake, west of the Des Plaines River and east of River Road, as that was the last area that had not been searched by their unit. The above mentioned area was searched by Mrs. Neseth and her team, supervised by Lt. Schwieson, this Officer and Officer Kaspar from approximately 1800 until 1715 hours with negative results.

Det. A. Adams

ILLINOIS UNIFORM CRIME REPORT
MANAGEMENT INFORMATION SYSTEM

MONTH OF REPORT: DEC 1978

DCN NO: 1 1 0 7 6 2 5 0 0

HOMICIDE

MURDER: X   **VOLUNTARY MANSLAUGHTER:** ___   **JUSTIFIABLE USE OF FORCE:** ___

Situation	Victim Age	Sex	Race	Offender Age	Sex	Race	Victim/Offender Relationship	Day of Mo.	Time of Day (24 Hour Clock)	Weapon	Circumstances Surrounding Death
A	15	M	W	36	M	W	NONE	11	2100	STRANGULATION	SEX ABUSE / MASS MURDER

SITUATIONS

A. SINGLE VICTIM - SINGLE OFFENDER
B. SINGLE VICTIM - UNKNOWN OFFENDER OR OFFENDERS
C. SINGLE VICTIM - MULTIPLE OFFENDERS
D. MULTIPLE VICTIMS - SINGLE OFFENDER
E. MULTIPLE VICTIMS - MULTIPLE OFFENDERS
F. MULTIPLE VICTIMS - UNKNOWN OFFENDER OR OFFENDERS

INVOLUNTARY MANSLAUGHTER AND RECKLESS HOMICIDE TOTAL

SUPPLEMENTARY REPORT / DES PLAINES POLICE

7 Apr 79 0900 Hours

Missing Person / Murder

Piest, Robert J.

NARRATIVE:

On the same time and date a state wide broadcast was teletyped to the following states, Illinois, Indiana, Missouri, Kentucky, Tennessee, Louisiana, Arkansas and Mississippi. The purpose of the message was to encompass the waterways south of Joliet, west to the Mississippi River, east to Indiana and south to the Gulf of Mexico, as information had been received that Robert Piest had been deposited in the river near Joliet shortly after the youth was reported missing. Directing the message to the above eight states will cover the Illinois River, the Des Plaines River, the ship canal, the Kankakee River and the Mississippi River. The message gives a brief description of the youth and advises that we have photos and dental charts of Robert Piest and request any information on individuals fitting the description of Robert Piest who have not been identified.

7 Apr 79

Det. R. Adams 157

78-35203

All terminals State of Illinois

Re missing youth: Information received that Robert Piest, D.O.B. 03-16-63, alleged victim of John Wayne Gacy, was deposited in the river near Joliet, Illinois, shortly after s/, youth was reported missing during December 1978. Youth entered into LEADS on December 11, 1978, Number W7857880.

Description of youth: M/W, 5O8, 140, Brn/Brn, Hair worn shag style.
Photos and dental charts available.
Requesting any information on individuals fitting the above description who have not been identified.

Any info please contact Det. R. Adams, Des Plaines Police Dept., Des Plaines, ...,
Tx (312)297-2131, Ext. 222.

Please direct the above message on a state wide basis to the following states.

      Illinois
      Indiana
      Missouri
      Kentucky
      Tenn.
      Louisiana
      Arkansas
      Mississippi

NOTED

APR 5 1979

DEPARTMENT OF LAW ENFORCEMENT
DIVISION OF SUPPORT SERVICES
JOHN G. LINDER - DEPUTY DIRECTOR

Bureau of Technical Field Services
315 N. Woodruff Road
Joliet, IL 60432
815-727-5301

April 13, 1979

TO: Honorable William D. Button
Sheriff of Grundy County
Grundy County Sheriff's Office
Morris, IL 60450

ATTENTION: LT. RON FOX

RE: CASE #J-79-120

VICTIM: ROBERT PIEST
OFFENSE: MURDER
SUBJECT: JOHN WAYNE GACY

REQUEST:

On April 9, 1979 at approximately 12:45 P.M. I received word that my assistance was needed by the Grundy County Sheriff's Office. I arrived at the crime scene at approximately 1:15 P.M. on that date where I met with Grundy County Detective Lieutenant Fox and Detective Sergeant Olson.

INVESTIGATION:

The crime scene consisted of a body lying face down in the Des Plaines River approximately 200 yards east of the Dresden Locks. This body was photographed at this time. The body was then removed and transferred to Kurtis Funeral Parlor in New Lenox.

At approximately 6:15 P.M. on that date the body was transferred to Silver Cross Hospital in Joliet for head X-rays. It was determined at this time that the victim was Robert Piest and the autopsy would be performed at the Cook County Morgue the following day.

At approximately 10:00 P.M. on that date I received word at my residence that because the autopsy was being performed at the Cook County Morgue my assistance would not be needed that following day.

Respectfully submitted,

Edward J. Konstanty
Crime Scene Technician

EJK:jm

cc: Detective Lawrence (Cook County S.O.)
Detective Paul Sabin (Cook County S.O.)
Detective R. Adams (Des Plaines P.D.) ✓

107 ARMORY BUILDING • SPRINGFIELD, ILLINOIS • 62706

CAS SUPPLEMENTARY REPORT / DES PLAINES POLICE

8 Jan 80

Missing Person — Murder

Piest, Robert

NARRATIVE:

On this date R/O provided ASA Sullivan the remaining recovered evidence that had been retained by this department. The evidence was given to ASA Egan & Mr Egan signed the Des Plaines recovered property receipt acknowledging receipt.

Also on this date was a scheduled court appearance of the defendant, Jhn Gacy. At this hearing Judge Garippo heard evidence from the defense on change of venue motion. After the presentation of evidence Garippo ruled that the selection of jurors would commence on January 28 in Winnebago County northwest of Cook County (Rockford area.) After the selection of jurors the trial would be transferred back to Cook County for the trial proceedings. Judge Garippo will preside over the jury selection in Winnebago County. Next court date will be January 28 in Winnebago County with an unspecified back date prior to this date.

All officers involved would be contacted by the states attorney's office for future instructions.

Accompanying this officer to 26th and California was Det. Robinson.

Det M Albrecht 209

Missing Person

Piest, Robert

NARRATIVE:

At 1115 hours this date John Wayne Gacy appeared before Judge Fitzgerald in Room #404 of the Criminal Courts Building and was arraigned on the previous 26 indictments. Each of the indictments was read by Judge Fitzgerald and at the termination Sam Amirante entered a not guilty plea to all 26 counts, which would include the individuals whose identity had been determined and in the case of the unidentified were referred to as John Doe. John Gacy was then brought before Judge Louis Garippo, at which time certain motions were entered, pretrial discovery was discussed, a list of witnesses was entered and A.S.A. Terry Sullivan presented Judge Garippo and Mr. Amirante with a notice of election pertaining to Indictment Number 79-65, in which case John Wayne Gacy was indicted for the murder of Robert Piest, and at that point Mr. Sullivan stated the State was ready for trial. Judge Garippo stated that he will enter a disposition regarding the vehicles belonging to John Wayne Gacy sometime prior to May 9, 1979. The motion made by the defense regarding discovery is to be filed by June 1, 1979. Judge Garippo stated that he wanted all motions filed by July 16, 1979, at which time he may establish a trial date.

On April 10, 1979 at approximately 0630 hours Captain Kozenczak and this Officer departed from the Des Plaines Police Station in route to the Forensic Institute of Science to attend the autopsy of a body that had been pulled from the Illinois River in Grundy County, which had been assigned Coroner's Case 231. Upon arriving at the Institute at 0730 hours, photos were taken by this officer and after completing the photos of the deceased, a member of the staff of the Institute x-rayed the body of the deceased. The autopsy which was conducted by Doctor Robert Stein and who was assisted by Doug Childress lasted until approximately 1015 hours. Present at the autopsy were head photographer Nicholas Grand, representing the Des Plaines Police Department were Captain J. Kozenczak and Detective R. Kaut and present from the Grundy County Sheriff's Department were Lt. Ron Fox and Sgt. Jim Olsen. The Cook County Sheriff's Police Department was represented by E.T. Ted Nagorski. Upon speaking with Doctor Stein, it was determined that the body of the deceased could be released to the Piest family, at which time we went to the Piest residence and advised the family of our conversation with Doctor Stein. Upon returning to the police station, the teletype message regarding Robert J. Piest, LEADS #W7857880, was cancelled at 1325 hours.

On _____ this date Captain _____ received a call from Sgt. _____, _____ at which time he advised that the _____ County Sheriff's Police _____ had removed a body from the Illinois River and the stature and weight of the body fit that of Robert Piest. The body had been removed from the north bank of the Illinois River approximately 200 yards north of the Dresden Locks. Lt. Fox, of the _____ County Sheriff's Police Department, made arrangements to have the body moved to the Kurtz Memorial Chapel, 102 East Francis Road, New Lenox, Illinois, tx 815-485-5460. Captain Kozenczak and this officer departed from the police station at approximately 1819 hours and met Assistant State's Attorney Terry Sullivan and State's Attorney Investigator Greg Bedoe and together we arrived at the Kurtz Memorial Chapel at approximately 1845 hours. The body of the deceased was removed from the Memorial Chapel and transported to the Silver Cross Hospital, in Joliet, at which time an xray of the skull was taken. Doctor Pavlik then compared the x-ray of the skull with the dental x-rays of Robert Piest and confirmed the fact that the body that had been removed from the river was, in fact, that of Robert Piest. Captain Kozenczak and this Officer then proceeded to the Piest residence, arriving at 2007 hours, at which time the Piests were advised that through the use of the head x-ray and Robert's dental x-rays, the body of the deceased that had been removed from the river had been positively identified as that of Robert Piest by Doctor Pavlik. Upon returning to the police station, a press release was prepared and released at 2030 hours by Captain Kozenczak.

9 Apr 79

Missing Person / **Murder**

Robert J. Piest

The following is a brief synopsis of the culmination on the criminal trial of John Wayne Gacy in regards to the Piest homicide. The jury selection in regards to this case took place in Rockford, Illinois during the month of January 1980. The jury involved in this trial consisted of seven men and five women. The actual trial in this matter started on February 6, 1980 and was held in the criminal courts building at 26th & California, Chicago, Illinois.

There were a total of 79 prosecution witnesses, along with 22 defense witnesses called in this matter.

The trial terminated on March 12, 1980. After a two hour deliberation by the jury, JOHN WAYNE GACY was found guilty of 22 murders, one of which included the murder of ROBERT J. PIEST and he was also found guilty of Deviate Sexual Assault and Taking Indecent Liberties with a Child, these charges stemming from ROBERT PIESTS murder.

After deliberation of the same jury the recommendation was made by them that JOHN WAYNE GACY be sentenced to die in the electric chair. On March 18, 1980 Judge LOUIS GARIPPO, presiding judge of the trial, sentenced JOHN WAYNE GACY to die in the electric chair on June 2, 1980. JOHN WAYNE GACY was remanded to the custody of the Illinois Department of Corrections and transported to the Menard State Penitentiary, to be held on Death Row, until his Appeal Process is exhausted.

Attached is a copy of the original Murder complaint signed by this officer.

J. KOZENCZAK

12/80

SAO-78-3-610

CLERK OF THE CIRCUIT COURT OF COOK COUNTY

FELONY

IN THE CIRCUIT COURT OF COOK COUNTY, ILLINOIS

The People of the State of Illinois
Plaintiff

v.

John W. Gacy Jr.
Defendant

COMPLAINT FOR PRELIMINARY EXAMINATION

No. 78-3-008020-01

Lt. Joseph Kozenczak, complainant, now appears before The Circuit Court of Cook County and states that John W. Gacy Jr. (Defendant) has, on or about December 11, 1978 (date) at 8213 W. Summerdale, Cook County, Illinois (Place of offense) committed the offense of Murder in that he killed Robert J. Piest without lawful justification by strangling him with a rope intended to kill said Robert J. Piest.

in violation of Chapter 38 Section 9 (A)(1)

ILLINOIS REVISED STATUTES

1420 Miner St., DesPlaines 297-2131
(Complainant Address) (Telephone No.)

STATE OF ILLINOIS }
COUNTY OF COOK   } ss.

Lt. Joseph Kozenczak
(Complainant's Name Printed or Typed)

being first duly sworn, on his oath, deposes and says that he has read the foregoing complaint by him subscribed and that the same is true.

Subscribed and sworn to before me December 22, 19 78

TO: RECORDS DIVISION COMMANDER
FROM: PATROL DIVISION COMMANDER
SUBJECT: TRANSFER OF GACY VEHICLES
DATE: 30 JANUARY 1979

RD #78-35203

The vehicles belonging to John Wayne Gacy will be transferred to the custody of the Cook County Sheriff's Department. Vehicle identification is as follows:

#1 Chevrolet Scottsdale - 20 - Black Pickup 1978
   VIN/CKL248J182155
   Plate - ILL. ▓▓▓▓▓ 1978

#2 Chevrolet Van - 20 - Black 1978
   VIN/CGL2584118817
   Plate - ILL. ▓▓▓▓▓ 1978

#3 Oldsmobile 4-DR Sedan - Black 1979
   VIN/3N69R9X105706
   Plate - ILL. ▓▓▓▓▓

RD. #78-35369

I hereby acknowledge receipt of the above vehicles all in driveable condition. No damage visible on any vehicle.

▓▓▓▓▓▓▓▓▓▓▓▓▓▓▓ 378. 30 JAN 79
Sheriff's Representative   DATE

LIEUTENANT AUG H. SCHWIESOW
PATROL DIVISION COMMANDER

9TH PRECINCT — **NORWOOD PARK TOWNSHIP**

JOHN GACY
DEMOCRATIC PRECINCT CAPTAIN

REPRESENTING
NORWOOD PARK TOWNSHIP
REG. DEMOCRATIC ORG.
ROBERT F. MARTWICK
COMMITTEEMAN

8213 SUMMERDALE AVENUE
NORWOOD PARK, ILL. 60656
PHONE 457-1614

CUSTOM DESIGN

P.D.M. Contractors
8213 W. SUMMERDALE
NORWOOD PARK, ILL. 60656
457-1614

JOHN GACY

457-1614
8213 SUMMERDALE
NORWOOD PARK, ILL. 60656

JOHN GACY

Painting Decorating Maintenance

AFFILIATED CONTRACTOR
AMERICAN HOME OWNER ASSOCIATION

CUSTOM DESIGN

P.D.M. Contractors
8213 W. SUMMERDALE
NORWOOD PARK, ILL. 60656
457-1614

JOHN GACY

RAPHCO INC.

Contractors/Developers

John W. Gacy
Vice President,
Operations

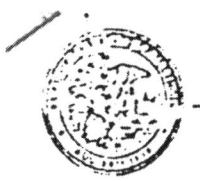

DEPARTMENT OF LAW ENFORCEMENT
DIVISION OF SUPPORT SERVICES
BUREAU OF IDENTIFICATION

515 East Woodruff Road,
Joliet, Illinois 60432

MAR 26 1980

24) L 9 U 000 14
L 4 MOI

9
3 M/W DOB. 03 17 42

The following record is furnished for official use only.

Illinois State Bureau Number 1377836

F.B.I. Number

vh

CONTRIBUTOR OF FINGERPRINTS	NAME AND NUMBER	ARRESTED OR RECEIVED	CHARGE	DISPOSITION
PD., Chgo., Ill.	John W. Gacy IR #273632	06 19 70 MP	PAROLED INTO ILLINOIS	
PD., Chgo., Ill.	John W. Gacy IR #273632	02 12 71	State disorderly	DWP 3-9-71
D., Northbrook, Ill.	John Wayne Gacy #7204499	06 22 72	Agg battery Reckless conduct	11-22-72 Agg bat Reck conduct-SOL
D., Chgo., Ill. 85289230	John W. Gacy Io #273632	07 15 78	Battery wrt.	
D., DesPlaines, Il. 00938497	John Wayne Gacy #A 6710	12 21 78	Poss cont subs-F Poss cannabis-M	
D., DesPlaines, Il. 00938500	John Wayne Gacy #A 6710	12 22 78	Murder-F	

CONFIDENTIAL
CJIS—OPER—0158—3/77

Due to the fact that you did not furnish fingerprints, we cannot guarantee that the enclosed record belongs to the subject of your inquiry.

Superintendent
State of Illinois
Bureau of Identification
CJIS-OPER-0157-3/77

For completion of our records, please supply dispositions to this Bureau in any of the foregoing cases where they do not appear.

UNITED STATES DEPARTMENT OF JUSTICE
FEDERAL BUREAU OF INVESTIGATION
WASHINGTON, D.C. 20537

The following FBI record, NUMBER **585 181 G**, is furnished FOR OFFICIAL USE ONLY. Information shown on this Identification Record represents data furnished FBI by fingerprint contributors. WHERE FINAL DISPOSITION IS NOT SHOWN OR FURTHER EXPLANATION OF CHARGE IS DESIRED, COMMUNICATE WITH AGENCY CONTRIBUTING THOSE FINGERPRINTS.

CONTRIBUTOR OF FINGERPRINTS	NAME AND NUMBER	ARRESTED OR RECEIVED	CHARGE	DISPOSITION
PD Waterloo Iowa	John Wayne Gacy #18022	5-20-68	Sodomy	10 yrs Ft Madison other chg dismissed
SO Waterloo Iowa	John Wayne Gacy #9988	9-9-68	Conspiracy aslt/w/int to commit a fel	
SO Waterloo Iowa	John Wayne Gacy #9-9-68	9-12-68	B & E	
en's Ref Anamosa Iowa	John Gacy #26526	12-11-68	BlackHawk Co sodomy	10 yrs Paroled 6-18 to Chgo Ill see supplem
PD Chicago Ill	John W Gary #273632	6-19-70	parole process	
PD Chicago Ill	John W. Gacy #273632	2-12-71	State Disord	
PD Northbrook Ill	John Wayne Gacy Jr. #7204499	FP 6-22-72	Aggravated battery Reckless conduct	disch S.O.L. moti to reinstat
PD Chicago IL	John W. Gacy 273632 SID 1377836	7-15-78	batt	
PD Des Plaines IL	John Wayne Gacy Jr A 6710 SID 1377836	FP 12-22-78	Murder	
PD Des Plaines IL	John Wayne Gacy A 6710 SID 1377836	Prt Rec 1-9-79	Poss Cont Substance Poss Cannabis	

Notations indicated by * are NOT based on fingerprints in FBI files but are listed only as investigative leads or possibly identical with subject of this record.

CITY OF CHICAGO / DEPARTMENT OF POLICE / 1121 South State Street
IDENTIFICATION SECT. Chicago, Illinois 60605

CRIMINAL HISTORY OF: GACY, John W. 281 M/W

DATE: 19 Jun 70 (22) (15

DATE OF BIRTH: 17 Mar 42

REVISED 4 Oct 78

I.R. NO.	FBI NO.	I.S.B. NO.
273632	585 181 G	1377836

NAME & ADDRESS	C.B. NO.	DATE OF ARREST / ARRESTING OFFICER & DIST. / CHARGE
in Wayne GACY	*	-20 May 68, PD Waterloo, Iowa, Sodomy, 10 yrs. at Madison other charge DISMISSED.
	*	-9 Sept 68, SO Waterloo, Iowa, Conspiracy, Aslt w/int to commit a felony.
in GACY	*	-12 Sept 68, SO Waterloo, Iowa, Burg. & Entry
	*	-11 Dec 68, Anamosa, Iowa. Mens Ref.#26526,(Blackhawk Co), Sodomy, 10 yrs.
in W. GACY	3036939	18 Jun 70, PAROLED to Chgo., 19 Oct 71, DISCH BY Exp. of Sent -19 Jun 70, PAROLED to Chgo, Ill, from Des Moines, Iowa #26426, Anamosa, Iowa. Sent for Sodomy, 3 Dec 68, 10 yrs, Served 18 months.
in Wayne GACY 43 N. Kedvale	3205798	-12 Feb 71, Off.Healy, 17th Dist., 9 Mar 71, Disord. Cond.(38-26-101), D.W.P., Judge Edelstein.
in Wayne GACY Jr.	*	-22 Jun 7., PD Northbrook, Ill, Agg.Battery, Reckless Conduct, DISCH., S.O.L.,
in GACY W. 13 W. Summerdale	5289230	-15 Jul 78, Off.Burke, 16th Dist,Battery,

5 JAN 79

MASTER 3-21-80 6 RDK

UNITED STATES DEPARTMENT OF JUSTICE
FEDERAL BUREAU OF INVESTIGATION
WASHINGTON, D.C. 20537

The following FBI record, NUMBER 585 1 2 G , is furnished FOR OFFICIAL USE ONLY.
Information shown on this Identification Record represents data furnished FBI by fingerprint contributors.
WHERE DISPOSITION IS NOT SHOWN OR FURTHER EXPLANATION OF CHARGE OR DISPOSITION IS
DESIRED, COMMUNICATE WITH AGENCY CONTRIBUTING THOSE FINGERPRINTS.

CONTRIBUTOR OF FINGERPRINTS	NAME AND NUMBER	ARRESTED OR RECEIVED	CHARGE	DISPOSITION
	#26526, 12-11-68		Disch. by Expiration of sentence 10-19-71 on charge of sodomy.	

SUPPLEMENT

		C.I.D. SUPPLEMENTARY REPORT / DES PLAINES POLICE		1. DATE/TIME THIS REPORT 10 Dec 79

2. ORIGINAL OFFENSE	3. OFFENSE CHANGED TO
Missing Person	

4. VICTIM	5. ADDRESS
Piest, Robert	2722 Craig

NARRATIVE:

Roll 9 of 10

Roll 9 Kodak Plus X 135-20   ASA 125

DATE	TEAM	DIRECTION	FRAME	SUBJECT	SHUTTER SPEED	APERATURE
	B	N/W	1	U.S. 41 & Westleigh Rd.	60	F 2.8
	B	N/W	2	6100 Cicero Polish Nat'l Alliance	60	F 2.8
	B	N/W	3	3420 Peterson Medical Center	60	F 1.8
	B	S	4	Prime House - Kedzie & Berteau	30	F 1.8
	B	S/E	5	Prime House Interior	60	F 8
	B	E	6	4623 Kenneth	15	F 1.8
	B	E	7	Jefferson Pk. Train Station	30	F 1.8
	B	N/W	8	Gale St. Inn 4914 Milwau.	30	F 1.8
	B	S/E	9	Gale St. Inn Interior	60	F 8
	B	W	10	Kennedy X-Way at Sayre	30	F 1.8
	B	N	11	7304 Collum Aunt's House	15	F 1.8
	B	N	12	7950 Lawrence	15	F 2.8
	B	N/W	13	Parking Lot - Ray's True Value - Lawrence & Cumb.	30	F 2.8
	B	E	14	Rear Ray's True Value Parking Lot	30	F 1.8
	B	N	15	Bruce & Ken's Pharmacy 8350 Lawrence	30	F 1.8
	B	W	16	Pittsburg Strong	15	F 1.8

R.D. # 78-35203

DPPD FORM # 211

A sample of developed photos of locations Gacy visited.

IMPRISONMENT & SUPPLEMENTAL MATERIALS

33 Slain

Jurors Find Gacy Guilty

Menard Correctional Center, Menard, Illinois.

Stateville Correctional Center, Crest Hill, Illinois.

Lance L

March 5th, 1993

Greetings Lance,

Thank you for your letter of no date. So you have 1589-220 Pogo the clown which was assigned to Shawn Jackson , who sold it to Mike Johnson in Buck town. now its in your ands and since you gave me the number I will register this painting to you.

I never know who buys them unless they write me and give me a number so that I can list them with the owners. all of my work is done on real canvas panles made by Fredrix's so Yes you have an original painting of mine as like all of them sold via agents. You did not mention what you paind for it but let's just say its higher then you would have paid direct or my man in Baton Rouge, La.

Yes I do commission painting by requests just as long as you send a photo of what your wanting, they are called commissioned works (one of a kind)and start at $225.00.

Rick Staton P.O. Box 45888 Baton Rouge, LA. 70895-4888 can send you a list other then portraits and commissioned work. He has the full line of my work and the HI Ho series you speak of while they last. I only do 50 of each of the HI HO years.

If your interested in writing me direct then I enclosed a bio sheet which you can fill out and reurn with a photo of you so that I can see who I am writing. then I will return the same with all my answers on it. On the art write Rick for a listing.

thanks again,

regards,

John Gacy

A sample of correspondence Gacy wrote. Notice his memory and attention to detail.

John Wayne Gacy N00921   Execute Justice... Not People!!!

Lock Box 711
Menard Illinois
USA 62259

Lance L

May 21st, 1993

HI HO Lance,

Thanks for your letter nice to hear from you, enclosed please find the photo of Pogo the clown. I have been keeping very busy trying to get out the special requests. Which by the way I just put your painting in a package yesterday and when the visit comes next week it will be mailed out to you. I had finished it and had to let it dry to touch so as to put the cover over it to mail it. Keep in mind oil painting should take up to six months to totally dry so always handle it with care the first year as thats the time it takes to harden.

Yes I heard about sleazy CBS 2 airing my art again thats file footage from May of 1992 May 4th I am told they had others making comments which mostly are not factual.

I trust that you will enjoy your custom painting as I found it interesting to do. I put a message on the back to you also.

I still never got the patches photo, so I am not sure how soon I will have any. The guy who was getting them for me, well we are parting company.

Hey take care for now have fun and if I can do anything for you let me know.

                             regards,

                             John

Bio Review

Full Name: John Wayne Michael Gacy **Date of Birth:** March 17th, 1942

Age, HT., Wt.: 50, 5'9", ~~220~~ 208 **Home:** Menard, Deathrow, Chester, Ill.

Maritial Status: Twice divorced **Family:** 2 sisters, 5 children

Wheels: last car 79 oldsmobile 4 dr. **Brothers:** none **Sisters:** two

Most Treasured Honor: 3 times man of the year Jaycees 3 different cities

Perfect woman or man: woman, independant, thinker, self starter, mind of her own. Man: Bright, bold, honest dependable says what he is thinking.

Childhood Hero: J.F. Kennedy, R.J. Daley **Current Hero:** M Cuomo, Donald Trump.

Favoirte TV shows: Unsolved Mysteries, National Gepgraphic specials

Favorite movies: Once Upon a time in American, Good fellas, Ten Commandments

Favorite song: Send in the clowns, amazing grace

Favorite singers: Judy Collins, Bob Dylan, Neil Diamond. Roy Orbison, Sha na na

Favorite Musicians: REO Speedwagon Elton John, Zamfir

Hobbies: Correspondance, oil painting, study of human interests.

Favorite Meals: Fried Chicken, deboned lake perch drawn in butter, salad. Tea.

Why you wrote JW Gacy: I don't I just answer for him.

Recommended Reading: Texas Connection, Question of Doubt

Last Book read: Naked Lunch and Wild boys William S Burroughs

Ideal Evening: Dinner and concert or live show, drinks and a quiet walk by lake

Every Jan1st I resolve: Correct things that I let go year before.

Nobody Knows I'm: a character who love to tease and joke around

My Biggest regret: being so trusting and gullible, taken advantage of.

It I were President I'd: Make sure the people of this country had jobs and a place to live before worrying about other countrie

My advice to children: Be yourself, think positive respect parents

What I don't like about People: Phonies, people who don't keep their word.

My Biggest Fear: Dying before I have a chance to clear my name with truth.

Pet Peeves: People who say things they have no intentions in doing.

Superstitions: none its for negative people

Friends like me because: I am outspoken and honest, fun loving, dependable

The questionnaire Gacy would send to the people he corresponded with. Gacy filled this one about himself.

page two

Behind my back they say: The bastard got it made and He Grandiose.

People in History I'd like to have met: Michelangelo, Leonardo, Di Vinci

If I were an animal I'd be: a Bear or an Eagle

Personal goals in Life: To see to it that my Children are provided for.

Personal interests: Reading, Writing meeting people, classic movies and music

Favorite color: __Red__   Favorite Number: __nine__

I view myself as: a positive thinker, self starter, open minded, non judgmental.

What I think of this country: Great, if people would work for it instead of against it, pointing the finger at others, the problem takes all races to make bett

Political views: Semi-Liberal Democrat, that one party doesn't have all winners.

Thoughts on Crime: Too much political corruption, and allowed drugs by governmen has off set the balance of judicial reform and punishment.

Thougts on Drugs: Make some legal, to avoid crime block all else to this country

Thoughts on Sex: Liberal, whatever the will of consenting adult people who are i control of their own well being, and lives.

I consider myself: Conservative _____ Moderate: _____ Liberal: __with values__

What I expect from Friendships: light hearted, fun loving, dependable, and Hones some one who is with you think and thin, good and bad. expecting nothing

Religious thinking: My faith is in God, Churches need to work on the family unit

What your thinking now: why the hell did I fill this out and who care what I hav to say.

Your artistic interests: To please myself first and hope that that expression i enjoyable to others with bold and brightness of colors
Art as in life is a journey not a destination, if you don' like it move on. Just like music to the ear, food to the smell and taste.

```
                                        JOHN GACY N00921
                                        BOX 711
                                        MENARD
                                        ILLINOIS
                                        U.S.A.
                                        62259
                                        October 31st, 1989
```

Dear Lindy,

Its been awhile, tried to get hold of you a couple of times. Enclosed is the drawing for Mike Albrecht, which should give him a good laugh. I wasn't too sure had I sent it to the Mayor of Des Plaines that they would let it go out, so thats why I am sending it to you. This way it may stay out of the Media, You know what a field day they have with me.

Enclosed a clipping from the Tribune also the early notice from the Tribune didn't think it was due already. Also the flyer on the book which just came out, thought you would like to see it.

Hey I hope Hugo didn't do any damage to your place down in the islands, I was thinking of you when I first heard of it hitting down that way. Had wondered if it even came into your area.

I read where Kozenczak was doing a book, "A Passing Acquaintance" from what I hear from publishing people they don't think it will get off the ground. And did you know he did a Screen play for TV. I just read it, you would laugh your ass off, this made for TV movie, has Kozenczak as a super cop with him as the big hero putting the whole case together, and him keeping everyone on the case when they were ready to give up. There going to shit blue bricks when the documentary movie comes out about my case, showing how sloppy the Des Plaines police were and how they covered up others involved, how my own attorney was having sex with his investigator, and Yes we have affidavits to support all of this. The three other suspects with links to the victims, etc.

By the way, my Mom isn't doing too well, Doctors say she will not live long she has been retaining fluids on her lungs, and they say its only a matter of time since they can't do anymore for her. you know she is 8½ 81½ now.

I trust that you have been well and things going good for you, let me know whats up stranger I haven't heard from you in a while. Tell Mike to thank you, because if it wasn't for you he would not have got the drawing.

                                        Later,
                                                John

Gacy hated the Des Plaines Police Department lead investigator, Joseph Kozenczak.

The origins of Gacy's asshole of the year originated from *Hustler* magazine, which had an "asshole of the month" in the magazine every month, critizing a public figure.

Pogo painting by Gacy. (Courtesy of Steve Giannangelo.)

Seven Dwarfs paintings by Gacy. (Courtesy of Steve Giannangelo.)

STATE OF ILLINOIS
MEDICAL EXAMINER'S – CORONER'S CERTIFICATE OF DEATH

STATE FILE NUMBER: 139771
PERMANENT CERTIFICATE: ☒
TEMPORARY CERTIFICATE: ☐
REGISTRATION DISTRICT NO.: 99.0
REGISTERED NUMBER: 001004

1. **Deceased Name:** JOHN WAYNE GACY
2. **Sex:** MALE
3. **Date of Death:** MAY 10, 1994
4. **County of Death:** WILL
5a. **Age – Last Birthday:** 52
5d. **Date of Birth:** MARCH 17, 1942
6a. **City, Town, Twp, or Road District:** LOCKPORT TOWNSHIP
6b. **Hospital or Other Institution:** STATEVILLE CORRECTIONAL CENTER
7. **Birthplace:** CHICAGO, ILLINOIS
8a. **Married, Never Married, Widowed, Divorced:** DIVORCED
9. **Was Deceased Ever in Armed Forces:** NO
10. **Social Security Number:** 344-34-3840
11a. **Usual Occupation:** CONTRACTOR
11b. **Kind of Business or Industry:** OWN BUSINESS
12. **Education:** 12 / 5+
13a. **Residence (Street and Number):** KASKASKIA STREET
13b. **City, Town, or Road District:** MENARD
13c. **Inside City:** YES
13d. **County:** RANDOLPH
13e. **State:** ILLINOIS
13f. **Zip Code:** 62259
14a. **Race:** WHITE
14b. **Hispanic Origin:** NO
15. **Father's Name:** JOHN STANLEY GACY
16. **Mother's Name:** MARION ROBERTSON SCOW
17a. **Informant's Name:** JOHN GREENLEES
17b. **Relationship:** LAWYER
17c. **Mailing Address:** 3039 W. IRVING PK. RD. CHICAGO, IL 60618

18. PART I. Cause of Death:
(a) ACUTE CONGESTIVE HEART FAILURE
DUE TO, OR AS A CONSEQUENCE OF
(b) LETHAL LEVELS OF POTASSIUM CHLORIDE
DUE TO, OR AS A CONSEQUENCE OF
(c) LETHAL INJECTION

19a. **Autopsy:** YES
19b. **Were Autopsy Findings Available Prior to Completion of Cause of Death:** YES
20a. **Manner of Death:** HOMICIDE
20b. **Date of Injury:** MAY 10, 1994
20c. **Hour:** 12:17 A.M.
20d. **How Injury Occurred:** victim injected with lethal drugs per judicial order
20e. **Injury at Work:** NO
20f. **Place of Injury:** STATE PRISON
20g. **Location:** LOCKPORT TWP, WILL COUNTY, ILLINOIS

21a. **Decedent Pronounced Dead on:** MAY 10, 1994
21c. **At:** 12:58 A.M.
22a. **Coroner's / Medical Examiner's Signature:** PATRICK K. O'NEIL
22b. **Date Signed:** JUNE 17, 1994

24a. **Burial, Cremation, Removal:** CREMATION
24b. **Cemetery or Crematory Name:** RIVER HILLS CREMATORY
24c. **Location:** BATAVIA, ILLINOIS
24d. **Date:** MAY 14, 1994
25a. **Funeral Home:** McKOWN-DUNN FUNERAL HOME, LTD., 210 MADISON STREET, OSWEGO, ILLINOIS 60543
25b. **Funeral Director:** WILLIAM F. DUNN
25c. **License Number:** 034-010714
26b. **Date Filed by Local Registrar:** JUN 24 1994

CERTIFICATION

STATE OF ILLINOIS
COUNTY OF WILL

DATE October 2, 1995

I, JAN GOULD, COUNTY CLERK, DO HEREBY CERTIFY THAT THIS DOCUMENT IS A TRUE AND CORRECT COPY OF THE ORIGINAL RECORD ON FILE IN THE WILL COUNTY CLERK'S OFFICE, JOLIET, ILLINOIS.

COUNTY CLERK, WILL COUNTY, ILLINOIS

DEPUTY

(COUNTY SEAL)

Gacy is executed

For any information pertaining to leads or questions in identifying further victims in the John Wayne Gacy case, contact the cook county sheriff's office:

cookcountysheriff.org

AFTERWORD: THE RIPPER CREW

by John Borowski

There are some questions involving the Gacy case that we may never know the answers to. One of the questions which is often speculated on is whether any of the members of the Ripper Crew ever involved with John Wayne Gacy. The Ripper Crew, A.K.A. The Chicago Rippers, were a four-man team who were suspected of 18 disappearances in Illinois in the early 1980's.

An urban legend was spawned that Robin Gecht, one of the members of the Ripper Crew, had worked for Gacy. This piece of false information most likely originated from an article in the Chicago Tribune newspaper (below) which states: "A friend quoted Gecht as saying 'The only mistake Gacy made was burying the bodies under his home.'". No connection whatsoever was ever established between Gacy and Gecht. The investigators in the case had recovered ALL of Gacy's business and personal records. Gacy collected and saved everything in his attic or garage.

There was also a brief defense attempt to tie Gacy to an international child porn and human trafficking network overseas. Child porn was not Gacy's thing. Ultimately the defense's attempt went nowhere, proved nothing and the prosecution investigators (with help from European law enforcement agencies including Interpol) found no possible connection.

> A friend quoted Gecht as saying, "The only mistake Gacy made was burying the bodies under his home."

Chicago Tribune newspaper (10-12-87, section 5 p. 2)

9-19-14.

Hello ▓▓▓
Thank you for your kind letter of 8-29-14. I don't mind at all - you've written me.
  So you read a book by Jennifer Furio? I hope you got your money back? Her inmates wrote her book - Not her! Pretty much all of them. Feed her the bullshit she wanted them to tell her by her lead-on questions - You don't see published.
  As to the back cover of her book where it states - I once worked for John Wayne Gacy. Is bull- Like internet. It's there to grab your attention! It sells copies!

  This started in 1982 when Detectives were questioning Andrew Kokuraties Re "murder." He was fucking with cops - (as always) And said, "Yea, He killed 17 people but wasn't stupid enough to bury them under his house like his friend Gacy. He nor I even knew

Letter written by Robin Gecht 9-9-14. Courtesy of Bruce LeMaster of *Killer's Crawlspace*.

2 | Gacy back in 82. As Gacy was in prison since 1978. So Detectives gave some b.s. to media - and the stories ran wild. They still do today - by online lost souls that need to be noticed. So they ad to a already B.S. Story. to sound better. It sells as well!
There's no truth as to I ever working or knowing Gacy! Until 1985 - When I heard Gacy was here. We never met but here at Menard. Andrew K become Gacy's cellmate on Death Row. That's all I ever know as to Gacy other then what you know of him - or his crimes.
So you work with someone who lived close to Gacy at one time? Small world huh? That must q been a shocker for your co-worker to realize he lived near a house q horror from what I've read or seen on T.V. Being from Chicago, I am aware where Du-page Co is. And where Gacy's house was. It's no longer there!

POLICE DEPT.
DES PLAINES, ILL.
78-467 12-22-78

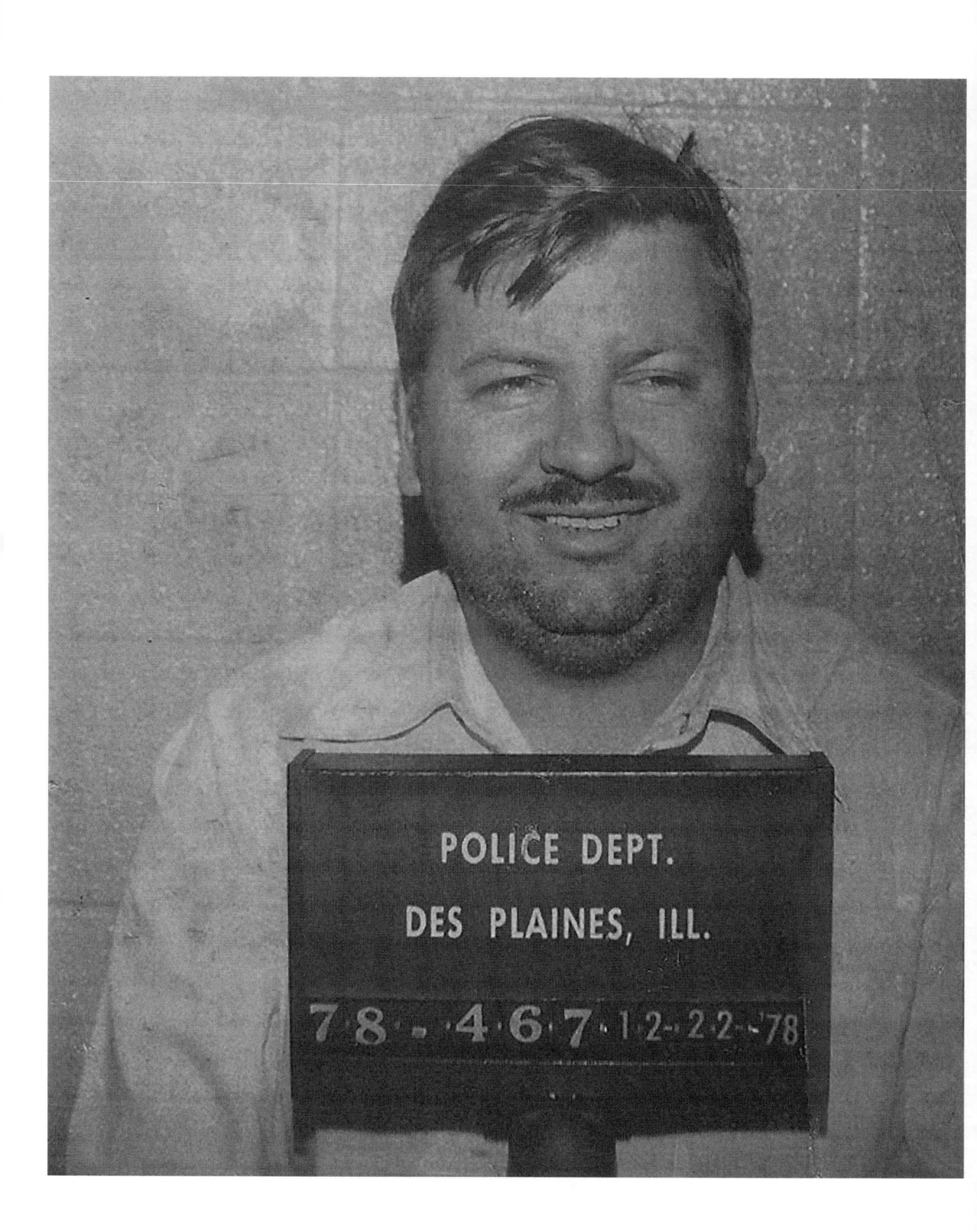

Printed in Great Britain
by Amazon